Computer Ethics

A Case-Based Approach

ROBERT N. BARGER

University of Notre Dame

CAMBRIDGE
UNIVERSITY PRESS

CAMBRIDGE UNIVERSITY PRESS
Cambridge, New York, Melbourne, Madrid, Cape Town, Singapore, São Paulo, Delhi

Cambridge University Press
32 Avenue of the Americas, New York, NY 10013-2473, USA

www.cambridge.org
Information on this title: www.cambridge.org/9780521709149

First published 2008

Printed in the United States of America

A catalog record for this publication is available from the British Library.

Library of Congress Cataloging in Publication Data

Barger, Robert N., 1938–
Computer ethics : a case-based approach / Robert N. Barger.
p.   cm.
Includes bibliographical references and index.
ISBN   978-0-521-88251-4 (hardback) – ISBN   978-0-521-70914-9 (pbk.)
1. Computers – Moral ethical aspects.   2. Information technology – Social aspects.   I. Title.
QA 76.9.M65B37 2008
303.48′33 – dc22   2007049088

ISBN   978-0-521-88251-4 hardback
ISBN   978-0-521-70914-9 paperback

This book is dedicated to my lovely wife, Jo,
with love and gratitude.

Contents

Preface

An Opening Orientation

The words "computer ethics" sometimes evoke the quip: "'Computer ethics . . . isn't that an oxymoron?" Indeed, the computer has received a great deal of bad press over the years because of its association with things like spam, fraud, and impersonalization, but the computer itself is not to blame for these things. Obviously, it is the people who misuse computers who are to blame. They are the unethical ones, not the computers. This book shows that there is indeed an ethics that governs the use of computers. It examines the basis for ethical decision-making and presents a methodology for reaching ethical decisions concerning computing matters. Finally, it concentrates on the theory and practice of computer ethics, using a case-based approach.

An Outline of This Book

Chapter 1 considers a brief history of computers and the Internet, the meaning of ethics, the distinction between law and ethics, the subjects of ethics, and whether computer ethics is a unique kind of ethics. This chapter, and the rest of the chapters in the book, ends with a chapter summary and a "your turn" section soliciting student response to material covered in the chapter.

Chapter 2 deals with the computer as a humanizing agent. This chapter shows that the computer is not – as it is sometimes accused of being – the antithesis of what it means to be human.

Chapter 3 gives a systems approach to ethics. Here you can study the philosophies of Idealism, Realism, Pragmatism, Existentialism, and Philosophical Analysis.

Chapter 4 provides the chance to identify your own philosophic worldview. First you can complete the Ross-Barger Philosophic Inventory. Then you will interpret its results and learn how the inventory was formulated and validated.

Chapter 5 pursues the question of whether a unifying ethical theory can be found for computer ethics. The efforts of James H. Moor in this regard are evaluated.

Chapter 6 provides a framework for making ethical decisions that you will use in solving computer ethics cases. The majority of these cases are be presented in the closing chapters of this book. Most of the cases used have arisen from the experience of computer professionals who have worked within this field for many years.

Chapter 7 goes beyond philosophy to consider psychological factors affecting computer ethics. Here we distinguish between philosophical ethical theories and moral development theories. Then we look at one of the leading theories of moral development made famous by Lawrence Kohlberg.

Chapter 8 gives a brief history of the professions. It then deals with the question of whether the field of computing can be considered a "true" profession.

As a follow-up to this chapter, Chapter 9 presents the codes of conduct used by leading professional associations. This chapter also considers the Ten Commandments of Computer Ethics, a code of ethics formulated by the Computer Ethics Institute, which is a project of the Brookings Institution in Washington, D.C.

Chapter 10 looks at the area of computer ethics as it affects international development. Documents from the World Summit on the Information Society are used for this purpose.

Chapter 11 considers roboethics. "Roboethics" is a name that has been proposed to refer to the area of ethics and robotics.

Chapter 12 covers topics in the area of computer theft and piracy.

Chapter 13 considers a number of cases concerning theft and piracy.

Chapter 14 considers topics in the area of computers and privacy.

Chapter 15 presents cases about computers and privacy.

Chapter 16 deals with topics related to the category of computers and power.

Chapter 17 considers cases about computers and power.

Chapter 18 provides a number of miscellaneous cases.

Chapter 19 considers parasitic computing – a truly unique case in computer ethics.

An appendix is attached, which lists topics suitable for presentations, discussions, and papers. The last entry in the book is an index. The book will be updated periodically by the addition of further cases on the Cambridge University Press Web site. These can be found at the following URL: http://www.cambridge.org/9780521709149.

Acknowledgments

The first person to be thanked for his contributions to this book is John Halleck. He is a computer administrator and programmer at the University of Utah. He began participating in my computer ethics class at Eastern Illinois University twenty years ago by way of a listserv. He was appointed an adjunct faculty member at Eastern for his work with the class. I have spoken with him on the phone and exchanged hundreds of e-mail messages with him, but still look forward to the opportunity of meeting him in person some day. You will soon see that the vast majority of the cases used in this book have been authored by John. The second person to be thanked is Thomas Lapp, also a participant from the beginning in our computer ethics class at Eastern (where he, too, was named to the adjunct faculty). He is a computer engineer. The cases he has contributed to this book reflect his interesting experiences in the field of business and industry. Besides our online communication, I have been fortunate to meet him in person. Heather Bergmann, computer science editor for Cambridge University Press, and her assistants, Pooja Jain and David Jou, have been most helpful in getting this book to press. Heather's gift for making the right suggestion at the right time is something at which I marvel. I am also grateful to Shana Meyer, project manager, and to Mary Kelly, copy editor, for their correction of my composition errors. Last, but certainly not least, I am more than grateful to my wife, Professor Jo Barger, for her encouragement and suggestions concerning this book.

ONE

Introduction

1.1 A Brief History of Computers and the Internet

At the beginning of a study of computer ethics we need to have some understanding of how computing has developed in society. In one sense, computers have been around for a long time, and in another, they are a fairly recent phenomenon. Historically, the first computers were simply fingers and toes – digital computers in the literal sense. They were simple tools used for counting. As calculation became more complex, other tools began to be used to leverage the calculating load. This technology developed along the lines of sticks and stones, then the abacus about 1000 BCE in China, and finally the machines produced during the period of formal mechanics.

Like the railroad, mechanical computers were invented in the United Kingdom. The inventor of the first mechanical computer was Charles Babbage (1791–1871). In the early 1820s he began work on a model of a machine he called the Difference Engine. The purpose of this machine was to calculate numbers for use in mathematical tables. In the early 1830s he turned his attention to work on a programmable Analytical Engine, which was intended to use punched cards. This machine, like the Difference Engine, never went into production. Part of the problem was Babbage's continual rethinking of his plans for the engines. The other part of the problem was the lack of available tools that would produce materials of the tolerance that he required. Though Babbage was never able to finish it, the Analytical Engine may be regarded as a prototype for the modern electronic computer.[1]

Figure 1.1. Herman Hollerith

George Boole (1815–1864) was a contemporary of Babbage. He was Professor of Mathematics at Queen's College (now University College Cork), in Cork City, Ireland. He formulated what today we call Boolean logic or Boolean algebra. It utilizes three basic operators: AND, OR, and NOT. Although Boole was not an inventor of any computing hardware, the logic that bears his name facilitates much of the computing that goes on today. It is by the use of his logic that search engines, for example, are able to do their work.

Herman Hollerith was another nineteenth century inventor who, unlike Charles Babbage, actually did use punched cards in computing. He designed a machine for the 1890 U.S. Census that, through a combination of the use of electricity and information punched into cards, greatly increased the speed with which census data could be tabulated. He later left the Census Bureau and founded a private company that eventually evolved to become IBM.[2]

The MARK series of computers at Harvard University was developed by Howard Aiken and Grace Hopper (the latter was known, because of her extraordinary achievements, as "Amazing Grace"). The MARK I, built in 1944, was a much different machine than the computers of today. It was fifty-five feet long and eight feet high, weighed five tons, and contained five hundred miles of wire. Despite its size, it was slow in processing speed, requiring three to five seconds to perform a multiplication operation. The Mark I was used by the Navy for gunnery and ballistic calculations. Grace Hopper, the first woman to become a Rear Admiral in the U.S. Navy, was a mathematician who developed validation software for the COBOL language. It was her idea that programs could be written in a human-type language rather than in machine code. She is also known for a remark in the Mark II log that she was "debugging" the computer because a moth had been found in it. She was awarded the first "Man of the Year" award by the Data Processing Management Association. Howard Aiken headed the team that worked on the Mark series. He published many articles on electronics and switching theory and went on to found Aiken Industries. He would seem to be a better scientist than prognosticator, since in 1947 he said, "Only six electronic digital computers would be required to satisfy the computing needs of the entire United States."[3]

The first electronic computer, ENIAC (an acronym for "Electronic Numerical Integrator and Computer"), began operating at the University of Pennsylvania in 1946. It was invented by John W. Mauchly and J. Presper Eckert. It used an external type of programming made up of cables and switches. There are still programmers working today who once used this type of "wiring board" to program their computers. Although it is apparently a myth that ENIAC dimmed the lights throughout Philadelphia when it was turned on, it did make use of a total of 18,000 vacuum tubes.[4] Computer hardware has progressed over the years from vacuum tubes to transistors to integrated circuits to microprocessors or microchips. These advances have made possible tremendous increases in speed of operation and in reduction of size. This "smaller but faster" technology allowed for the development of personal computers in the 1970s and 1980s.

ENIAC was an early form of digital computer. Digital means that data is represented as discrete units. Analog, on the other hand, means that data is represented as continuous quantity. An example of analog representation would be a timepiece with smoothly sweeping hour, minute,

Figure 1.2. ENIAC (U.S. Army photo)

and second hands. An example of digital representation would be a time-piece with hours, minutes, and seconds that change by discrete numbers. It is interesting that these different representations make for a different "conception" of time. For instance, a person wearing an analog watch is likely to report the time as being "a quarter to eleven," whereas the wearer of a digital watch – because of the discrete digits that appear on the face of the watch – might say that the time was "ten forty-five."

An interesting hallmark in the development of interactive software occurred in 1963 when Joseph Weizenbaum, a Professor of Computer Science at the Massachusetts Institute of Technology (MIT), created a program called "Eliza." This program functioned like a Rogerian psychotherapist, basically reflecting a patient's comment back to the patient and getting the patient to develop it further. Weizenbaum once told me that he was amazed and appalled that some people were actually using this program as if it were really capable of achieving a psychotheraputic result. Weizenbaum is also famous for the following joke he loved to tell, emphasizing the divide between science and the humanities. It seems a college student was shopping in a supermarket located between the campuses of Harvard and MIT. He pulled his very full cart into a checkout lane that had a sign saying, "Eight items or less." The cashier glanced at the overflowing cart, then at the sign, and finally at the student. Then with a pained expression the cashier asked, "Are you from Harvard and can't count or from MIT and can't read?"

A quantum leap in computing occurred with the development of communication between distant computers. The initial work on this type of communication was done in the late 1960s by a U.S. Defense Department agency known as the Advanced Research Projects Agency (ARPA). It constructed a computer network between contractors working for the Defense Department, which was known as the ARPANET. A major concern in the development of this network was to insure that if a node on the network were obliterated by an atomic attack, messages could be routed around this node so that communication with the rest of the network would not be disrupted. The ARPANET was followed in the 1970s by the development of the Internet, which was essentially a network of networks. The Internet made it possible for virtually an infinite number of servers to communicate with one another. Its development was enabled by the invention of the Transmission Control Protocol and the Internet Protocol, known by the acronym TCP/IP. These protocols were invented by Vinton Cerf and Robert Kahn. These TCP/IP protocols will be explained in detail in Chapter 19 in the context of the parasitic computing case. The most recent major development in worldwide computer communication was the Hypertext Transfer Protocol (http). It was invented in 1989 by Tim Berners-Lee while he was working at the European Particle Physics Laboratory in Switzerland. The http protocol facilitates exchange of hypertext documents by a browser with servers on the World Wide Web (www). The Web, although often thought of as synonymous with the Internet, is actually a subset of it.

A list of other highlights in hardware and software development in the last quarter of the twentieth century concludes this section:

1975 – The first personal computer (PC) appeared on the market. It was sold as a kit through *Popular Electronics* magazine. It enabled programming through the use of the BASIC language.

1976 – Steve Jobs and Steve Wozniak built the first Apple computer.

1976 – The Cray-1, the first supercomputer, was built by Cray Research.

1977 – Bill Gates and Paul Allen founded Microsoft.

1977 – PCs manufactured by Tandy and by Commodore appeared on the market.

1979 – VisiCalc was marketed, becoming the first electronic spreadsheet program.

1982 – The Compaq computer entered the marketplace.

1983 – IBM produced its own spreadsheet program, Lotus 1–2–3.

1984 – Apple introduced the Macintosh computer.

1984 – The CD-ROM, making possible greater storage capacity, was produced by Sony and Philips.

1988 – Robert Morris, Jr., released the Internet Worm, contending that he meant it to expose security risks on the Internet.

1995 – The Java language was developed by Sun Microsystems.[5]

1.2 The Meaning of Ethics

Ethics is defined by *Webster's Third International Unabridged Dictionary of the English Language* as "the discipline dealing with what is good and bad or right and wrong or with moral duty and obligation." Ethics is a part of philosophy, not science. As John Horgan, noted science journalist and author, says: "Science tells us that there are limits to our knowledge. Relativity theory prohibits travel or communication faster than light. Quantum mechanics and chaos theory constrain our predictive ability. Evolutionary biology keeps reminding us that we are animals, designed by natural selection, not for discovering deep truths of nature, but for breeding. The most important barrier to future progress in science – and especially pure science – is its past success."[6] Philosophy, on the other hand, does not place limitations on our knowledge. It deals with questions of quality, not quantity. It is not so much concerned with measuring amounts of things as it is with understanding ideas and concepts. A more rigorous investigation of ethics will be undertaken in Chapter 3, but for now let us conclude by saying that the words "computer ethics" do not denote the oxymoron spoken of in the Preface of this book. Rather, they symbolize the hope that dilemmas involving one of the world's most complex machines, the computer, can be analyzed with a systematic use of normative value theory. This investigation will not be an easy task. Heinz von Foerster, late Professor Emeritus of Biophysics and Electrical Engineering at the University of Illinois at Urbana-Champaign, has suggested the difficulty of such a study. He said: "The hard sciences are successful because they deal with the soft problems; the soft sciences are struggling because they deal with the hard problems."[7]

1.3 The Distinction between Law and Ethics

An assumption is often made that what is right is also what is legal and that what is legal is also what is right. However, it is possible for an act to be ethical but illegal, or, conversely, unethical but legal. An example of the former might be the case of objection to fighting in a war by a person who truly has a conscientious objection to participating in violent actions, but where that person's government has not provided for excusing such an individual from service. An example of the latter might be the case of a government sanctioning capital punishment when a majority of its citizens believe capital punishment to be an immoral means of punishment.

You will find that computing dilemmas will be analyzed in this textbook more from the standpoint of ethics than from the standpoint of law. I sometimes ask a professor of law to visit my computer ethics class and comment on computer ethics dilemmas. Of course the professor's comments tend to be legally based rather than philosophically based. While I do believe that law is very important and that our society could not survive without it, I always remind my students that – as indicated in the previous paragraph – ethics and law are not the same thing. It is true that often the law requires what ethics requires, but not always. It is also true that often ethics requires what the law requires, but not always. It is my belief that computer ethics dilemmas should be analyzed and solved on the basis of enduring ethical principles, even if there is an argument about which of these principles should enjoy priority. I do not believe that computer ethics dilemmas should be analyzed and solved primarily on the basis of legal precedents that change with time, shifting majorities, and revisions of law.

1.4 The Subjects of Ethics

By "subjects of ethics," I mean those persons to whom ethics applies. As might be concluded from a statement in the Preface of this book that it is people who are unethical and not computers, the subjects of ethics are basically individual human beings. Human beings are the subjects of ethics because they are free in their actions and therefore are responsible. To the extent that a person's actions or choices are constrained in some way, then to that same extent a person is not acting or choosing freely. Such persons are therefore limited in the responsibility that they have for their actions or choices. Thus, those actions or choices cannot be called fully ethical or unethical.

Besides individuals, moral or corporate persons may also be the subjects of ethics. What this means is that institutions and organizations must bear responsibility for their corporate activity just as individuals bear responsibility for their individual activity. Corporations may have a broader scope of activity that may not be as easy to isolate as the activity of individuals, but they bear the same degree of responsibility for the effects of their actions as do individuals.

Finally, we sometimes speak of "good" weather or "bad" weather, but we do not really mean this in a moral sense. Although we might colloquially "blame" Mother Nature for the state of the elements, there clearly is no choice or responsibility implied in our manner of speaking.

1.5 Computer Ethics as a Unique Kind of Ethics

A word of acknowledgment should be given at the start of this section to James H. Moor, a philosopher at Dartmouth College, for his groundbreaking article in 1985 on computer ethics.[8] In that article Moor spoke of computers as "logically malleable," in other words, as able to occasion all sorts of new possibilities for human action and hence also able to create "policy vacuums" (absence of policies for dealing with these new possibilities). He saw computer ethics as a way to analyze these policy vacuums and to formulate appropriate policies.

Since Moor's article, other questions have arisen concerning the field of computer ethics. A central question has been whether computer ethics is essentially different from other kinds of ethics. Traditional computer ethicists maintain that the principles of ethics are relatively constant, no matter to what areas of activity they might be applied. That is to say, the principles of medical ethics, legal ethics, and computer ethics are all the same. They do not differ from one professional field to another. Another way to put this is: theft is theft, no matter whether it is accomplished at the point of a gun or by means of a computer. Some computer ethicists, such as Deborah G. Johnson, suggest that new circumstances occasioned by the use of a computer make for new questions about how ethical principles are to be applied. For example, she points out that computers have brought about the creation of new kinds of things that have never existed before, such as microchips. As she says, "The activity of encoding ideas on silicon chips could not have been conceived of sixty years ago."[9] Undoubtedly, the unique features of computers and the way in which they operate have created new ethical problems. These problems, if not "new" in the sense of a new genus of problem, are at least new in the sense of a new species. This is true because of the change in the scope and scale of the "old" problem brought about by the way in which the computer operates. Consider the following problems as examples:

- Speed/reflex behavior

Computers have facilitated an increasingly speedy form of communication. An example where this speed can cause unique problems is the "flame" phenomenon. This occurs when a person immediately responds by e-mail to a posting, using an immoderate tone, which the person would not use if he or she had taken the time to write a traditional letter or had contacted the recipient in person or by phone.

- Storage/privacy

Massive numbers of files can be retained on a computer for indefinite periods of time. Once information is recorded in these files and shared with other computers at lightning rates of speed, information about people (whether accurate or inaccurate) can take on a life of its own and invade people's privacy in a way never before possible.

- Identity theft

It is possible, using a computer, literally to steal another person's identity. People who have been victims of such theft have found that a great amount of time and trouble is necessary to recover from it.

- Internationality

Computer transmissions do not stop at national boundaries. For example, material that is considered obscene (and perhaps illegal) in one country can be sent into that country from another country in which there is no such prohibition.

- Copying/stealing

In a few seconds with a few clicks of a mouse, images and text can be stolen using a computer. They can then be applied out of context, or without attribution to their true author.

- Perversion
  - Pornography: Pornographic sites exist that display material without regard to the age of the viewer and that can be disguised to avoid detection by pornography filters.
  - Gambling: Sites exist (some of which are located offshore) where one can remotely gamble for money, using a credit card. This gambling is usually done against computer programs rather than against human beings. These gambling sites may use unfair odds and may not pay off a player's winnings.
  - Stalking: Stalking with a computer involves unauthorized persistent surveillance. It is illustrated in the "Fingering" case in Chapter 15 of this book.
- Social issues
  - Gender: Computer science is still a male-dominated field. Research indicates that this is the result of social inequities.[10]
  - Race and social class: Consider these statistics from a 1998 study published by Henry Jay Becker of the University of California, Irvine. Only about 22% of children in families with annual incomes of less than $20,000 have access to a home computer, compared with 91% of children in families with incomes of more than $75,000.[11] Clearly, the rich have more access to computing

resources than do the poor. But is this not similar to saying that the rich have more access to all the more expensive things in life? After all, this is the way things work in a capitalist society. However, can it not be argued that the computer is such a basic tool in modern life that it is morally wrong for the poor not to have equal access to it?

- Privacy
  - Selling private data: Is it fair for someone to harvest e-mail addresses on the Web, along with other information about the holders of these e-mail addresses such as their browsing interests and purchasing activity, and then sell this information to mass marketers who will send unwanted spam to these addresses?
  - Opt-in versus opt-out for solicitation: Is it unfair to marketers to prevent them by law from sending e-mail except to those who have requested it in some way?

Besides the "new" ethical problems mentioned above that are caused by a change in scope and scale of old problems, there is also the question of whether new features of computer technology can raise moral dilemmas that amount to a new genus of problem rather than just a new species. This issue has already been raised by Deborah Johnson, but Herman Tavani speaks of it in more detail in an article on the uniqueness debate in computer ethics. He points out that there are two basic views on the question. The first view is held by traditionalists who believe that we can use traditional categories to analyze any issue, old or new, and that computing dilemmas are not therefore unique. In other words, a new kind of ethics is not needed to address these kinds of new dilemmas. The second view holds that computing dilemmas are at least somewhat unique. This is because some issues related to computers are old and some are essentially new, that is, belonging to a new category. Others holding the second view believe that, beyond the question of uniqueness, some dilemmas in computing simply cannot be analyzed adequately within our conventional moral framework.[12] Questions concerning changes in ethics occasioned by new computer features will be further addressed in Chapter 19. In that chapter a unique computer ethics case called parasitic computing will be examined.

As noted in the last paragraph, new and different dilemmas can also raise the question of whether new ethical systems might be required for their solution. This possibility has been addressed by Luciano Floridi and J. W. Sanders in a proposal for a new ethical system known as Information Ethics.[13]

This proposal is similar to that of certain environmental ethicists in the sense that the proposal would grant moral consideration to entities and objects besides human beings. Besides human beings, it would grant moral status to animals and the environment, and even to nonbiologic entities, such as information. Understanding this proposal is difficult. Let us consider an extended summary of the argument of Floridi and Sanders as presented by Herman Tavani.

Drawing from certain analogies involving ecology and the "ecosphere," and the recent attention such notions have received from environmental ethicists, Floridi and Sanders suggest that we should explore a domain that they refer to as the "infosphere." Their recommendation that the "infosphere" be viewed as an analog to the "ecosphere" is instructive in the following sense. Floridi and Sanders (2002) point out that research in environmental ethics has introduced new moral entities or what we earlier referred to as new "objects of moral consideration." The authors point to the example of "land ethics," which some environmental ethicists have argued shows the need to broaden the sphere of moral consideration to include entities in addition to humans and animals, i.e., entities such as trees, ecosystems, etc.

Floridi and Sanders also note that when ethicists began to analyze moral issues involving the environment, some argued that none of the standard ethical theories – e.g., utilitarian, Kantian, and virtue ethics theories – were adequate. For example, whereas virtue ethics is "agent oriented" in that it focuses on the moral character development of individual agents (i.e., persons), utilitarianism and Kantianism are "action oriented" in that they are concerned with the consequences and motives of individuals engaged in moral decisions. While action-oriented theories focus primarily on agents and the actions of those agents, those theories attend only minimally to the "recipients" (or objects) or moral actions. Floridi and Sanders acknowledge that action-oriented theories are "relational" in the sense that those theories consider both the act of the agent and the impact of the act on recipients (objects) of the actions. However, the authors also believe that these "standard" ethical theories are deficient because they do not accord sufficient attention or consideration to the recipient or what Floridi and Sanders refer to as the "patient" involved in the moral action. The authors also believe that the improvement with the macroethical theory used by some in the fields of environmental ethics, bioethics, and medical ethics is that it is "patient oriented" – i.e., because that theory takes into account as potential recipients or patients certain kinds of "entities" in addition to human beings and animals. For example, such "patients" can include trees, ecosystems, etc., as entities deserving moral consideration. Floridi and Sanders (2002) argue that a shortcoming of the environmental macroethical theory, and the primary reason why that theory will not work for computer ethics, is that it limits the kinds of "patients" that qualify for moral consideration to biologic life forms. Hence, the bias in that macroethical theory for the environment and biological life forms, which Floridi and Sanders describe as a theory that is "biocentric."

Whereas environmental ethics is "biocentric" with respect to which objects it is willing to extend the status of moral consideration, Floridi and Sanders point out that Information Ethics (or IE) is "ontocentric." IE is ontocentric because it grants moral status to inanimate objects – i.e., to nonbiologic objects or entities – as well as to entities that can be regarded as standard life forms. Floridi and Sanders (2001) argue that moral good and evil can be "determined even in the absence of biologically sentient participants."[14]

It might seem that this proposal tests the boundaries of ethics, since ethics has until now been anthropocentric. That is, it has been concerned only with human beings. The eighteenth-century philosopher Immanuel Kant, for instance, did not believe that animals had rights.

Clearly the computer, as a tool, has raised new problems for society. Some would claim that it is more than a tool simply because of its widespread impact on society. I agree indeed that the computer is having a radical impact on society, but I maintain that the computer is simply a tool. The fact that it can be employed in many different areas of life, inside or outside the workplace, does not stand in the way of its being understood basically as a tool. Its great utility and its great potential for social good or evil comes from the fact that it is a very fundamental kind of tool, as James H. Moor has said. We might think of it as an extension of the human nervous system with input, processing, and output functions. Its potential comes from the fact that it is so similar to human operation. Its processing ability, which enables it to do programmed decision making, makes it a unique extension of the human person. This is a topic that will be considered in the next chapter.

In conclusion, on the question of computer ethics as a unique kind of ethics, like Professor Deborah Johnson, I do not believe that computer ethics are qualitatively different from medical ethics or legal ethics or any other kind of professional ethics. Like her also, I believe that the nature of the computer and its operation gives certain dilemmas in computing a difference in degree that approximates a difference in kind and that certainly makes computer ethics a unique field of study.

1.6 Chapter Summary

A brief history of computers and the Internet covered primitive computing, Charles Babbage, George Boole, Herman Hollerith, the MARK series of computers, ENIAC and its inventors John W. Mauchly and Presper Eckert, Eliza, ARPANET, and the Internet and Web as enabled by the invention of the Transmission Control Protocol, the Internet Protocol, and the Hypertext Transfer Protocol. This recount of computer history ended with a list of highlights in the development of hardware and software that occurred in the last quarter of the twentieth century. Next, the meaning of ethics was explored. It was noted that ethics was part of philosophy rather than science, that it dealt with questions of quality rather than quantity, and that it provided a means to analyze dilemmas with a systematic use of normative value theory. Following that, the distinction between law and ethics was considered. Ethics and law are not the same thing. It is possible for an action to be ethical and illegal or unethical and legal. Of course, it is also possible for an action to be ethical and legal or unethical and illegal. Next followed a treatment of the subjects of ethics. These subjects are the individual and the corporate person.

It was stated that the computer has created new species of problems in the following areas: speed/reflex, storage/privacy, identity theft, internationality, copying/stealing, pornography, gambling, stalking, gender, race and social class, selling private data, and opt-in versus opt-out for solicitation. This list does not exhaust the possibilities for new species of problems.

On the question of whether computer ethics is unique as a form of ethics, it is fair to say that computer ethics does not have different principles than do other kinds of ethics. However, the nature of the computer does give many dilemmas concerning it a difference in degree that approximates a difference in kind and makes computer ethics a unique field of study.

1.7 Your Turn

Question 1. Can you think of any other notable occurrences in the history of computers and the Internet that you think should have been included in Section 1.1 of this chapter?

Question 2. Can you give other examples, besides those provided in Section 1.3, where an action may be legal but unethical or where an action may be illegal but ethical?

Question 3. Can you think of other kinds of problems, besides those noted in Section 1.5, where the computer has raised a unique dilemma not seen in previous ethical experience?

Question 4. Do you agree that the nature of the computer and its effect on the scope and scale of problems associated with it makes computer ethics a unique field of study?

TWO

The Computer as a Humanizing Agent

2.1 Introduction

In many ways, ethics is concerned with authentic human development. In this regard, we will look at the different ethical systems in Chapter 3 and the topic of psychology and computer ethics in Chapter 7. Before we do that, a sketch is presented here of the relationship between computers and a humanistic view of human development.

From the beginning of time until 1980 there had only been about one million computers in existence. Even considering that the first electronic computer was produced in 1946, the exponential increase in the production of computers in the last few decades has been nothing short of incredible. It seems that the computer revolution is having an impact on our society equal to that of the Industrial Revolution.

Consider this prediction made in 1979 by Alfred Bork, a physics professor at the University of California at Irvine who has done pioneering work with educational computers: "By the year 2000 the major way of learning at all levels, and in almost all subject areas will be through the interactive use of computers."[1] What is it about the computer that made Professor Bork think that, within two decades, the computer would become the major instrument of learning?

I believe the reason is that, physiologically and psychologically, the computer is the most natural of human learning instruments. Consider that the computer is basically a replica of the human nervous system. It has an electrical system that provides input and output, much as does the human neural system, which is electrical and chemical in its operation. The computer's central processing unit and its memory are patterned on the human brain, which is essentially an information processing, regulating, and storage device. Indeed, we may soon have a combination of the brain and the computer. For, with rapidly developing technology, it may soon be possible to surgically implant in the brain a chip that contains encyclopedic amounts of knowledge. Although this may sound incredible at present, this development could be as easily accepted by society as were the developments of the contact lens and the pacemaker.

Computers are currently portrayed as the antithesis of what it means to be human. They are shown as cold steel structures driven by high-technology electronics, able to perform incredible feats with lightning speed. They evidence no emotion. They do not tire. And, as computer experts are fond of saying, they never make mistakes. What could be less human?

The personification of the inhuman computer is "Hal," the villain of the now-classic film *2001: A Space Odyssey*. As the on-board computer for a space flight at the turn of the twenty-first century, Hal begins to take on a life of his own and is only stopped from subverting the flight's mission when the human crew wins a hard-fought battle against him and succeeds in "pulling his plug." It is a thrilling story, worthy of rank with the triumphal sagas of humanity against the elements, humanity against the organization, and now, finally, humanity against that ultimate machine, the computer.

Such is the myth of the computer. But I believe that the myth is wrong. The computer is not the natural enemy of humanity. Quite the opposite is true. Many humanists will consider what I am about to say to be heresy. But let me state the "heresy" boldly. Properly programmed, the computer can show people what it means to be human and can help them become more human. I want to emphasize, however, that the element of human control over the computer is critically important. Computer hardware can never be better than its designer and computer software can never be better than its programmer.

Now, if I am to escape the fires of a humanistic auto-da-fe, I must list what I consider to be the essential characteristics of the human condition and show how these characteristics can be enhanced by the computer.

To make this a bit more practical, I will use the field of education as an example.

I think that being fully human means possessing the traits of autonomy, individuality, rationality, affectivity, responsiveness, and creativity. I will examine each of these traits in turn to see how they might be enhanced by the computer.

2.2 Autonomy

Computers have become as omnipresent as telephones and television sets. This means that a facility in their use will be necessary for human autonomy. By autonomy I mean control of one's own aims and purposes. Plato said that a slave is one who carries out another's purposes. Jefferson, at the beginning of the American Republic, stated that a basically educated citizenry is necessary to safeguard that citizenry's freedom. If a technical elite is not to gain tyranny over the common person, much as literary elites have done in earlier times, then computer "literacy" will be as essential to human autonomy in the future as was a knowledge of reading and writing in the past. Perhaps what we need today is another Horace Mann (the pioneer of the American public school system) to promote education about computers.

Also, the meaning of what it is to "know" has changed in this era of the information explosion. What you "knew" previously meant what you had in your memory. Now what you "know" is what you have the ability to access from inside or outside of yourself. In this environment, an ignorance of the computer and its use may mean the sacrifice of human autonomy.

2.3 Individuality

All students do not learn at the same rate. Unfortunately, traditional classroom instruction cannot easily take this fact into account, but the computer can. With the computer, students can pace themselves. They can linger over material that they need more time to absorb or they can speed through material that they readily understand. In fact, with the computer it is possible to branch a student to remedial material or to move a student ahead to more advanced material on the basis of the student's responses. Also with the computer, students can be allowed choice regarding the path they take through a lesson and the format in which they study it. In traditional instruction, the instructor might use different examples each semester in a course, or might teach the course in a radically different manner each time, but the students could only experience it in that one way during any given semester. However with the computer, students could be offered a number of optional approaches to the same material.

Some educators worry that the computer might promote social isolation since it is such a one-to-one instrument. This concern does not seem to be born out in fact. Many teachers say that contrary to their initial expectations, computers tend to promote conversation and cooperation among students rather than isolation and introspection, especially if the computers are placed in clusters. Invariably, an underground network will develop in which students pass around interesting programs and computer tricks that they have discovered.

A final point concerning individuality involves the time and place for instruction. Instead of being restricted to a scheduled time and place, as is the case with traditional classroom instruction, the student can use computer-assisted instruction at almost any hour and any place. Given the advances in computing platforms (cell phones, BlackBerrys, etc.), the limits of time and space have virtually disappeared.

2.4 Rationality

Computers are valuable tools for teaching students how to think. In order to program a computer, a student must begin by schematically outlining the steps for the operation that the computer is to perform. Then the student must decide how to code these steps into lines of instruction in a language that the computer can understand. All of this involves the use of the problem-solving method or, to put it more simply, logical thinking. This does not mean, be it noted, an exercise in abstract theorizing. The student is involved in solving a concrete programming problem. If it is true, as educators from Johann Pestalozzi to John Dewey have claimed, that students learn by using a combination of thinking and doing, then the computer is a most efficient tool for helping students to sharpen their intellectual skills.

There is currently a discussion among educators as to whether students need only be taught how to operate computers or whether they also need to be taught how to program them. Even for students who are not going into computer science – perhaps especially for students who are not going into computer science – it would be helpful to teach some minimum programming skills. For, to teach a student how to operate a computer without also teaching programming is like teaching a student how to read without also teaching writing. There is an old saying that says, "give someone a fish and they will eat for a day, but teach someone how to fish and they will eat for a lifetime." A similar situation exists in teaching programming skills. The need for a modicum of independence and autonomy in the coming programmer-dominated age makes this skill – or at least an acquaintance with this skill – a necessity. Thus, it seems that some minimal programming ability should be included in the understanding of what it is to be fully computer literate in today's world.

2.5 Affectivity

Affectivity, as used here, means the quality of possessing emotions. It is this human quality that connects with the educational concerns of interest and motivation. Clearly, the computer is a good motivator. Many teachers regularly allow use of it as a means of reward for students. In the days before computers were omnipresent in our society, students were known to break into school after hours in order to use them. What is it about the computer that motivates students so highly? One thing seems to be its ability to involve students. It appeals to a number of the senses, most often those of sight, touch, and sound. In particular, the graphics capability of the computer is a powerful motivator. If a picture is worth a thousand words, and if many students are more visually oriented than aurally oriented,[2] then it is easy to see why this aspect of the computer is so engaging. Moreover, computer graphics need not be presented ready-made and static, as in a book. They can be drawn by the computer as the student watches, or even participates in the drawing. It is this dynamic aspect of the computer that is one of its most appealing features.

2.6 Responsiveness

It has often been said that learning is an active process. The teacher can teach all day, but if there is no response on the part of the student then no learning will take place. In the traditional classroom it is possible for the student to avoid this dialogical process, but on the computer it is not. The student must enter a response through the computer terminal at critical points in the program or most programs will not proceed. It is no accident that the premier computer education system in the 1970s was named PLATO after that famous teacher who, along with his mentor Socrates, believed in awakening learning in the student through a process of dialogue.

The student is not the only one who learns through computer dialogue. In writing a computer dialogue, the instructor may learn even more than the student who uses it. In the process of building a dialogue, the instructor must visualize the lesson from the students' viewpoint and must think of program responses to all possible wrong answers that might be given by the student as well as responses to right answers. In fact, in writing a good dialogue the instructor will probably spend more time programming responses for wrong answers than for right ones. This can be a learning experience even for the instructor who is quite advanced in her or his subject area. Also, the practice of soliciting student critique on the instructor's programs can be an occasion for added learning for both the student and the instructor.

Another aspect of responsiveness on the computer is that students get immediate feedback on their answers. In giving tests on the computer, incorrect answers can be immediately remedied. This allows testing to become a learning process for the student, rather than simply an evaluation process so that the instructor can arrive at a grade. Also, correct answers can be immediately reinforced and the student can be psychologically rewarded and encouraged to continue. Whether the answers are correct or incorrect, the student's response is instantly evaluated and immediate branching is possible to either remedial or advanced material consistent with the student's demonstrated ability.

The solution of computer-posed problems on a step-by-step basis also allows the student to obtain information as he or she sees the need for it. This is in keeping with the concept of "just-in-time" learning. According to this concept, information should be given to the student only within the context of an immediate problem, when the student can see the need for the information.

Finally, the computer can provide simulations of situations. The student can then experiment with these situations. This is particularly valuable because of the expense, difficulty, or danger of creating these situations in real life. Examples would include learning to fly an airplane, learning to control environmental pollution, and learning to perform surgery on a patient. In these and other cases, mistakes can be made in a simulated situation rather than in real life.

2.7 Creativity

The computer encourages creativity because it is open to a great variety of programming possibilities. Not only does it give students a number of options for handling learning material and doing their own creative programming, but it also gives instructors a wide choice of possibilities for presenting material. The multisensory capabilities of the computer that were previously discussed could be mentioned again here. Also, the computer indirectly encourages creativity by taking care of "drudge" work such as drills and record keeping and thus frees time for more creative work.

2.8 Conclusion

If the computer fits in so well with human traits, why are some teachers wary of it? Two basic responses could answer this question.

First, some teachers are still unaware of the humanizing possibilities of the computer. They may be familiar with the shortcomings of teaching machines in the past and may feel that the computer is just one more of these machines. If the foregoing observations have not been persuasive of an opposite view, perhaps a comment by the noted computer scientist and educator Thomas Dwyer might have an impact. He said, "We have found that computing, placed in the hands of well-supported teachers and students, can be an agent for catalyzing educational accomplishment of a kind that is without precedent. We believe that there has simply been no other tool like it in the history of education."[3]

Second, some teachers have themselves been highly successful under the traditional instructional system and hence tend to react to what they suspect might make for radical changes in this system. The computer may indeed make for radical changes, but if these changes will result in more effective learning and a more humanized style of education then the computer is not to be feared.

2.9 Chapter Summary

This chapter presented a sketch of the relationship between computers and a humanistic view of human development. First, it was postulated that the computer is very similar to the human being in its design and method of operation since both act according to the model of input, processing, and output. People, however, often see the computer as the antithesis of what it means to be human. On the contrary, the computer can enhance characteristics needed to be fully human. The computer can help one control one's own aims and purposes, thus supporting the human characteristic of autonomy. It can support the characteristic of individuality by allowing humans to gain knowledge in their own uniquely chosen ways. The computer relates to the characteristic of rationality by helping people learn how to think using the problem-solving method. The characteristic of affectivity is promoted by the computer since it serves as a good motivator of people, appealing to the senses with its graphics. The computer promotes the characteristic of responsiveness by involving people in dialogue and providing simulations and immediate feedback. Finally, the computer encourages the characteristic of creativity because it is open to a variety of programming possibilities and because it can free up time by taking care of drudgery such as drills and record keeping.

2.10 Your Turn

Question 1. Are there any human characteristics mentioned in this chapter (i.e., autonomy, individuality, rationality, affectivity, responsiveness, and creativity) that you do not agree are characteristics of what it means to be fully human? If so, why do you not agree?

Question 2. Are there other characteristics of what it means to be fully human that you would like to add, besides those mentioned in this chapter?

THREE

Philosophic Belief Systems

3.1 Introduction

Almost everyone would agree on the need for ethical standards. The problem comes in determining how those standards are to be derived. The area of philosophy known as "metaethics" is helpful in this task. However, metaethics is subject to misunderstanding. William Halverson regards metaethics as "The generic name for inquiries that have as their object the language of moral appraisal."[1] This definition reflects the viewpoint of a philosophy known as Philosophical Analysis. Metaethics is perhaps better conceived of as the generic name for inquiries about the source of moral judgments (i.e., about the foundation of moral judgments) and how such judgments can be justified. Taken in this sense, metaethics is not about isolated individual judgments concerning whether certain actions are right or wrong. It is about how a particular worldview – or more precisely, a weltanschauung – underlies and determines the formulation of such ethical judgments. This is an abstract way of saying, "What you think the meaning of life is, determines how you live it."

Before one can make a judgment on whether a particular action is right or wrong, one must have adopted a weltanschauung, that is, have made an assumption that life and reality have a particular meaning. After that, one can ask whether a particular action is in harmony with one's basic understanding of the meaning of life and reality and thus one can judge whether that action is right or wrong. In philosophy, the study of the basic meaning of reality is called metaphysics. A person's metaphysics is basically a statement of that person's belief about fundamental reality. It is a "belief" because it is the most fundamental of all assumptions one can make. As such, this assumption cannot be proven. The ancients defined metaphysics as "first principles" because only once one assumes a ground of meaning, or a worldview, can one go on to interpret the meaning of particular things and actions within that larger universe of meaning. Perhaps the reason that there exists a multiplicity of metaphysical theories is that each person must ultimately give a personal explanation of the meaning of life and reality – and there are a number of such possible meanings. Once a person adopts a metaphysical worldview, that worldview will necessarily govern that person's decisions about ethical matters – assuming that the person is ethically consistent. To put this another way, a person's viewpoint on reality will determine that person's viewpoint on value questions.

This chapter is titled "Philosophic Belief Systems." A system is a unified whole made up of interdependent parts. A part is said to be interdependent if it is necessary for the performance of the unit's functions. To be interdependent, it must depend on the other parts and the other parts must depend on it. Take, for example, a microcomputer system. In order for a microcomputer to work, the following parts are needed: 1) An input device (e.g., a keyboard) to supply data to the computer; 2) A microprocessor to compare or to change the data (i.e., to process it in some way); 3) An output device (e.g., a monitor, printer, or storage disk) to receive and/or display the results of the data processing. Notice that each part of this trio (input device, processor, and output device) depends on the other parts to do its job. If one of the parts is removed, no results will be received/displayed. It is also worth noting that the parts must be "compatible." That is, they must interface, or work together, properly. You cannot, for example, run a Windows software package on a LINUX operating system (at least not without using an implementation like "Wine") because they are not designed to work together.

There are philosophic systems, just as there are computer systems. There are essentially four such systems in philosophy. These are Idealism, Realism, Pragmatism (sometimes known as Consequentialism or Utilitarianism), and Existentialism. Other systems are sometimes mentioned, but all of them can be subsumed under these four philosophies (e.g., Virtue Ethics is essentially a form of Realism, while Act Utilitarianism and Rule Utilitarianism are essentially forms of Pragmatism). A synopsis of each of these four basic systems will be given. Idealism and Realism are absolutist philosophies. That is, these philosophies assume reality does not depend on external relationships. This is true whether reality is conceived to be spiritual or mental (as with the Idealists) or whether it is conceived to be material (as with the Realists). Pragmatism and Existentialism are relativist philosophies. That is, these philosophies assume that reality does depend on external relationships. This is true whether these relationships are consequences (as with the Pragmatists) or one's own subjective outlook (as with the Existentialists). Additional notes on a nonsystem called Philosophical Analysis (also known as Logical Analysis or Linguistic Analysis) will be given. Philosophic systems, like other kinds of systems, are composed of interdependent parts. The parts of a philosophic system are metaphysics (practically indistinguishable from what is sometimes called ontology), epistemology, and axiology. Axiology is, in turn, divided into ethics and aesthetics.

Metaphysics is the theory of the ultimate nature of reality. It asks the question: what is real, or put another way, what does reality mean? It is the starting point for all other philosophical questions and determines a person's views on knowledge and value.

Epistemology is the theory of truth or knowledge. It asks the question: what is true, and how do we come to know that truth? We will consider epistemology only briefly here to see how it fits into each philosophy. Metaphysics, however, is what basically influences ethics.

Axiology is the theory of value or worth. It asks the questions: what is good and what is bad? Axiology is made up of two categories: ethics, which is the theory of the goodness or badness of human behavior, and aesthetics, which is the theory of the goodness or badness of visual appearance or audible sound (expressed in terms of beauty or ugliness). We will give only a brief consideration to aesthetics in this analysis of computer ethics since aesthetics is a different category of value than ethics. It is not concerned with the rightness or wrongness of human actions.

The parts of a philosophic system must be compatible with one another, just as the parts in a computer system must be compatible with one another. A person's view of reality (metaphysics) must be consistent with how that person thinks reality is known (epistemology) and how that person thinks reality is to be valued (axiology). As will be seen, it would be incompatible for a person with, for instance, an Idealistic view of reality to adopt a Pragmatic view of value.

Metaphysics (one's explanation of reality) is the fundamental, or controlling, element of philosophy. Metaphysics determines epistemology and axiology. That is, the way you explain reality will determine how you explain knowledge and value. In other words, if you tell me what your view of reality is (i.e., what you think the meaning of life and the universe is) then I can predict how you will think knowledge is to be gained and what you will think is of value.

3.2 Idealism

Idealist Metaphysics

The person with an Idealist worldview believes that reality is basically mental, rather than physical. For the Idealist, the idea is more real than the thing, since the thing only reflects or represents the idea. The world of spirit or idea (i.e., the immaterial world) is static (it does not change) and absolute (it is not defined in relation to anything else). Socrates (470–399 BCE) and Plato (ca. 427–ca. 327 BCE) are perhaps the best-known ancient representatives of this view.

Plato's parable of the Cave illustrates the Idealist view of what reality is. In his dialogue titled *The Republic*, Socrates is dialoging with Glaucon (whose comments, like all of Socrates' respondents, are usually limited to phrases like, "But of course, Socrates!"). Socrates asks Glaucon to image a cave where people have been chained since their childhood so that it is only possible for them to see the wall of the cave straight in front of them. They cannot turn around and see that, behind them, people are moving back and forth. But there is a fire burning behind these people that causes their shadows to be cast on the wall and the chained people can see these shadows. Also the voices of the moving people behind those who are chained echo off the wall and are heard by the chained people, giving the impression to them that the voices are coming from the shadows on the wall. Socrates concludes, with Glaucon's consent of course, that the chained people will believe that reality consists of the

Figure 3.1. Plato

shadows that they see on the wall and the echoes that they hear coming from it. Imagine their surprise, says Socrates, if the chained people were released and were able to turn around and face the light. They would be confused and would at first prefer to go back to the shadows rather than to face the reality that was causing the shadows. They would be even more surprised if they were reluctantly dragged out of the cave and forced to look at the sun itself. It would take them quite a while to become accustomed to the real world, but eventually they would come to understand that the world of light is to be preferred to the world of shadows.

Socrates goes on to explain that in the world of knowledge the idea of the Good appears last of all and is seen only with much effort. But when it is seen, it is understood to be the author of all things beautiful and right. Thus, Socrates concludes, ultimate reality is not to be found in this world of shadows that our senses experience. It is to be found in the world of ideas, which only our minds can experience.[2]

Idealist Epistemology

Since reality is mental or "spiritual," Idealists believe that knowledge results from the mind grasping reality. Since the mind and the ideas that it knows are immaterial, the process of knowing is entirely abstract. Use of reason is thus a primary concern for the Idealist.

Idealist Ethics

For the Idealist, goodness is found in the ideal, that is, in perfection. It is found on the immaterial level, that is, in the perfect concept, or notion, or idea, of something. Thus, perfect goodness is never to be found in the material world. Evil, for the Idealist, consists of the absence or distortion of the ideal. It is a breaking of the eternal law. Goodness involves conformity to the ideal. Since ideals can never change (because they are static and absolute), moral imperatives concerning them do not admit of exceptions. That is, these imperatives are stated in terms of "always" or "never." For example: "Always tell the truth" or (put negatively) "Never tell a lie." Since truth is the knowledge of ideal reality and a lie is a distortion of that reality, truth must always be told and lying can never be fully justified. Idealists judge solely on the action itself and not on the results of the action. If an action is wrong then it may not be performed even if its performance results in a great deal of good. Sometimes an Idealist might excuse the performance of a wrong action on the grounds that it is the "lesser of two evils." For example, breaking into a computer to get vital medical information might be justified if it was necessary to save a life. This would not make the action good, but would be a lesser evil than allowing a person to die if the vital medical information was not obtained.

Immanuel Kant (1724–1804) was a relatively modern Idealist. Consult Geoffrey Sayre-McCord's commentary on "Kant's Grounding for the Metaphysics of Morals" for an introduction on Kant's ethical theory.[3] Kant believed that moral principle could be summed up in what he called the Categorical Imperative. He had two formulations of this Imperative, each of which he considered equivalent to the other. The first was: "Act only according to that maxim by which you can at the same time will that it should become a universal law." This is very close to the Golden Rule enunciated by Jesus: "Do to others what you would want them to do to you." The great Rabbi Hillel put this same thought in negative form during the first century of the Common Era when he said: "That which is hateful to you, do not do to your fellow." The second formulation of Kant's Categorical Imperative was: "Act so that you treat humanity, whether in your own person or in that of another, always as an end and never as a means only."[4] Notice that Kant does not say simply "never as a means," but rather "never as a means *only*." The Categorical Imperative is not influenced by any conditions or circumstances or achievement of results. It is to be done simply because a person has a duty to do it and not for the reason of any good results that might come from doing it. It is to be done simply because it is the right thing to do. If something that is done is to be judged good, then it must be done for reasons that would be acceptable to any person. If it is good to do, then it must be good for everyone to do. The demands of this imperative are universal and thus the requirement that everyone be treated the same.

An Illustration of Idealist Ethics

This illustration is taken from Plato's dialogue known as the *Crito*.[5] The setting is a prison where Socrates had been kept while awaiting execution after his conviction by the citizens of Athens for misleading the Athenian youth. He is visited by Crito, who tells Socrates that he and his friends have made plans for Socrates' escape from prison so that he may avoid the death penalty. The dialogue then continues between Crito and Socrates:

Socr. Why have you come at this hour, Crito? Is it not very early?

Cri. It is.

Socr. About what time?

Cri. Scarce day-break.

Socr. I wonder how the keeper of the prison came to admit you.

Cri. He is familiar with me, Socrates, from my having frequently come hither; and he is under some obligations to me.

Socr. Have you just now come, or some time since?

Cri. A considerable time since.

Socr. Why, then, did you not wake me at once, instead of sitting down by me in silence?

Cri. By Jupiter! Socrates, I should not myself like to be so long awake, and in such affliction. But I have been for some time wondering at you, perceiving how sweetly you slept; and I purposely did not awake you, that you might pass your time as pleasantly as possible. And, indeed, I have often before throughout your whole life considered you happy in your disposition, but far more so in the present calamity, seeing how easily and meekly you bear it.

Socr. However, Crito, it would be disconsonant for a man at my time of life to repine because he must needs die.

Cri. But others, Socrates, at your age have been involved in similar calamities, yet their age has not hindered their repining at their present fortune.

Socr. So it is. But why did you come so early?

Cri. Bringing sad tidings, Socrates, not sad to you, as it appears, but to me, and all your friends, sad and heavy, and which I, I think, shall bear worst of all.

Socr. What tidings? Has the ship arrived from Delos, on the arrival of which I must die?

Cri. It has not yet arrived, but it appears to me that it will come today, from what certain persons report who have come from Sunium, and left it there. It is clear, therefore, from these messengers, that it will come today, and consequently it will be necessary, Socrates, for you to die tomorrow.

Socr. But with good fortune, Crito, and if so it please the gods, so be it. I do not think, however, that it will come today.

Cri. Whence do you form this conjecture?

Socr. I will tell you. I must die on the day after that on which the ship arrives.

Cri. So they say who have the control of these things.

Socr. I do not think, then, that it will come today, but tomorrow. I conjecture this from a dream which I had this very night, not long ago, and you seem very opportunely to have refrained from waking me.

Cri. But what was this dream?

Socr. A beautiful and majestic woman, clad in white garments seemed to approach me, and to call to me and say, "Socrates, three days hence you will reach fertile Pythia."

Cri. What a strange dream, Socrates!

Socr. Very clear, however, as it appears to me, Crito.

Cri. Very much so, as it seems. But, my dear Socrates, even now be persuaded by me, and save yourself. For if you die, not only a single calamity will befall me, but, besides being deprived of such a friend as I shall never meet with again, I shall also appear to many who do not know you and me well, when I might have saved you had I been willing to spend my money, to have neglected to do so. And what character can be more disgraceful than this – to appear to value one's riches more than one's friends? For the generality of men will not be persuaded that you were unwilling to depart hence, when we urged you to it.

Socr. But why, my dear Crito, should we care so much for the opinion of the many? For the most worthy men, whom we ought rather to regard, will think that matters have transpired as they really have.

Cri. Yet you see, Socrates, that it is necessary to attend to the opinion of the many. For the very circumstances of the present case show that the multitude are able to effect not only the smallest evils, but even the greatest, if any one is calumniated to them.

Socr. Would, O Crito that the multitude could effect the greatest evils, that they might also effect the greatest good, for then it would be well. But now they can do neither; for they can make a man neither wise nor foolish; but they do whatever chances.

Cri. So let it be, then. But answer me this, Socrates: are you not anxious for me and other friends, lest, if you should escape from hence, informers should give us trouble, as having secretly carried you off, and so we should be compelled either to lose all our property, or a very large sum, or to suffer something else besides this? For, if you fear any thing of the kind, dismiss your fears; for we are justified in running the risk to save you – and, if need be, even a greater risk than this. But be persuaded by me, and do not refuse.

Socr. I am anxious about this, Crito, and about many other things.

Cri. Do not fear this, however; for the sum is not large on receipt of which certain persons are willing to save you, and take you hence. In the next place, do you not see how cheap these informers are, so that there would be no need of a large sum for them? My fortune is at your service, sufficient, I think, for the purpose; then if, out of regard to me, you do not think right to spend my money, these strangers here are ready to spend theirs. One of them, Simmias the Theban, has brought with him a sufficient sum for the very purpose. Cebes, too, is ready, and very many others. So that, as I said, do not, through fears of this kind, hesitate to save yourself, nor let what you said in court give you any trouble, that if you went from hence you would not know what to do with yourself. For in many places, and wherever you go, men will love you; and if you are disposed to go to Thessaly, I have friends there who will esteem you very highly, and will insure your safety, so that no one in Thessaly will molest you.

Moreover, Socrates, you do not appear to me to pursue a just course in giving yourself up when you might be saved; and you press on the very results with respect to yourself which your enemies would press, and have pressed, in their anxiety to destroy you. Besides this, too, you appear to me to betray your own sons, whom, when it is in your power to rear and educate them, you will abandon, and, so far as you are concerned, they will meet with such a fate as chance brings them, and, as is probable, they will meet with such things as orphans are wont to experience in a state of orphanage. Surely one ought not to have children, or one should go through the toil of rearing and instructing them. But you appear to me to have chosen the most indolent course; though you ought to have chosen such a course as a good and brave man would have done, since you profess to have made virtue your study through the whole of your life; so that I am ashamed both for you and for us who are your friends, lest this whole affair of yours should seem to be the effect of cowardice on our part – your appearing to stand your trial in the court, since you appeared when it was in your power not to have done so, the very manner in which the trial was conducted, and this last circumstance, as it were, a ridiculous consummation of the whole business; your appearing to have escaped from us through our indolence and cowardice, who did not save you; nor did you save yourself, when it was practicable and possible, had we but exerted ourselves a little. Think of these things, therefore, Socrates, and beware, lest, besides the evil that will result, they be disgraceful both to you and to us; advise, then, with yourself; though, indeed, there is no longer time for advising – your resolve should be already made. And there is but one plan; for in the following night the whole must be accomplished. If we delay, it will be impossible and no longer practicable. By all means, therefore, Socrates, be persuaded by me, and on no account refuse.

Socr. My dear Crito, your zeal would be very commendable were it united with right principle; otherwise, by how much the more earnest it is, by so much is it the more sad. We must consider, therefore, whether this plan should be adopted or not. For I not now only, but always, am a person who will obey nothing within me but reason, according as it appears to me on mature deliberation to be best. And the reasons which I formerly professed I can not now reject, because this misfortune has befallen me; but they appear to me in much the same light, and I respect and honor them as before; so that if we are unable to adduce any better at the present time, be assured that I shall not give in to you, even though the power of the multitude should endeavor to terrify us like children, by threatening more than it does now, bonds and death, and confiscation of property. How, therefore, may we consider the matter most conveniently? First of all, if we recur to the argument which you used about opinions, whether on former occasions it was rightly resolved or not, that we ought to pay attention to some opinions, and to others not; or whether, before it was necessary that I should die, it was rightly resolved; but now it has become clear that it was said idly for argument's sake, though in reality it was merely jest and trifling. I desire then, Crito, to consider, in common with you, whether it will appear to me in a different light, now that I am in this condition, or the same, and whether we shall give it up or yield to it. It was said, I think, on former occasions, by those who were thought to speak seriously, as I just now observed, that of the opinions which men entertain some should be very highly esteemed and others not. By the gods! Crito, does not this appear to you to be well said? For you, in all human probability, are out of all danger of dying tomorrow, and the present calamity will not lead your judgment astray. Consider, then; does it not appear to you to have been rightly settled that we ought not to respect all the opinions of men, but some we should, and others not? Nor yet the opinions of all men, but of some we should, and of others not? What say you? Is not this rightly resolved?

Cri. It is.

Socr. Therefore we should respect the good, but not the bad?

Cri. Yes.

Socr. And are not the good those of the wise, and the bad those of the foolish?

Cri. How can it be otherwise?

Socr. Come, then: how, again, were the following points settled? Does a man who practices gymnastic exercises and applies himself to them, pay attention to the praise and censure and opinion of every one, or of that one man only who happens to be a physician, or teacher of the exercises?

Cri. Of that one only.

Socr. He ought, therefore, to fear the censures and covet the praises of that one, but not those of the multitude.

Cri. Clearly.

Socr. He ought, therefore, so to practice and exercise himself, and to eat and drink, as seems fitting to the one who presides and knows, rather than to all others together.

Cri. It is so.

Socr. Well, then, if he disobeys the one, and disregards his opinion and praise, but respects that of the multitude and of those who know nothing, will he not suffer some evil?

Cri. How should he not?

Socr. But what is this evil? Whither does it tend, and on what part of him that disobeys will it fall?

Cri. Clearly on his body, for this it ruins.

Socr. You say well. The case is the same, too, Crito, with all other things, not to go through them all. With respect then, to things just and unjust, base and honorable, good and evil, about which we are now consulting, ought we to follow the opinion of the multitude, and to respect it, or that of one, if there is any one who understands, whom we ought to reverence and respect rather than all others together? And if we do not obey him, shall we not corrupt and injure that part of ourselves which becomes better by justice, but is ruined by injustice? Or is this nothing?

Cri. I agree with you, Socrates.

Socr. Come, then, if we destroy that which becomes better by what is wholesome, but is impaired by what is unwholesome, through being persuaded by those who do not understand, can we enjoy life when that is impaired? And this is the body we are speaking of, is it not?

Cri. Yes.

Socr. Can we, then, enjoy life with a diseased and impaired body?

Cri. By no means.

Socr. But can we enjoy life when that is impaired which injustice ruins but justice benefits? Or do we think that to be of less value than the body, whatever part of us it may be, about which injustice and justice are concerned?

Cri. By no means.

Socr. But of more value?

Cri. Much more.

Socr. We must not then, my excellent friend, so much regard what the multitude will say of us, but what he will say who understands the just and the unjust, the one, even truth itself. So that at first you did not set out with a right principle, when you laid it down that we ought to regard the opinion of the multitude with respect to things just and honorable and good, and their contraries. How ever, some one may say, are not the multitude able to put us to death?

Cri. This, too, is clear, Socrates, any one might say so.

Socr. You say truly. But, my admirable friend, this principle which we have just discussed appears to me to be the same as it was before. And consider this, moreover, whether it still holds good with us or not, that we are not to be anxious about living but about living well.

Cri. It does hold good.

Socr. And does this hold good or not, that to live well and Honorable [sic] and justly are the same thing?

Cri. It does.

Socr. From what has been admitted, then, this consideration arises, whether it is just or not that I should endeavor to leave this place without the permission of the Athenians. And should it appear to be just, we will make the attempt, but if not, we will give it up. But as to the considerations which you mention, of an outlay of money, reputation, and the education of children, beware, Crito, lest such considerations as these in reality belong to these multitudes, who rashly put one to death, and would restore one to life, if they could do so, without any reason at all. But we, since reason so requires, must consider nothing else than what we just now mentioned, whether we shall act justly in paying money and contracting obligations to those who will lead me hence, as well they who lead me as we who are led hence, or whether, in truth, we shall not act unjustly in doing all these things. And if we should appear in so doing to be acting unjustly, observe that we must not consider whether from remaining here and continuing quiet we must needs die, or suffer any thing else, rather than whether we shall be acting unjustly.

Cri. You appear to me to speak wisely, Socrates, but see what we are to do.

Socr. Let us consider the matter together, my friend, and if you have any thing to object to what I say, make good your objection, and I will yield to you, but if not, cease, my excellent friend, to urge upon me the same thing so often, that I ought to depart hence against the will of the Athenians. For I highly esteem your endeavors to persuade me thus to act, so long as it is not against my will. Consider, then, the beginning of our inquiry, whether it is stated to your entire satisfaction, and endeavor to answer the question put to you exactly as you think right.

Cri. I will endeavor to do so.

Socr. Say we, then, that we should on no account deliberately commit injustice, or may we commit injustice under certain circumstances, under others not? Or is it on no account either good or honorable to commit injustice, as we have often agreed on former occasions, and as we just now said? Or have all those our former admissions been dissipated in these few days, and have we, Crito, old men as we are, been for a long time seriously conversing with each other without knowing that we in no respect differ from children? Or does the case, beyond all question, stand as we then determined? Whether the multitude allow it or not, and whether we must suffer a more severe or a milder punishment than this, still is injustice on every account both evil and disgraceful to him who commits it? Do we admit this, or not?

Cri. We do admit it.

Socr. On no account, therefore, ought we to act unjustly.

Cri. Surely not.

Socr. Neither ought one who is injured to return the injury, as the multitude think, since it is on no account right to act unjustly.

Cri. It appears not.

Socr. What, then? Is it right to do evil, Crito, or not?

Cri. Surely it is not right, Socrates.

Socr. But what? To do evil in return when one has been evil-entreated, is that right, or not?

Cri. By no means.

Socr. For to do evil to men differs in no respect from committing injustice.

Cri. You say truly.

Socr. It is not right, therefore, to return an injury, or to do evil to any man, however one may have suffered from him. But take care, Crito, that in allowing these things you do not allow them contrary to your opinion, for I know that to some few only these things both do appear, and will appear, to be true. They, then, to whom these things appear true, and they to whom they do not, have no sentiment in common, and must needs despise each other, while they look to each other's opinions. Consider well, then, whether you coincide and think with me, and whether we can begin our deliberations from this point – that it is never right either to do an injury or to return an injury, or when one has been evil-entreated, to revenge one's self by doing evil in return, or do you dissent from, and not coincide in this principle? For so it appears to me, both long since and now, but if you in any respect think otherwise, say so and inform me. But if you persist in your former opinions, hear what follows.

Cri. I do persist in them, and think with you. Speak on, then.

Socr. I say next, then, or rather I ask; whether when a man has promised to do things that are just he ought to do them, or evade his promise?

Cri. He ought to do them.

Socr. Observe, then, what follows. By departing hence without the leave of the city, are we not doing evil to some, and that to those to whom we ought least of all to do it, or not? And do we abide by what we agreed on as being just, or do we not?

Cri. I am unable to answer your question, Socrates; for I do not understand it.

Socr. Then, consider it thus. If, while we were preparing to run away, or by whatever name we should call it, the laws and commonwealth should come, and, presenting themselves before us, should say, "Tell me, Socrates, what do you purpose doing? Do you design any thing else by this proceeding in which you are engaged than to destroy us, the laws, and the whole city, so far as you are able? Or do you think it possible for that city any longer to subsist, and not be subverted, in which judgments that are passed have no force, but are set aside and destroyed by private persons?" – what should we say, Crito, to these and similar remonstrances? For any one, especially an orator, would have much to say on the violation of the law, which enjoins that judgments passed shall be enforced. Shall we say to them that the city has done us an injustice, and not passed a right sentence? Shall we say this, or what else?

Cri. This, by Jupiter! Socrates.

Socr. What, then, if the laws should say, "Socrates, was it not agreed between us that you should abide by the judgments which the city should pronounce?" And if we should wonder at their speaking thus, perhaps they would say, "Wonder not, Socrates, at what we say, but answer, since you are accustomed to make use of questions and answers. For, come, what charge have you against us and the city, that you attempt to destroy us? Did we not first give you being? and did not your father, through us, take your mother to wife and beget you? Say, then, do you find fault with those laws among us that relate to marriage as being bad?" I should say, "I do not find fault with them." "Do you with those that relate to your nurture when born, and the education with which you were instructed? Or did not the laws, ordained on this point, enjoin rightly, in requiring your father to instruct you in music and gymnastic exercises?" I should say, rightly.

Well, then, since you were born, nurtured, and educated through our means, can you say, first of all, that you are not both our offspring and our slave, as well you as your ancestors? And if this be so, do you think that there are equal rights between us? and whatever we attempt to do to you, do you think you may justly do to us in turn? Or had you not equal rights with your father, or master, if you happened to have one, so as to return what you suffered, neither to retort when found fault with, nor, when stricken, to strike again, nor many other things of the kind; but that with your country and the laws you may do so; so that if we attempt to destroy you, thinking it to be just, you also should endeavor, so far as you are able, in return, to destroy us, the laws, and your country; and in doing this will you say that you act justly – you who, in reality, make virtue your chief object? Or are you so wise as not to know that one's country is more honorable, venerable, and sacred, and more highly prized both by gods, and men possessed of understanding, than mother and father, and all other progenitors; and that one ought to reverence, submit to, and appease one's country, when angry, rather than one's father; and either persuade it or do what it orders, and to suffer quietly if it bids one suffer, whether to be beaten, or put in bonds; or if it sends one out to battle there to be wounded or slain, this must be done; for justice so requires, and one must not give way, or retreat, or leave one's post; but that both in war and in a court of justice, and everywhere one must do what one's city and country enjoin, or persuade it in such manner as justice allows; but that to offer violence either to one's mother or father is not holy, much less to one's country? What shall we say to these things, Crito? That the laws speak the truth, or not?

Cri. It seems so to me.

Socr. "Consider, then, Socrates," the laws perhaps might say, "whether we say truly that in what you are now attempting you are attempting to do what is not just toward us. For we, having given you birth, nurtured, instructed you, and having imparted to you and all other citizens all the good in our power, still proclaim, by giving the power to every Athenian who pleases, when he has arrived at years of discretion, and become acquainted with the business of the state, and us, the laws, that any one who is not satisfied with us may take his property, and go wherever he pleases. And if any one of you wishes to go to a colony, if he is not satisfied with us and the city, or to migrate and settle in another country, none of us, the laws, hinder or forbid him going whithersoever he pleases, taking with him all his property. But whoever continues with us after he has seen the manner in which we administer justice, and in other respects govern the city, we now say that he has in fact entered into a compact with us to do what we order; and we affirm that he who does not obey is in three respects guilty of injustice – because he does not obey us who gave him being, and because he does not obey us who nurtured him, and because, having made a compact that he would obey us, he neither does so, nor does he persuade us if we do any thing wrongly; though we propose for his consideration, and do not rigidly command him to do what we order, but leave him the choice of one of two things, either to persuade us, or to do what we require, and yet he does neither of these."

Idealist Aesthetics

When an Idealist wants to visually or audibly represent an idea, his or her approach will be to get that idea across to the viewer or listener. The Idealist is not overly interested in specific or concrete instances, since reality is in the general idea of something, and less in a particular representation of that idea. An Idealist painter, for example, will therefore try to paint the "perfect" person – to bring out the person's inner identity. If the person in the painting had cut herself or himself and had a scar on her/his face, the painter would leave the scar out (or at least idealize it) because the scar is an imperfection – something that should not ideally be there.

3.3 Realism

Realist Metaphysics

The person with a Realist worldview believes that reality is basically matter (i.e., the physical universe), rather than spirit. For the Realist, the thing is more real than the idea. Whatever exists is therefore

Figure 3.2. John Locke

primarily material, natural, and physical. "Whatever exists at all exists in some amount" (as Edward Lee Thorndike, one of the first experimental psychologists, has said).[6] It exists independently of any mind and is governed by the laws of nature, primary among which are the laws of cause and effect. The universe, according to the Realist, is one of natural design and order. Aristotle (384–322 BCE) was an early representative of this view. John Locke exemplified this philosophy in the seventeenth century.

Professor John Searle (1932–) of the University of California, Berkeley, is a contemporary Realist. He holds the position that mental states are merely variable states of neuron firing, that consciousness is a feature of the brain, and that brains cause minds. In other words, thinking is just neurons firing.[7] I once asked Marvin Minsky, one of the pioneers of artificial intelligence, if his own position that mental states were a matter of setting switches in the brain wasn't close to Searle's position. His reply follows:

Yes, except that terms like 'just' or 'merely' miss the incredible complexity of the relations between cells, switches, or atoms. That's like saying that the world is just atoms or literature is just words. There should be a better word than "reductionism" to describe the view that a system's properties depend on the relationships between the parts. There's a nice statement that I quoted in my book, *The Society of Mind*: "It has been the persuasion of an immense majority of human beings that sensibility and thought [as distinguished from matter] are, in their own nature, less susceptible of division and decay, and that, when the body is resolved into its elements, the principle which animated it will remain perpetual and unchanged. However, it is probable that what we call thought is not an actual being, but no more than the relation between certain parts of that infinitely varied mass, of which the rest of the universe is composed, and which ceases to exist as soon as those parts change their position with respect to each other. – Percy Bysshe Shelley[8]

Realist Epistemology

For the Realist, knowledge is gained through the senses. Reality exists in the material object, not in the immaterial mind. Therefore, it is the mind that must conform to the object – not the object to the mind. This conformity of the mind to the object is done through the senses and is an entirely physical process. Science is thus a primary concern for the Realist.

Realist Ethics

For the Realist, the baseline of value is that which is natural, that is, that which is in conformity with nature. Nature is good. One need not look beyond nature to some immaterial ideal for a standard of right and wrong. Rather, goodness will be found by living a life of virtue in harmony with nature. Evil, for the Realist, is a departure from this natural norm either in the direction of excess or defect (i.e., having, or doing, too much or too little of something which is naturally good). It is a breaking of the natural law.

An Illustration of Realist Ethics

This illustration consists of two paragraphs, one from Book I and one from Book II of Aristotle's *Nicomachean Ethics*.

With those who identify happiness with virtue or some one virtue our account is in harmony; for to virtue belongs virtuous activity. But it makes, perhaps, no small difference whether we place the chief good in possession or in use, in state of mind or in activity. For the state of mind may exist without producing any good result, as in a man who is asleep or in some other way quite inactive, but the activity cannot; for one who has the activity will of necessity be acting, and acting well. And as in the Olympic Games it is not the most beautiful and the strongest that are crowned but those who compete (for it is some of these that are victorious), so those who act win, and rightly win, the noble and good things in life.[9]

That moral virtue is a mean, then, and in what sense it is so, and that it is a mean between two vices, the one involving excess, the other deficiency, and that it is such because its character is to aim at what is intermediate in passions and in actions, has been sufficiently stated. Hence also it is no easy task to be good. For in everything it is no easy task to find the middle, e.g. to find the middle of a circle is not for every one but for him who knows; so, too, any one can get angry – that is easy – or give or spend money; but to do this to the right person, to the right extent, at the right time, with the right motive, and in the right way, that is not for every one, nor is it easy; wherefore goodness is both rare and laudable and noble.[10]

Realist Aesthetics

In seeking good appearance, or sound, the Realist will look to nature as the standard. Thus, for the Realist, art should imitate nature. If a Realist is painting a portrait of a person who has a facial scar, the Realist will paint the scar because reality includes imperfection.

3.4 Pragmatism

Pragmatist Metaphysics

For the Pragmatist, reality is not so easily pinpointed as it is for the Idealist and Realist. Reality is neither an idea nor is it matter. It would

Figure 3.3. John Dewey

be a mistake to view reality as either a spiritual or physical "something." Rather, the Pragmatist believes that reality is a *process*. It is a dynamic coming-to-be rather than a static, fixed being. It is change, happening, activity, and interaction. In short, it is experience. Reality is more like a verb than a noun. It is flux and flow where the concentration is not so much on the things as on the relationship between the things. Since everything changes, nothing can have any permanent essence or identity. An ancient Greek Pragmatist used to say in this regard: "You can't step in the same river twice." For the Pragmatist, everything is essentially relative. The only constant is change. The only absolute is that there are no absolutes. The British authors Jeremy Bentham (1748–1832) and John Stuart Mill (1806–1873) and the Americans William James (1842–1910) and John Dewey (1859–1952) are representatives of this view.

Pragmatism is essentially a form of Consequentialism or Utilitarianism. Note that William James dedicated his book *Pragmatism* to John Stuart Mill, the father of Utilitarianism, saying that he fancied that Mill would be "our leader were he alive today."[11] It might be helpful to quote from William James here on the subject of Pragmatist metaphysics:

It is astonishing to see how many philosophical disputes collapse into insignificance the moment you subject them to this simple test of tracing a concrete consequence. There can BE no difference anywhere that doesn't MAKE a difference elsewhere – no difference in abstract truth that doesn't express itself in a difference in concrete fact and in conduct consequent upon that fact, imposed on somebody, somehow, somewhere and somewhen. The whole function of philosophy ought to be to find out what definite difference it will make to you and me, at definite instants of our life, if this world-formula or that world-formula be the true one.

There is absolutely nothing new in the pragmatic method. Socrates was an adept at it. Aristotle used it methodically. Locke, Berkeley, and Hume made momentous contributions to truth by its means. Shadworth Hodgson keeps insisting that realities are only what they are 'known-as.' But these forerunners of pragmatism used it in fragments: they were preluders only. Not until in our time has it generalized itself, become conscious of a universal mission, pretended to a conquering destiny. I believe in that destiny, and I hope I may end by inspiring you with my belief.

Pragmatism represents a perfectly familiar attitude in philosophy, the empiricist attitude, but it represents it, as it seems to me, both in a more radical and in a less objectionable form than it has ever yet assumed. A pragmatist turns his back resolutely and once for all upon a lot of inveterate habits dear to professional philosophers. He turns away from abstraction and insufficiency, from verbal solutions, from bad a priori reasons, from fixed principles, closed systems, and pretended absolutes and origins. He turns towards concreteness and adequacy, towards facts, towards action, and towards power. That means the empiricist temper regnant, and the rationalist temper sincerely given up. It means the open air and possibilities of nature, as against dogma, artificiality and the pretence of finality in truth.

At the same time it does not stand for any special results. It is a method only. But the general triumph of that method would mean an enormous change in what I called in my last lecture the 'temperament' of philosophy. Teachers of the ultra-rationalistic type would be frozen out, much as the courtier type is frozen out in republics, as the ultramontane type of priest is frozen out in protestant lands. Science and metaphysics would come much nearer together, would in fact work absolutely hand in hand.

Metaphysics has usually followed a very primitive kind of quest. You know how men have always hankered after unlawful magic, and you know what a great part, in magic, WORDS have always played. If you have his name, or the formula of incantation that binds him, you can control the spirit, genie, afrite, or whatever the power may be.

Solomon knew the names of all the spirits, and having their names, he held them subject to his will. So the universe has always appeared to the natural mind as a kind of enigma, of which the key must be sought in the shape of some illuminating or power-bringing word or name. That word names the universe's PRINCIPLE, and to possess it is, after a fashion, to possess the universe itself.

'God,' 'Matter,' 'Reason,' 'the Absolute,' 'Energy,' are so many solving names. You can rest when you have them. You are at the end of your metaphysical quest.

But if you follow the pragmatic method, you cannot look on any such word as closing your quest. You must bring out of each word its practical cash-value, set it at work within the stream of your experience. It appears less as a solution, then, than as a program for more work, and more particularly as an indication of the ways in which existing realities may be CHANGED.

THEORIES THUS BECOME INSTRUMENTS, NOT ANSWERS TO ENIG-MAS, IN WHICH WE CAN REST. We don't lie back upon them, we move forward, and, on occasion, make nature over again by their aid. Pragmatism unstiffens all our theories, limbers them up and sets each one at work. Being nothing essentially new, it harmonizes with many ancient philosophic tenden-cies. It agrees with nominalism for instance, in always appealing to particulars; with utilitarianism in emphasizing practical aspects; with positivism in its dis-dain for verbal solutions, useless questions, and metaphysical abstractions.

All these, you see, are ANTI-INTELLECTUALIST tendencies. Against ratio-nalism as a pretension and a method, pragmatism is fully armed and militant. But, at the outset, at least, it stands for no particular results. It has no dogmas, and no doctrines save its method. As the young Italian pragmatist Papini has well said, it lies in the midst of our theories, like a corridor in a hotel. Innumer-able chambers open out of it. In one you may find a man writing an atheistic volume; in the next someone on his knees praying for faith and strength; in a third a chemist investigating a body's properties. In a fourth a system of idealistic metaphysics is being excogitated; in a fifth the impossibility of metaphysics is being shown. But they all own the corridor, and all must pass through it if they want a practicable way of getting into or out of their respective rooms.

No particular results then, so far, but only an attitude of orientation, is what the pragmatic method means. THE ATTITUDE OF LOOKING AWAY FROM FIRST THINGS, PRINCIPLES, 'CATEGORIES,' SUPPOSED NECESSITIES; AND OF LOOKING TOWARDS LAST THINGS, FRUITS, CONSEQUENCES, FACTS.[12]

Pragmatist Epistemology

Given the Pragmatic understanding of reality, the question of knowl-edge becomes somewhat problematic. The mind can certainly not be depended on for knowledge. Even the senses cannot be totally trusted, since things may not be – or continue to be – what they seem to be. The only sure route to knowledge in a world of constant change is to test things and see if they work. There is no fixed and permanent truth. Rather, truth "happens" to a thing. If it is found to work (i.e., to be useful in achieving some end), then it becomes true. When it no longer works toward achieving an end, then it ceases to be true. This testing of knowledge is a "public" test. That is, it is open to anyone's inspection. It must be able to be replicated. If it works for you, it must be able to work for me. Thus, truth is the result of a consensual process. It is an agreement reached by the group (or at least by a majority of the group). It is also tentative, since it is only held as long as it proves to be true (i.e., as long as it is found to be useful). Finally, truth is relative. It is relative to the end or goal to which it is thought to be useful, and it is relative in the sense that it is not always true, but is true only so long as it is useful. Society's judgment is thus a primary concern for the Pragmatist.

Pragmatist Ethics

The Pragmatist believes that value claims must be tested and proven in practice. In the Pragmatist's view, things are value-neutral in themselves. There is nothing that is always good, nor is there anything that is always bad. Thus, the Pragmatist believes that moral judgments should not be based on the action that is done, but rather on the results of that action. It is possible that a Pragmatist might be a pacifist (believing that killing is always wrong). But if a particular Pragmatist would believe that killing is always wrong it would be because that Pragmatist believes that killing always leads to worse consequences than any other action that could be performed, and not because that Pragmatist believes that killing is intrinsically wrong. The value of anything is determined solely in terms of its usefulness in achieving some end. In answer to the question, "Is that good?" a Pragmatist would probably reply, "Is it good for what?" Pragmatist ethics are relativistic, that is, relative to the end to be achieved. Thus, the Pragmatist believes that the end justifies the means. That is, if something is useful for achieving some end or goal, then it becomes good. To state this another way, a means gets its positive value from being an efficient route to the achievement of an end. The more efficient a means is in bringing about an end, the better it is. Thus, a means is not valued for its own sake, but only in relation to its usefulness for achieving some end. Results or consequences are the ultimate measure of goodness for a Pragmatist. The usefulness of a means to an end can only be judged after the fact, by its efficiency in bringing about an end. Thus, for the Pragmatist, there can be no assurance that something is good until it is tried. Even then, it can only be held tentatively as good, since a thing is good only as long as it continues to work. Evil, for the Pragmatist, is that which is counterproductive. It is (usually) a breaking of a civil or criminal law.

There can be a dispute about which means are more effective for achieving an end. So there can be a dispute about which ends should, in fact, be pursued. Thus, the Pragmatist looks for guidance to society. The reasons for this are metaphysical: reality is experience, but it is the experience of the whole (the group). For the Pragmatist, the whole is greater than the sum of its parts. This means that the whole is more valuable than any of its parts. Thus, in the field of value judgments, the group's collective wisdom is to be more highly esteemed than the wisdom of any individual within the group. Also, a Pragmatist will base moral judgments on what is best for the greatest number of people. This means that the Pragmatist attempts to achieve "the greatest good for the greatest number." The Pragmatist thus hopes to achieve a mathematical optimization of good results over a minimum of bad results in looking at what should be done in the context of any given group. Pragmatists like Bentham recommended a measure of pleasure over pain as a way of making this calculation. If the alternatives in a situation all seemed to produce varying degrees of bad outcomes, then Bentham recommended choosing the alternative that would produce the least amount of undesirable results.

An Illustration of Pragmatist Ethics

This illustration of Pragmatist ethics is taken from the article "The Moral Philosopher and the Moral Life" by William James.

> On the whole, then, we must conclude that no philosophy of ethics is possible in the old-fashioned absolute sense of the term. Everywhere the ethical philosopher must wait on facts. The thinkers who create the ideals come he knows not whence; their sensibilities are evolved he knows not how; and the question as to which of two conflicting ideals will give the best universe then and there, can be answered

by him only through the aid of the experience of other men. I said some time ago, in treating of the "first" question, that the intuitional moralists deserve credit for keeping most clearly to the psychological facts. They do much to spoil this merit on the whole, however, by mixing with it that dogmatic temper which, by absolute distinctions and unconditional "thou shalt nots," changes a growing, elastic, and continuous life into a superstitious system of relics and dead bones. In point of fact, there are no absolute evils, and there are no non-moral goods; and the *highest* ethical life – however few may be called to bear its burdens – consists at all times in the breaking of rules which have grown too narrow for the actual case. There is but one unconditional commandment, which is that thou shalt seek incessantly, with fear and trembling, so to vote and to act as to bring about the very largest total universe of good which thou canst see.[13]

Pragmatist Aesthetics

In keeping with the Pragmatist value theory, there is no appearance or sound that is, in itself, good or bad. Appearances or sounds take their value from their relationships to group goals. Thus, in the realm of art, values will be determined by the majority view and in relation to the social benefit of the art in question.

3.5 Existentialism

Existentialist Metaphysics

The Existentialist joins with the Pragmatist in rejecting the belief that reality is fixed and static. But instead of believing that reality is a process whose meaning is defined primarily by the controlling group, the Existentialist believes that reality must be determined by each autonomous individual. An atheistic Existentialist, for example, Jean-Paul Sartre (1905–1980), would find the world to be "absurd," that is, literally "without meaning." The meaning of things must be chosen by the individual, and that meaning will hold only for that individual. A theistic Existentialist, for example, Gabriel Marcel (1889–1973), would say that meaning is not so

Figure 3.4. Fyodor Dostoevsky

much chosen as it is "recognized." Either way, each person's world, as well as each person's own identity, is the product of that person's subjective choice or willful perception. Each person is self-defined and each person's world is essentially what that person views it to be. Thus, reality is different for each individual. We each live in our own world and we are who we decide to be. The founder of Existentialism is considered to be the Danish Christian philosopher, Soren Kierkegaard (1813–1855). Fyodor Dostoevsky (1821–1881) was a widely published nineteenth-century Russian Existentialist writer.

Existentialist Epistemology

For the Existentialist, knowledge is an individual matter. An individual must choose his/her own truth. The individual does not discover ideas, but rather creates them. This results in multiple truths – even contradictory truths. The Idealist or Realist, and even the Pragmatist, would call this crazy. But since, in the Existentialist view, each person is the designer of her/his own scheme of truth there is no problem if your view of truth does not agree with mine. What is true for you is not necessarily true for me. We each must choose our own truth. We may, in fact, agree on truth, but we will have independently arrived at this agreement.

Existentialist Ethics

Individual choice and responsibility are primary concerns for the Existentialist. The individual must create his/her own value. There is no escape from the necessity of creating values. Not to decide *is* to decide (that is, not deciding is a matter of *deciding* not to decide). The individual must express her/his own preferences about things. In making choices, or defining values, the individual becomes responsible for those choices. The individual cannot deflect praise or blame for those choices onto others. If the choices were freely made, then responsibility for them must be accepted. While heredity, environment, and society might influence what choices an individual makes, the Existentialist believes there is a zone of freedom within each individual that cannot be conditioned or predetermined. Evil, for the Existentialist, is being false to oneself. It is a breaking of one's personal law. An Existentialist is not necessarily a nonconformist, but if an Existentialist conforms to the values of a group it will be because that person has freely chosen to do so – not because that person has been pressured to do so by the group. An Idealist, a Realist, a Pragmatist, and an Existentialist may all agree upon the morality of a particular action, but they would do so for different reasons. The Idealist because the action conforms to some ideal, the Realist because it is natural, the Pragmatist because it is socially useful, and the Existentialist because she/he has decided (through whatever personal process) that it is good. Individual choice and responsibility are thus primary concerns for the Existentialist.

Existentialism is not necessarily a "selfish" type of philosophy. It is not primarily concerned with one's own interests, but rather with one's own conscience. Far from being a "candy stick" type of philosophy, it is perhaps the hardest philosophy to follow. The Idealist has ideals or divine commands as a guide, the Realist has nature to follow, the Pragmatist has the guidance of the group, but the Existentialist has only himself or herself as the basis for ethical decisions.

An Illustration of Existentialist Ethics

This illustration of Existentialist ethics is a summary of Chapter 5, The Grand Inquisitor, from *The Brothers Karamazov* by Fyodor Dostoevsky.[14] It actually illustrates Existentialism by negation since Dostoevsky, an Existentialist, uses as his main character the Grand Inquisitor, who is the exact opposite of an Existentialist.

In this chapter, Ivan, one of the Karamazov brothers, creates a legend that is set in sixteenth-century Spain during the height of the Inquisition. He describes the Grand Inquisitor as walking down a street one day with his henchmen. He sees in the distance a man who is healing the sick and raising the dead. A crowd gathers and, recognizing the man by his works, the crowd begins to shout: "It is He! It is He!" Immediately understanding what is happening, the Grand Inquisitor orders his henchmen to arrest that man. That night the Grand Inquisitor visits the man in his dungeon cell. He says: "I know who you are, or at least whom you seem to be. You came once before, but you failed man. I have corrected your work. I have chosen to serve man better." He continues by explaining, "the one thing that man cannot bear is his freedom. But instead of taking this awful burden away from him, you only made it worse. You made his responsibility for decisions total, forever binding. But I have lifted this burden from his shoulders. I have freed man from his freedom. In this way, I have protected weak man from himself." Although Dostoevsky's Grand Inquisitor is pictured as being well intentioned and wanting to make humans happy, for the Existentialist he is the greatest of all heretics because his goal is to take away human freedom.

Existentialist Aesthetics

The question of what is good in appearance or sound will be determined, in Existentialist terms, solely by each individual. Value, like reality and truth, must be created by the person. It is not found preexisting, or determined by group consensus. Thus, how value is portrayed will be a

Figure 3.5. Rudolf Carnap

matter of individual preference. What is good art for you may be bad art for me, and vice versa.

3.6 Philosophical Analysis

Philosophical Analysis (also known as Logical Analysis or Linguistic Analysis) is not a true philosophic system. It has no interdependent parts. It might even be considered an antisystem because it holds that the only valid consideration in philosophy is epistemology. It does not believe that metaphysics and axiology can be discussed, for reasons that will be seen. The person most often associated with the formulation of this philosophic view is Ludwig Wittgenstein (1899–1951). Another twentieth-century exponent of this view was Rudolf Carnap (1891–1970).

According to Philosophical Analysis, knowledge may be determined (i.e., verified) in two ways – and only two ways. Those ways are by the use of logic and by the use of sense experience. Logical verification is possible when the predicate of a sentence is contained in the subject of the sentence (e.g., "The black cat is black."). This type of verification is also called analytic verification because the predicate is "analyzed out" of the subject. Sense experience verification is possible when the predicate has no logical relationship to the subject, but when sense observation can establish the truth or falsity of the statement (e.g., "The black cat is wet."). This type of verification is also called synthetic verification because the predicate is observed as being "synthesized" or "joined" to the subject rather than being inherent in it. Logic and sense observation are thus primary concerns for the philosophical analyst.

Since questions of right or wrong are not subject to analysis by logic or by sense experience, those questions are beyond the bounds of verifiable (i.e., logical or sensible) discussion. According to Philosophical Analysis, there are indeed questions of value but they simply cannot be talked about in a logical or sensible way. In this regard, Ludwig Wittgenstein once said that philosophy leaves the essential problems of human life untouched. Axiology is important, but it cannot be discussed. Wittgenstein has written: "What we cannot speak about, we must pass over in silence."[15] Analysts would say that when people speak of something as "good," they are really just expressing their feeling about it. Hence, analysts call these sorts of statements "emotive" statements.

An Illustration of Philosophical Analysis

This illustration of Philosophical Analysis is composed of a series of propositions from Wittgenstein's *Tractatus Logico-Philosophicus*[16]:

6.4 All propositions are of equal value

6.41 The sense of the world must lie outside the world. In the world everything is as it is, and everything happens as it does happen: *in* it no value exists – and if it did exist, it would have no value.

If there is any value that does have value, it must lie outside the whole sphere of what happens and is the case. For all that happens and is the case is accidental.

What makes it non-accidental cannot lie *within* the world, since if it did it would itself be accidental.

It must lie outside the world.

6.42 And so it is impossible for there to be propositions of ethics. Propositions can express nothing that is higher.

6.421 It is clear that ethics cannot be put into words.
Ethics is transcendental.
(Ethics and aesthetics are one and the same.)

6.422 When an ethical law of the form, "Thou shalt . . . ", is laid down, one's first thought is, "And what if I do not do it?" It is clear, however, that ethics has nothing to do with punishment and reward in the usual sense of the terms. So our question about the *consequences* of an action must be unimportant – At least those consequences should not be events. For there must be something right about the question we posed. There must indeed be some kind of ethical reward and ethical punishment, but they must reside in the action itself.

(And it is also clear that the reward must be something pleasant and the punishment something unpleasant.)

3.7 Conclusion

The outline of philosophical views might appear to oversimplify the basis for ethical decision making. I would agree that ethical decision making in real time is a much more difficult process than might appear from the summaries. For instance, our research has found that students had a measurable preference for philosophic views (as will be shown in the next chapter). While most of the students surveyed had a predominant leaning toward one of the four systematic philosophies described, they also had concomitant lesser leanings toward all or most of the other three philosophies. In other words, nobody is one-hundred percent an Idealist, Realist, Pragmatist, or Existentialist.

This means that simply knowing a person's dominant philosophical outlook will not allow assured prediction of how that person might act in response to a given ethical situation. This is true for two reasons: 1) sympathies with other philosophical views besides one's dominant view might end up controlling action in this or that particular situation, and 2) the fact that people do not always act conscientiously in a manner consistent with their beliefs. That is, they might fail to follow through in a particular situation on what they actually believe is the right thing to do.

3.8 Chapter Summary

This chapter begins with a treatment of metaethics, which is the study of the foundation of moral judgments, and then considers the parts of a philosophic system: metaphysics, epistemology, and axiology. Metaphysics is the study of the basic meaning of reality. Epistemology is the study of truth and how we know it. Axiology is the study of value. The chapter then considers the metaphysics and ethics of each of the four basic philosophic views: Idealism, Realism, Pragmatism, and Existentialism. Idealism believes reality is mental or spiritual in nature and therefore that goodness is found in the ideal. Realism believes that reality is material in nature and therefore that goodness is found in following what is natural. Pragmatism believes that reality is a process and therefore that goodness is found by trying things out and finding out what works. Existentialism believes that reality must be defined by each autonomous individual. At the conclusion of each philosophic view an illustration of that view is given using the writings of a philosopher associated with that view. The chapter concludes with a consideration of a nonsystematic philosophy known as Philosophical Analysis. This philosophy believes that the nature of ultimate reality is beyond the ability of language to discuss and therefore that goodness, which depends upon an understanding of reality, is not able to be discussed either.

3.9 Your Turn

Question 1. Do you think one philosophy is better than another? Explain.

Question 2. How would you decide which philosophy you believe is best?

Question 3. Do you see a problem in a person having equal sympathy with both an absolutist philosophy (Idealism or Realism) and a relativist philosophy (Pragmatism or Existentialism)?

FOUR

A Philosophic Inventory

4.1 Introduction

In this chapter you will have the opportunity to complete a philosophic inventory and learn with which philosophic theories you are most in agreement. Answer each of the questions as follows: if you strongly agree, put 2; if you agree, put 1; if you are undecided, put 0; if you disagree, put −1; and if you strongly disagree, put −2.

4.2 Inventory Questions

1. Learning is a process of interacting with people and things around us. It leads to new understandings which can then be used to solve social problems.
2. The human person is primarily a nervous system that is influenced by interaction with the physical environment along lines recognized by science.
3. Education should lead a person to spiritual understanding.
4. Knowledge involves successful adaptation to our surroundings.
5. Knowledge is accurate if it reflects physical, material reality.
6. The human person is basically a spiritual being.
7. The human person discovers knowledge from the physical, material world.
8. Knowledge is meant to be used. It is ultimately a means to survival.
9. Education is basically a process of spiritual growth.
10. Good is anything that results in achieving a goal agreed upon by society.

11. Knowledge is found by considering the practical implications of ideas.

12. The human mind is simply the brain at work.

13. Learning is a process of choosing our identity.

14. The mind is a spiritual entity that determines what reality is (rather than reality determining what the mind is).

15. All true knowledge engages the feelings of the knower.

16. The most important thing in reality is the ability to choose or decide.

17. Intelligence is the ability to know physical, material facts.

18. A person is nobody until she/he takes action. It is in acting (choosing) that a person determines who she/he is.

19. Intelligence is the ability to formulate and test out new solutions to problems.

20. Reality results from God holding the universe in existence by the power of God's thought.

21. The test of any theory or belief must be its effect on us, that is, its practical consequences.

22. Knowledge is objective (rather than subjective), that is, it is in accord with the teachings of physical science concerning the nature of material reality.

23. A person is really the sum of that person's choices up to the current point in that person's life.

24. God is the spiritual summit of reality.

25. Reality basically consists of dealing with questions of love, choice, freedom, personal relationships, and death.

26. Education is a process of stimulating students to search themselves for their identity.

27. True ideas are those we can assimilate, validate, corroborate, and verify experimentally.

28. Knowledge ultimately comes from a supernatural (that is, a divine) source.

29. Since a person acts freely, he/she is responsible for his/her actions.

30. A person must reach beyond this material world to fulfill her/his spiritual destiny.

31. The physical world as experienced by our senses is basically factual, objective reality.
32. Knowledge is that which is useful in achieving a solution to some problem.
33. Reality has its basis and origin in the material, physical world.
34. Obtaining knowledge is basically a process of searching the physical universe for objective facts.
35. People receive knowledge by revelation from God.
36. People can reconstruct (remake) solutions to problems and this results in new knowledge.
37. Reality occurs when a person chooses to face a situation and make a commitment.
38. The mind is biological in origin and can be explained in physical, material terms.
39. The laws by which human conduct is judged are determined by God.
40. Reality ultimately exists in the individual person.

4.3 Inventory Scoring

After answering all of the questions, figure your sub-score for each philosophic theory in this manner: Total the numbers for the ten items that are shown as keyed to Idealism. Then do the same for each set of Realism, Pragmatism, and Existentialism items.

Idealism item numbers are: 3, 6, 9, 14, 20, 24, 28, 30, 35, 39
Realism item numbers are: 2, 5, 7, 12, 17, 22, 31, 33, 34, 38
Pragmatism item numbers are: 1, 4, 8, 10, 11, 19, 21, 27, 32, 36
Existentialism item numbers are: 13, 15, 16, 18, 23, 25, 26, 29, 37, 40

Keep a record of your four sub-scores for Idealism, Realism, Pragmatism, and Existentialism.

Now that you have completed and scored the inventory, you may be interested in how it was composed, how it was validated, and what it means to you. The inventory was derived from a series of eighty philosophical statements first published in 1970 by Colvin Ross of the University of Connecticut. Of the eighty statements, twenty were associated with each of the four basic philosophic views: Idealism, Realism, Pragmatism, and Existentialism. Professor Ross did extensive item analysis on this inventory and tested it for reliability and validity.[1] The eighty statements were later reduced to forty as a result of subsequent research by Josephine C. Barger, Robert N. Barger, and John J. Rearden. This reduction was accomplished by computing internal consistency correlations for each item in the four philosophic scales and then factoring only the items that maximized the corrected item-total correlations for each scale.[2]

4.4 Significance of Scores

You will note that your completion of the inventory has produced four sub-scores. The higher your sub-score for each philosophy (on a scale of +20 to −20), the more agreement you can assume that you have with that philosophic view. If one sub-score is ten or more points above the next highest sub-score (e.g., Idealism = +8, Realism = −2, Pragmatism = −2, Existentialism = −2) that is indicative of a significant difference. In this case you would most probably be more of an Idealist than a Realist, Pragmatist, or Existentialist. On the other hand, if your sub-scores are Idealism = +20, Realism = −20, Pragmatism = −20, Existentialism = −20, you can be very sure that you are a thoroughgoing Idealist. Sometimes a person's sub-scores are all very similar (e.g., Idealism = +10, Realism = +10, Pragmatism = +10, Existentialism = +10). This is often indicative of a broad sympathy with all of the philosophic views, since there is no dominant view indicated.

We learned in the last chapter that Idealism and Realism are absolutist philosophies, while Pragmatism and Existentialism are relativist philosophies. By totaling your Idealism and Realism sub-scores and your Pragmatism and Existentialism sub-scores, you may see on which side of the absolute/relative divide your sympathies rest. If your combined sub-scores for Idealism and Realism total ten or more points above your combined sub-scores for Pragmatism and Existentialism, that is a significant indication that you are an absolutist. If your combined sub-scores for Pragmatism and Existentialism total ten or more points above your combined sub-scores for Idealism and Realism, that is a significant indication that you are a relativist.

A word of caution needs to be given about the sub-scores. As noted in Chapter 1, the things that philosophy deals with are not as objective, quantifiable, and measurable as the things with which science deals. So the sub-scores are perhaps best thought of as indicators of philosophic leanings, not as absolute assurances. This is particularly true of the sub-score for Existentialism. With the exception of Philosophical Analysis, Existentialism is the least systematic of all philosophies. Some of its most famous adherents have even denied that they were Existentialists (e.g., Albert Camus) because they did not want it to seem that Existentialists can be categorized and are predictable. But even though Existentialism shares a number of concerns with the other philosophies (such as a concern for choice, responsibility, and individual identity), most philosophers still believe that it is best considered as a separate philosophic view.

4.5 Conclusion

In conclusion, there is no one correct philosophic view (. . . although the higher your absolutist score, the more you might be inclined to disagree with this statement). The correct philosophic view for you is the one that best explains the meaning of the world, as you understand it. Of course, this will vary from individual to individual. Even though you will likely have your own favorite philosophic view, it will be helpful for you to understand the other philosophic views which are held by people for whom you work and with whom you work. Understanding their philosophies – although not necessarily agreeing with them – will go a long way toward helping you understand why these people do the things they do and why they believe the things that they believe.

4.6 Chapter Summary

This chapter presented the philosophic inventory and gave you the opportunity to complete it and find out your sub-scores for Idealism, Realism,

Pragmatism, and Existentialism, as well as your scores for absolutism and relativism. You also learned how the inventory was composed, how it was validated, and what the scores mean for you.

4.7 Your Turn

Question 1. Having studied the four basic systematic philosophical views in the last chapter and having completed the philosophic inventory in this chapter, do you think that the sub-scores that the inventory yielded are accurate? That is, do these sub-scores accurately reflect your philosophic views? Give reasons for your answer to this question.

FIVE

The Possibility of a Unifying Ethical Theory

5.1 Introduction

In Chapter 3 on Philosophic Belief Systems, it was mentioned that people of different philosophic viewpoints might agree on a common solution to an ethical dilemma. They would, however, do so for different reasons. Let us recall the outlooks of the four basic philosophies. The Idealist believes that reality lies ultimately in the ideal, nonmaterial dimension and so goodness would involve conformity to the ideal. The Realist believes that reality is found in nature and so goodness involves acting in accord with what is natural. The Pragmatist believes that reality is not an idea or a thing but rather an ongoing experience (i.e., the flow of life) and so goodness is concerned with the production of socially desirable results. The Existentialist believes that reality is self-defined and so goodness is concerned with whatever one's own conscience dictates.

To illustrate, let us take the case of murder. The Idealist would say that murder is wrong because all life is sacred. The Realist would say that murder is wrong because people should die only of natural causes. The Pragmatist would say that murder is wrong because it is disruptive of the good of society. The Existentialist would say that murder is wrong simply because the Existentialist believes it is wrong (probably out of respect for other people's autonomy and integrity). The adherents of the different philosophic worldviews might agree on a common ethical stance, as in the disapproval of murder, but is there the further possibility that they could agree on a single unifying ethical theory as the rationale for this stance? Albert Einstein spent the last thirty years of his life searching for

Figure 5.1. James H. Moor

a unifying field theory that would describe all the forces of nature. He failed. Can ethicists hope to do better in their field?

5.2 The Argument of James H. Moor

James H. Moor, the philosopher who did groundbreaking work with an article entitled "What Is Computer Ethics" in 1985, has written a more recent article with the thesis that a unifying ethical theory is possible.[1]

Moor begins by admitting that "consequentialist theories and deontological theories are often presented as hopelessly incompatible."[2] By "consequentialist" he means Pragmatist and by "deontological" he means Idealist. These theories would indeed seem to be incompatible since the first is relativist (i.e., depending on some external thing or circumstance) and the second is absolutist (i.e., depending on nothing else). How does Moor reconcile these two apparently contradictory theories?

Moor says, "Among other objections consequentialism seems to be insensitive to issues of justice. I believe there may be a unifying ethical theory that allows us to take into account the consequences of policies while at the same time making sure that these policies are constrained by principles of justice."[3] He then posits that there are several core values that pertain to all people. These are human life, happiness, and autonomy. He says that it is the task of justice to protect these values. But, he says, sometimes it is necessary to intrude on even these core values (e.g., while dispensing just punishment or in defending oneself). Some principle is needed to justify this intrusion. He turns to Bernard Gert[4] for this principle, which is: "people are allowed to harm (within limits) other people who are unjustly harming them. A rational, impartial person could accept such a policy in that others could be allowed to follow it as well. Others following such a policy will not harm you unless you harm them first."[5] What Moor seems to be advocating here – although he does not mention Kant explicitly – is the invocation of Kant's Categorical Imperative which says, "Act only according to that maxim by which you can at the same time will that it should become a universal law."

Moor thinks that justice can be insured if everyone agreed to universalize their actions, that is, to do only those things that they would want done to them. Conversely, they would also agree not to do those things that they would not want done to them. It is at this point that Gert's "blindfold of justice" comes into play. Like Rawls' "veil of ignorance," the "blindfold" prevents those who are blindfolded from knowing who will benefit from their choices and who will be harmed. The difference between Gert's "blindfold" and Rawls' "veil" is that Gert allows those who are blindfolded to assign different weights to the list of potential benefits and harms. Moor thinks this will result in some computing policies being judged as unjust by all rational, impartial people, and other policies being judged as just, and still other policies as being in dispute. He thinks that once people can agree on what is unjust, and hence to be avoided, they can go on from there to select computing policies on a consequentialist basis (i.e., by considering the results of these computing policies).

Moor's proposal sounds appealing, but it must be asked if what he is proposing is truly a unifying theory. The first part of Moor's theory is clearly Kantian/Idealistic/deontological. It is concerned with seeing that evil things are not done, that is, ensuring justice by seeing that no one is harmed who does not deserve to be harmed (e.g., that a person is not harmed except by just punishment or in the process of self-defense). By using Gert's "blindfold of justice" one can learn what the things are that should not be done. The second part of his theory is clearly Pragmatic/consequentialist, that is, deciding the most effective policy to follow from among those that have previously been determined to be just.

This theory seems, in fact, to be a combination of two theories. The first is an Idealistic theory used to judge what should not be done. The second is a Pragmatic theory used to judge what should be done from among the possibilities left after the first theory has been applied. Does Moor's proposal contribute anything truly novel then? I believe that it does. In proposing the tandem use of these two theories, Moor discovers a way, first, to avoid injustice and, second, a way to go on to decide the most efficient solution to the problem. However the two theories essentially deal with two related, but not identical, problems. The first is what should not be done (so that an injustice may be avoided), and the second is what should be done (in order to solve the problem efficiently after the question of justice has been considered). Innovative as this is, the use of Idealism to avoid injustice, followed by the use of Pragmatism to efficiently solve the problem involves the use of two different theories and so cannot strictly be called a unifying ethical theory.

If a unifying theory were ever to be found, it would probably have to be based on absolutism rather than relativism – perhaps combining the Idealist and Realist points of view. This is because absolutists believe that ethical theory must ultimately be based upon fixed principles. It would seem difficult, if not impossible, for Idealists and/or Realists to unite in a theory with Pragmatists and/or Existentialists who do not believe in fixed principles. Likewise there is the same difficulty, if not impossibility, for Pragmatists and/or Existentialists to unite in a theory with Idealists and/or Realists who do believe in fixed principles.

5.3 Chapter Summary

This chapter reviewed the beliefs of the four basic philosophies. It then summarized the argument of James H. Moor who attempted to develop a unifying ethical theory. Moor's argument was then critiqued. Moor's proposal seems to involve two theories, one Idealist and the other Pragmatist, rather than one unifying theory. The chapter concluded by suggesting that if a unifying ethical theory were ever to be found, it would have to be based on absolutism rather than relativism.

5.4 Your Turn

Question 1. It was suggested in this chapter that, if there were ever to be a unifying ethical theory, it might involve a combination of the Idealist and Realist views. What would be the major problem in trying to produce a unifying ethical theory involving a combination of the Pragmatist and Existentialist views?

SIX

The Ethical Decision-Making Process

6.1 Steps in the Ethical Decision-Making Process

There are eight steps involving questions to be answered in resolving computer ethics dilemmas. It may be asked whether this process actually facilitates one's ability to make the most ethical decisions or whether it simply encourages people to better document their own instinctive positions. Although it cannot be proven, the answer to this question is probably the former. Even if it were the latter, the process should still prove to be a valuable exercise.

The steps are:

Step 1. Briefly describe the ethical issues in this case.

Be aware that there may be multiple ethical issues in the case. Make sure that all of the issues are clearly articulated. Also, be aware that different issues may apply to the different people involved in the case.

Step 2. Identify the stakeholders in this case and tell what you think each of them would like to see as an outcome.

Empathy is needed here in order to put yourself in the place of each of the parties involved and state what each would presumably like to see done in keeping with each one's interests.

Step 3. A) Propose three possible solutions to the case (two extremes and a compromise). Mark them a), b), and c). B) Give a best-case and worst-case outcome for each solution and, for each solution, indicate whether you could tolerate the worst-case outcome. C) Which of the three solutions would you choose?

I am grateful to Professor Tom Bivins of the University of Oregon School of Journalism and Communications for the idea of including this three-solution step in the ethical decision-making process. This step is meant to present the full range of potential solutions to the case. The compromise solution is not necessarily the solution you should choose. You might end up picking the compromise or you might pick one at either extreme from the compromise, depending upon your philosophic outlook. You should, however, be able to tolerate the worst-case outcome for whatever solution you choose.

Step 4. A) Would you be willing for everyone to be permitted to use the solution you chose? Explain. B) Does this solution treat people as ends rather than as means only? Explain.

Step 4 is meant to test for an Idealist grounding to the solution. Part A asks, in keeping with Kant's first formulation of the Categorical Imperative, whether you would be willing to make your solution into a universal law. Part B asks, in accord with Kant's second formulation of the Categorical Imperative, whether your solution respects the humanity of people rather than simply using them as a means to an end (see Chapter 3).

Step 5. A) Is this solution in accord with what is natural (e.g., in accord with human nature, the environment, or the inherent purpose of anything else involved in the case)? Explain. B) Is this solution balanced between an approach that might be excessive on the one hand and deficient on the other? Explain.

Step 5 tests for a Realist grounding to the solution. It is meant to explore whether the solution is a balanced, "real world" solution as opposed to a utopian, idealistic one.

Step 6. A) Would there be majority agreement that this solution is the most efficient means to the end? Explain. B) Will it produce the greatest good for the greatest number of people? Explain.

Step 6 tests for a Pragmatist grounding to the solution. Part A asks about two things: whether this solution is the most efficient means to the end, and whether a majority of those in decision-making positions believe that it is the most efficient means to the end. Part B is John Stuart Mill's question about achieving the most net gain over net loss for the greatest number of people (see Chapter 3).

> *Step 7. A) Is this solution the one you feel most committed to in your own conscience, regardless of whether or not it benefits you personally? Explain. B) Do you choose this solution in an autonomous manner, as the final arbiter of the good, free from the influence of others? Explain.*

Step 7 tests for an Existentialist grounding to the solution. Part A asks whether you are personally committed to it regardless of whether you gain or lose from it. This part of the question might seem to be similar to John Rawls' "veil of ignorance" theory (see Chapter 5). In Rawls' theory, people are asked to decide on the justness of a social situation when they do not know ahead of time what their own socioeconomic status would be were they to be placed in that situation.[1] Here however the question is whether the person is committed to the solution, even knowing ahead of time that she or he might personally suffer from it. Part B asks whether your decision is personally, individually made, independent of any pressure from a group.

Adherents of all four philosophic views may be unselfish and hence could say "yes" to the first part of Step 7. Your response to the "Explain" part of the question should make clear that your support of this solution is being given despite any gain or loss that might affect you personally as a result of it.

> *Step 8. Which philosophy do you feel was most influential in your solution to this case? Why?*

Question 8 asks which philosophy was most influential in your solution. You may also wish to indicate other philosophies that you feel played a lesser role in your solution.

6.2 The Culture Clash on the Net Case

Let us examine a case called "Culture Clash on the Net," © 2007 by John Halleck, used with permission.

This problem was originally posed many years ago, when Utah had only one Internet Service Provider, and it was comparatively expensive and not a choice many students could make. Today telling the student to "just go somewhere else" is not the painful choice that it was at that time. There are still issues, but they are now somewhat moot.

There was a user at our university who was from some tribe in a small African country. He had an antagonist out on the network from another tribe in that country. There was a war going on and the antagonists were from tribes on opposite sides of the war – and they weren't known for getting along before that.

They were both using a network newsgroup (soc.culture.[that-country-name]) as a forum for their views. However, both of them were choosing the vilest, most offensive, crudest, threatening language possible for this "dialog."

Every time our user posted one of these we would get twenty or so complaints about our user's language and tone and, often, inappropriateness. We assumed that the other side received the same when their guy posted. Since this happened every day, there were twenty or so complaints every day, which tied up someone's morning every day.

The messages unquestionably violated the published rules for the accounts, and the user even admitted this. He was told that, if he didn't cease these violations, his account would be terminated. He continued, and his account was terminated four times, with a lecture from a different person here every time before his account was reactivated.

His point of view in all of this is actually quite defensible: 1) He is only replying to things directed at him, and replying in exactly the same language and tone as that which was used against him. 2) His family honor, his personal honor, and his tribal honor have been dragged through the mud, and he feels he has a right to defend himself and his family and tribe. 3) Since they are both doing this, he feels that it is unfair to have his account terminated and not that of the other person also. 4) We are effectively allowing someone else to insult him and lie about him publicly, worldwide (and therefore in his homeland), while denying him any chance to respond.

Our view is close to: 1) He is causing us extra work, and is violating the rules to do so. 2) He can defend himself. He just can't do it in an obscene objectionable way (even if that might be culturally accepted in his country as the appropriate response to an attack that is obscene and objectionable). 3) We can't terminate the other person since we have no control over any other site. That person may not, in fact, be violating the rules of the site that he uses. 4) We can't afford to keep dealing with the complaints. As long as the complaints are valid, we have a responsibility to fix that part of the problem to which we have access. If he continues to use objectionable language, we can't let him continue.

There are a number of interesting problems here, with many tied up in our forcing this student/tribesman to comply with our cultural norms, in a manner that is offensive to him. Please note that being a "tribesman" does NOT mean being "primitive." He was a student here at Desert State University. He was well educated, and very articulate. His being a member of a tribe is a cultural fact, relevant to the conflict, not a statement of anything else. This statement is made because some students have assumed all kinds of insulting things based on his being a tribesman.

6.3 A Sample Solution to the Culture Clash on the Net Case

Step 1. Briefly describe the ethical issues in this case.

One issue is that a rival tribesman on the Net is attacking a student/ tribesman's culture. Another issue is that this student/tribesman's defense is found to be offensive by other users on the Net. A third issue is that inordinate amounts of staff time are being consumed by this situation.

Step 2. Who are the interested parties and what do you suppose each of them would like to see as an outcome?

The interested parties are the student/tribesman and Desert State University's computer network users and administration. The student/tribesman would like to continue his defense of his culture unfettered. The computer network users and administration would like him to conform to the rules established for the computer network.

Step 3. A) Propose three possible solutions to the case (two extremes and a compromise). Mark them a), b), and c). B) Give a best-case and worst-case outcome for each solution and, for each solution, indicate whether you could tolerate the worst-case outcome. C) Which of the three solutions would you choose?

   a) As one extreme solution, I would suggest permanently removing the student/tribesman's university access to the network. The best-case outcome would be that the student/tribesman can no longer make obscene and inflammatory remarks and so the complaints would cease. The worst-case outcome would be that the student/tribesman fails his classwork due to nonaccess to the network and is unable to graduate. I could not tolerate this outcome.

b) As the other extreme solution, I would suggest the administration do nothing. The best-case outcome is that either the war ends and the mutual recrimination stops or the rival tribesmen get tired of exchanging insults and the complaints stop. The worst-case outcome is that, lacking any intervention by the administration, things just get worst. I could not tolerate this outcome.

c) As a compromise solution, I would suggest that the student/ tribesman be allowed to reply to the insults, but that he do so by first submitting his reply for screening to someone designated by the computer network administration. This person could edit the reply and delete any obscene or inflammatory language before posting it or allowing it to be posted. The best-case outcome is that the student/tribesman still has a means to reply to the insults (although perhaps not with the same verve which he would have liked), the complaints stop, and the staff no longer has to spend inordinate amounts of time on the situation. The worst-case outcome is that the student/tribesman feels that he is being discriminated against by not being allowed the same latitude in posting as his rival is being given on whatever network the rival happens to be located. I could tolerate this outcome. I would choose solution "c" – the solution that has a tolerable worst-case outcome.

Step 4. A) Would you be willing for everyone to be permitted to use the solution you chose? Explain.

I would be willing to see solution "c" used in any similar case (i.e., in any case where someone was posting with the same kind of disrespect for the network rules and the sensitivities of fellow users as the student/tribesman exhibited in this case).

Step 4. B) Does this solution treat people as ends rather than as means only? Explain.

Solution "c" does seem basically to treat the student/tribesman as an end by continuing to allow him to post, although in a restricted way. The first extreme solution (permanently removing the student's access to the network) would be close to treating him as a means only.

> *Step 5. A) Is this solution in accord with what is natural (e.g., in accord with human nature, the environment, or the inherent purpose of anything else involved in the case)? Explain.*

Clearly there is a clash of "cultures" at the root of this case, but there does not appear to be any violation of any type of "nature" involved in the solution.

> *Step 5. B) Is this solution balanced between an approach that is excessive on the one hand and deficient on the other?*

Yes, as a compromise solution it is situated between the extremes of permanently taking away the student/tribesman's access to the network on the one hand and doing nothing at all on the other.

> *Step 6. A) Would there be majority agreement that this solution is the most efficient means to the end? Explain.*

The universe to be considered here is made up of the network users at Desert State University. Their majority interests are assumed to be represented by the computer network administration. The rival tribesman, his fellow users, and the administration of his network do not count toward a majority since Desert State University has no authority over them. They are simply the population of a different node on the Internet. Assuming that the Desert State University computer network administration does represent their users' interests, then their decision expresses majority agreement on what is judged to be the most efficient means to the end. Of course, with Pragmatism, this will have to be tried to find out if it is indeed the most efficient solution.

> *Step 6. B) Will it produce the greatest good for the greatest number of people? Explain.*

Again, as to the consequences, it remains to be seen whether this solution will benefit the greatest number of people. Time will tell, but the hypothesis is that it will produce the greatest good for the greatest number of people.

Step 7. A) Is this solution the one you feel most committed to in your own conscience, regardless of whether or not it benefits you personally? Explain.

I am conscientiously committed to this solution. Since I am not personally involved in the situation, there is no gain or loss that would affect me personally as a result of it.

Step 7. B) Do you choose this solution in an autonomous manner, as the final arbiter of the good, free from any influence of others? Explain.

This decision is solely mine. I take total responsibility for it.

Step 8. Which philosophy do you feel was most influential in your solution to this case? Why?

This solution is fairly consonant with all of the philosophical views. It is closest to the Pragmatist part of the spectrum. It involves a compromise and, as such, aims to provide the most workable means in producing the greatest good for the greatest number of people.

Note that there is no "right" philosophical view to be used in solving this, or any, case. The "right" view will vary according to the personal worldview (or views) of each individual who analyzes the case and offers a preferred solution.

6.4 Chapter Summary

This chapter explained the eight steps in the ethical decision-making process. These steps are: 1. Briefly describe the ethical issues in this case. 2. Who are the interested parties and what do you suppose each of them would like to see as an outcome? 3. Propose three possible solutions (two extremes and a compromise). Mark them a), b), and c). Give a best-case and worst-case outcome for each solution and indicate whether you could tolerate the worst-case outcome. Which of the three solutions would you choose? Answer the following questions for the solution that you chose as best: 4. A) Would you be willing for everyone to be permitted to use the solution you chose? Explain. B) Does this solution treat people as ends rather than as means only? Explain. 5. A) Is this solution in accord with what is natural (e.g., in accord with human nature, the environment, the inherent purpose of any related mechanisms)? Explain. B) Is this solution balanced between an approach that is excessive on the one hand and deficient on the other? 6. A) Would there be majority agreement that this solution is the most efficient means to the end? Explain. B) Will it produce the greatest good for the greatest number of people? Explain. 7. A) Is this solution the one you feel most committed to in your own conscience, regardless of whether or not it benefits you personally? Explain. B) Do you choose this solution in an autonomous manner, as the final arbiter of the good, free from the influence of others? 8. Which philosophy do you feel was most influential in your solution to this case? Why?

A sample case (Culture Clash on the Net case) together with a sample solution, using the eight steps of the ethical decision-making process, concluded the chapter.

6.5 Your Turn

Question 1. Use the ethical decision-making process to analyze and solve the following case, which is called the False Images in Broadcasts case. It was condensed from a news article in the January 13, 2000, issue of *The New York Times*. All quotations are from that article.[2]

CBS Television wanted to cover the New Year's celebration in Times Square on New Year's Eve – December 31, 1999. There was only one problem. NBC happened to have a sign in Times Square that would have shown up in CBS' coverage. CBS decided to solve the problem by superimposing a digitally created CBS logo over the NBC sign, thereby blocking it out. CBS had used such electronic technology before, making it appear in their morning "Early Show" telecasts that CBS promotional signs existed at locations in downtown Manhattan when, in fact, they did not. The difference was that the superimposition of the CBS logo over the NBC sign was being done on a news program.

Dan Rather, the CBS news anchor, was not in agreement with the use of the digital logo. He said, "There is no excuse for it. I did not grasp the possible ethical implications of this and that was wrong on my part. At the very least we should have pointed out to viewers that we were doing it."

Andrew Heyward, President of CBS News, admitted that using the logo on the evening news was "a closer call" than using it during the Early Show to promote CBS, but said that he did not see the ethical problem that Rather did. He mentioned that Rather had not been part of the discussion about using this technique and said that "reasonable people could disagree on whether this was an appropriate use of digital technology." The President of CBS Television was more direct, saying: "Anytime there's an NBC logo up on our network we'll block it again." ABC and NBC have not used this technology. A spokesman for ABC said: "It's been discussed at length. We wouldn't use it here." The executive producer of NBC's Today show said: "We were offered the same technology and we passed because we didn't think it was appropriate."

SEVEN

Psychology and Computer Ethics

7.1 Introduction

In previous chapters we have looked at the question of right and wrong behavior from the viewpoint of philosophical ethics. Now we will compare this approach with another way of looking at right and wrong behavior – the approach of developmental psychology.

Psychology takes a scientific approach to the study of human behavior. It uses experimental investigative procedures to study how human behavior develops. Psychologists examine questions of right and wrong in the branch of psychology known as moral development. One of the most famous researchers in this branch was Lawrence Kohlberg. A brief review of his work follows.

7.2 Lawrence Kohlberg's Stages of Moral Development

Lawrence Kohlberg was, for many years, a professor at Harvard University and director of its Center for Moral Education. He became famous for his research on moral development, which began in the early 1970s. He started as a developmental psychologist and then moved to the field of moral education. He was particularly well known for his theory of moral development that he popularized through research studies. He believed that justice was a central concept in moral education and he spent a good deal of time experimenting with how to make schools into "just communities" by having students make decisions through the use of democratic processes.

Table 7.1. *Kohlberg's stages of moral development*

Level	Stage	Social orientation
	1	Obedience and Punishment
Pre-conventional (child)	2	Individualism/Instrumentalism
	3	"Good boy/Good girl"
Conventional (adolescent)	4	Law and Order
	5	Social Contract
Post-conventional (adult)	6	Principled Conscience

His theory of moral development was dependent on the thinking of the Swiss psychologist Jean Piaget and the American philosopher John Dewey. He was also inspired by the work of James Mark Baldwin, an early developmental psychologist. These men had emphasized that human beings develop philosophically and psychologically in a progressive fashion. That is, just as people grow up physically, they also grow up psychologically.

Kohlberg believed, and was able to demonstrate through studies, that people progressed in their moral reasoning (i.e., in their rationales for ethical behavior) through a series of stages. He believed that there were six identifiable stages that could be more generally classified into three levels. Kohlberg's classification is outlined in Table 7.1.

The first level of moral thinking is that generally found at the elementary school level and is known as the pre-conventional level. In the first stage of this level, people behave according to socially acceptable norms because they are told to do so by some authority figure (e.g., parent/guardian or teacher). This obedience is compelled by the threat or application of punishment. The second stage of this level is characterized by a view that right behavior means acting in one's own best interests.

The second level of moral thinking is that generally found throughout society. It is called the "conventional" level because people at this level behave according to certain social conventions. They make trades, exchange favors, and set punishments according to values held by the social majority. The first stage of this level (stage 3) is characterized by an attitude that seeks to do what will gain the approval of others and will meet social expectations. The second stage of this level (stage 4) is one oriented to abiding by the law (conforming to legal codes) and responding to the obligations of duty.

The third level of moral thinking, the post-conventional level, is one that Kohlberg felt is not reached by the majority of adults. Its first stage (stage 5) is an understanding of social mutuality and a genuine interest in the welfare of others. The second stage of this level (stage 6) is based on respect for universal principle and the demands of individual conscience. While Kohlberg always believed in the existence of stage 6 and had some nominees for it, he could never get enough subjects to define it, much less observe their longitudinal movement into it.

Kohlberg believed that individuals could only progress through these stages one stage at a time. That is, they could not "jump" stages. They could not, for example, move from an orientation of selfishness up to the law and order stage without passing through the good boy/good girl stage. They could only come to a comprehension of a moral rationale one stage above their own. Thus, according to Kohlberg, it was important to present them with moral dilemmas for discussion that would help them to see the reasonableness of a "higher stage" morality and encourage their development in that direction. This is the reason for Kohlberg's moral discussion approach. He saw this as one of the ways in which moral development can be promoted through formal education. Kohlberg believed, as did Piaget, that most moral development occurs through social interaction. The discussion approach is based on the insight that individuals develop as a result of cognitive conflicts at their current stage. [I wish to express my gratitude to Professor F. Clark Power of the University of Notre Dame (a former student of Kohlberg's) and Professor Steve Chilton of the University of Minnesota for their suggestions while I was preparing the foregoing summary.]

7.3 Morality at Premier Software Story

An example of a story that might provide the basis for discussion about moral development is given. It is known as the Morality at Premier Software story, © 2007 by Robert Newton Barger.

Once upon a time there lived a computer programmer named Marie. She was Vice President of Programming at a large software manufacturer named Premier Software. Her boss, the President of Premier, was named Harriet. One day Harriet called Marie into her office. She told Marie that she was going to retire in three months. Furthermore, she said that she had been told by the Chairperson of Premier's Board of Directors that she would receive a bonus of 5,000 shares of stock if, before she retired, she could ship the next version of Premier's operating system (O.S.). Harriet explained that Marie's help would be crucial in meeting this deadline. If she could shorten the beta testing so that the new O.S. version could be shipped in three months, Harriet said that she would recommend Marie as her replacement. Marie was troubled by this proposal. She told Harriet that she certainly wanted to help her and that she was very appreciative of her offer, but there was no way this side of the Styx river that she could possibly have the beta testing finished in three months. Harriet told Marie that she sympathized with her dilemma and that Marie might just give it some further consideration and get back to Harriet by the close of business that day. Marie hurried off to talk to Bill, her Associate Vice President of Programming. Marie shared with Bill what Harriet had told her. Bill responded that Marie had done the right thing in saying that the beta testing could never be completed in time for Harriet's retirement and that it would be wrong to try to complete it by then. Marie felt reassured by this response and told Harriet that she could not ship the new O.S. before Harriet's retirement date. The first thing next morning, Bill made an appointment to see Harriet and told her that Marie had mentioned Harriet's offer to him. He said that the three-month deadline could indeed be met by cutting down on the scope of the beta testing and that if any "issues" were discovered after release they could be dealt with then. He said he would be glad to meet the deadline in this manner if Harriet would recommend him to replace her. In the meantime, Marie felt upset at the position in which Harriet had placed her and made an appointment to see the Chairperson of the Board. She told the Chairperson about how Harriet wanted to shorten the beta testing of the new O.S. for her own selfish purposes. The Chairperson called Harriet in and fired her on the spot, not only ending any hope of her stock bonus but also of her receiving any retirement benefits.

7.4 Chapter Summary

This chapter explained that questions of right and wrong can be examined by the branch of psychology known as moral development, as well as by traditional philosophical ethics. Lawrence Kohlberg's Stages of Moral Development were then explained. The chapter closed with the Morality at Premier Software story which presents a series of dilemmas in the field of software development.

7.5 Your Turn

Question 1. In the Morality at Premier Software story, rank Marie, Harriet, Bill, and the Chairperson according to whom were the most immoral in their actions. Also, indicate their stage of moral development (if you feel you have enough information to determine it). Explain why you ranked the people in the order that you did.

EIGHT

The Computing Field as a Profession

8.1 Introduction

Four traits have traditionally characterized a profession: expert knowledge, autonomy in conducting one's practice, internal governance of one's professional field, and service to society. Each of these will be examined.

8.2 Expert Knowledge

Expert knowledge is special technical knowledge that is certified by some authority and is not possessed by the layperson. George Bernard Shaw once said that every profession is a conspiracy against the laity. Expert knowledge is related to skill, which may be learned "on the job." Indeed, in earlier times some professions were learned in an apprenticeship manner. Would-be lawyers "read law" in law offices and would-be physicians went along on house calls with doctors and assisted them in their practices. The practice of going on "hospital rounds" is still a part of medical education today.

8.3 Autonomy

Autonomy involves independence in conducting one's professional practice in the areas of diagnosis, treatment, and follow-up – to use the language of the medical profession. Diagnosis deals with finding the root of the problem that needs to be treated. Treatment involves discovering what should be done to alleviate the problem. Follow-up is concerned with evaluation, that is, checking to see if the treatment was effective.

8.4 Internal Governance

Internal governance means that one's professional field is controlled by its practitioners rather than by some external authority. It includes the setting of entrance requirements and the handling of the discipline of one's errant colleagues.

8.5 Service to Society

Historically, service to society has involved some kind of humanitarian service, for example, spiritual ministration, the curing of illness, or the defense of the wrongly accused.

8.6 A History of the Professions

The first professions were recognized in the Middle Ages to be Divinity (Theology), Law, and Medicine. The most defining characteristic of these professions was specialized knowledge, that is, knowledge beyond what the layperson (the noncleric, the nonlawyer, and the nonphysician) possessed. Since this knowledge was not meant for the layperson, it was dealt with in a special language that only professionals used, namely, Latin. In Theology, this was evident enough. Until recent years, Latin was used in theological training in Roman Catholic seminaries and in the liturgy of that church – the dominant church in the Western world during the Middle Ages. In Medicine, bones were named in Latin and prescriptions were written in Latin. A vestigial form of Latin is still used by physicians in writing prescriptions today (e.g., the abbreviation "q.i.d." means "quater in die" – [take] four times a day). In Law, legal briefs were written in Latin and Latin terminology still survives in current practice from the time of English case law (e.g., habeas corpus, corpus delecti, de facto, de jure).

Next in importance after specialized knowledge is the characteristic of autonomy. If one decides what needs to be done, how to do it, and how the results should be evaluated, then one is practicing as a professional. If any of those things are missing (one's control of diagnosis, treatment, or follow-up) then one is not a professional in the historic sense of the term.

After autonomy comes the characteristic of self-governance. This can be difficult to assess, given the control that government agencies exercise today in the fields of law and medicine. Remember that it took the adoption of the Establishment clause of the First Amendment of the United States Constitution to prevent government involvement with religion. Some of the states continued to have established religions until the Bill of Rights was applied to the states by the Fourteenth Amendment. It is therefore difficult for an attorney or physician today to maintain that she or he is completely independent, or self-governing, despite the activities of county, state, and national medical and legal associations.

Public service probably would rank last as a characteristic of a profession. The professions were originally more concerned with service to humanity than with the accumulation of wealth. They are still widely committed to this type of service. For instance, many physicians, surgeons, and nurses volunteer their time in medical service to the poor.

8.7 Computing Considered as a Profession

Can it be said that other fields of endeavor, and in particular the field of computing and information technology, have achieved the status of professions since the time of the beginning of the three traditional professions of Divinity, Law, and Medicine in the Middle Ages? Since specialized knowledge is seen as the most defining characteristic of a profession, one can look at advanced education (i.e., graduate education) as it is offered in universities today for a possible answer. There are colleges and schools of engineering, architecture, education, and information science, as well as many others, in contemporary universities. They prepare their students to enter their particular fields through curricula approved by the fields' professional boards. Clearly, the material studied in these curricula qualifies as expert knowledge. It may be assumed that certified practitioners exercise a fair degree of autonomy in their practice, thus meeting the autonomy characteristic of a profession. Colleges and schools also prepare their students to pass the board examinations that are administered by the professional boards of those fields (e.g., the Bar exam, the Medical Boards, and the Certified Public Accountant exam). This control over entrance to a professional field is an example of the internal governance characteristic of a profession. Most, if not all, professions have established codes of ethics to stipulate the kind of behavior and obligations that are incumbent on practitioners in their field. This also relates to the characteristic of internal governance. Most, if not all, of these codes of ethics point out the obligations of the practitioners of the field to have concern for society and to engage in public service, which is the final characteristic of a profession.

It would appear, then, that many positions in organized fields of knowledge and practice today do deserve the title of profession. Among those would be a number of positions in the field of computing and information technology. These fields require specialized knowledge. It can be assumed that many of the practitioners in these fields exercise a fair degree of autonomy in their work. These fields' professional organizations, such as the Association for Computing Machinery (ACM), exercise functions of internal governance. The fields qualify on the final point of service to society by providing and maintaining the computational infrastructure for most of the fundamental activities in which society engages today. Think, for instance, of what the world would be without the Internet!

8.8 Chapter Summary

This chapter provided a description of the four basic characteristics of a profession: expert knowledge, autonomy, internal governance, and service to society. Next it provided a brief history of the professions. Included in this history were the more recent professions, one of which is the field of computing and information technology. It concluded with the judgment that many of these recent professions, including computing and information technology, could be considered true professions.

8.9 Your Turn

Question 1. Name specific positions (i.e., occupational titles or roles) in the field of computing that would involve expert knowledge, autonomy, internal governance, and service to the community.

Question 2. Tell how one of these positions that you have named in response to Question 1 involves expert knowledge, autonomy, internal governance, and service to the community.

NINE

Computer-Related Codes of Ethics

The Center for the Study of Ethics at the Illinois Institute of Technology lists on its Web site forty-seven current codes of ethics relating to computing and information systems.[1] Two of these codes that pertain to large numbers of professionals in the computing field are the ACM (Association for Computing Machinery) Code of Ethics and Professional Conduct and the Software Engineering Code of Ethics and Professional Practice. The latter code is a joint project of the ACM and the Institute of Electrical and Electronics Engineers, Inc. (IEEE). A third document presented in this chapter, the Ten Commandments of Computer Ethics, is an early computer ethics code meant for popular consumption. It was produced by the Computer Ethics Institute, a project of the Brookings Institution located in Washington, D.C.

9.1 ACM Code of Ethics and Professional Conduct

Adopted by ACM Council 10/16/92.

Preamble

Commitment to ethical professional conduct is expected of every member (voting members, associate members, and student members) of the Association for Computing Machinery (ACM).

This Code, consisting of 24 imperatives formulated as statements of personal responsibility, identifies the elements of such a commitment. It contains many, but not all, issues professionals are likely to face. Section 1 outlines fundamental ethical considerations, while Section 2 addresses additional, more specific considerations of professional conduct. Statements in Section 3 pertain more specifically to individuals who have a leadership role, whether in the workplace or in a volunteer capacity such as with organizations like ACM. Principles involving compliance with this Code are given in Section 4.

The Code shall be supplemented by a set of Guidelines, which provide explanation to assist members in dealing with the various issues contained in the Code. It is expected that the Guidelines will be changed more frequently than the Code.

The Code and its supplemented Guidelines are intended to serve as a basis for ethical decision making in the conduct of professional work. Secondarily, they may serve as a basis for judging the merit of a formal complaint pertaining to violation of professional ethical standards.

It should be noted that although computing is not mentioned in the imperatives of Section 1, the Code is concerned with how these fundamental imperatives apply to one's conduct as a computing professional. These imperatives are expressed in a general form to emphasize that ethical principles which apply to computer ethics are derived from more general ethical principles.

It is understood that some words and phrases in a code of ethics are subject to varying interpretations, and that any ethical principle may conflict with other ethical principles in specific situations. Questions related to ethical conflicts can best be answered by thoughtful consideration of fundamental principles, rather than reliance on detailed regulations.

Contents & Guidelines

1. GENERAL MORAL IMPERATIVES.
   As an ACM member I will . . . .
   1.1 Contribute to society and human well-being.
      This principle concerning the quality of life of all people affirms an obligation to protect fundamental human rights and to respect the diversity of all cultures. An essential aim of computing professionals is to minimize negative consequences of computing systems, including threats to health and safety. When designing or implementing systems, computing professionals must attempt to ensure that the products of their efforts will be used in socially responsible ways, will meet social needs, and will avoid harmful effects to health and welfare.

      In addition to a safe social environment, human well-being includes a safe natural environment. Therefore, computing professionals who design and develop systems must be alert to, and make others aware of, any potential damage to the local or global environment.
   1.2 Avoid harm to others.
      "Harm" means injury or negative consequences, such as undesirable loss of information, loss of property, property damage, or unwanted environmental impacts. This principle prohibits use of computing technology in ways that result in harm to any of the following: users, the general public, employees, employers. Harmful actions include intentional destruction or modification of files and programs leading to serious loss of resources or unnecessary expenditure of human

resources such as the time and effort required to purge systems of "computer viruses."

Well-intended actions, including those that accomplish assigned duties, may lead to harm unexpectedly. In such an event the responsible person or persons are obligated to undo or mitigate the negative consequences as much as possible. One way to avoid unintentional harm is to carefully consider potential impacts on all those affected by decisions made during design and implementation.

To minimize the possibility of indirectly harming others, computing professionals must minimize malfunctions by following generally accepted standards for system design and testing. Furthermore, it is often necessary to assess the social consequences of systems to project the likelihood of any serious harm to others. If system features are misrepresented to users, coworkers, or supervisors, the individual computing professional is responsible for any resulting injury.

In the work environment the computing professional has the additional obligation to report any signs of system dangers that might result in serious personal or social damage. If one's superiors do not act to curtail or mitigate such dangers, it may be necessary to "blow the whistle" to help correct the problem or reduce the risk. However, capricious or misguided reporting of violations can, itself, be harmful. Before reporting violations, all relevant aspects of the incident must be thoroughly assessed. In particular, the assessment of risk and responsibility must be credible. It is suggested that advice be sought from other computing professionals. See principle 2.5 regarding thorough evaluations.

1.3   Be honest and trustworthy.

Honesty is an essential component of trust. Without trust an organization cannot function effectively. The honest computing professional will not make deliberately false or deceptive claims about a system or system design, but will instead provide full disclosure of all pertinent system limitations and problems.

A computer professional has a duty to be honest about his or her own qualifications, and about any circumstances that might lead to conflicts of interest.

Membership in volunteer organizations such as ACM may at times place individuals in situations where their statements or actions could be interpreted as carrying the "weight" of a larger group of professionals. An ACM member will exercise care to not misrepresent ACM or positions and policies of ACM or any ACM units.

1.4 Be fair and take action not to discriminate.

The values of equality, tolerance, respect for others, and the principles of equal justice govern this imperative. Discrimination on the basis of race, sex, religion, age, disability, national origin, or other such factors is an explicit violation of ACM policy and will not be tolerated.

Inequities between different groups of people may result from the use or misuse of information and technology. In a fair society, all individuals would have equal opportunity to participate in, or benefit from, the use of computer resources regardless of race, sex, religion, age, disability, national origin or other such similar factors. However, these ideals do not justify unauthorized use of computer resources nor do they provide an adequate basis for violation of any other ethical imperatives of this code.

1.5 Honor property rights including copyrights and patent.

Violation of copyrights, patents, trade secrets and the terms of license agreements is prohibited by law in most circumstances. Even when software is not so protected, such violations are contrary to professional behavior. Copies of software should be made only with proper authorization. Unauthorized duplication of materials must not be condoned.

1.6 Give proper credit for intellectual property.

Computing professionals are obligated to protect the integrity of intellectual property. Specifically, one must not take credit for other's ideas or work, even in cases where the work has not been explicitly protected by copyright, patent, etc.

1.7 Respect the privacy of others.

Computing and communication technology enables the collection and exchange of personal information on a scale unprecedented in the history of civilization. Thus there is increased potential for violating the privacy of individuals and groups. It is the responsibility of professionals to maintain the privacy and integrity of data describing individuals. This includes taking precautions to ensure the accuracy of data, as well as protecting it from unauthorized access or accidental disclosure to inappropriate individuals. Furthermore, procedures must be established to allow individuals to review their records and correct inaccuracies.

This imperative implies that only the necessary amount of personal information be collected in a system, that retention and disposal periods for that information be clearly defined and enforced, and that personal information gathered for a specific purpose not be used for other purposes without consent of the individual(s). These principles apply to electronic communications, including electronic mail, and prohibit procedures that capture or monitor electronic user data, including messages, without the permission of users or bona fide authorization related to system operation and maintenance. User data observed during the normal duties of system operation and maintenance must be treated with strictest confidentiality, except in cases where it is evidence for the violation of law, organizational regulations, or this Code. In these cases, the nature or contents of that information must be disclosed only to proper authorities.

1.8 Honor confidentiality.

The principle of honesty extends to issues of confidentiality of information whenever one has made an explicit promise to honor confidentiality or, implicitly, when private information not directly related to the performance of one's duties becomes available. The ethical concern is to respect all obligations of confidentiality to employers, clients, and users unless discharged from such obligations by requirements of the law or other principles of this Code.

2. MORE SPECIFIC PROFESSIONAL RESPONSIBILITIES.

As an ACM computing professional I will . . . .

2.1 Strive to achieve the highest quality, effectiveness and dignity in both the process and products of professional work.

Excellence is perhaps the most important obligation of a professional. The computing professional must strive to achieve quality and to be cognizant of the serious negative consequences that may result from poor quality in a system.

2.2 Acquire and maintain professional competence.

Excellence depends on individuals who take responsibility for acquiring and maintaining professional competence. A professional must participate in setting standards for appropriate levels of competence, and strive to achieve those standards. Upgrading technical knowledge and competence can be achieved in several ways: doing independent study; attending seminars, conferences, or courses; and being involved in professional organizations.

2.3 Know and respect existing laws pertaining to professional work.

ACM members must obey existing local, state, province, national, and international laws unless there is a compelling ethical basis not to do so. Policies and procedures of the organizations in which one participates must also be obeyed. But compliance must be balanced with the recognition that sometimes existing laws and rules may be immoral or inappropriate and, therefore, must be challenged. Violation of a law or regulation may be ethical when that law or rule has inadequate moral basis or when it conflicts with another law judged to be more important. If one decides to violate a law or rule because it is viewed as unethical, or for any other reason, one must fully accept responsibility for one's actions and for the consequences.

2.4 Accept and provide appropriate professional review.

Quality professional work, especially in the computing profession, depends on professional reviewing and critiquing. Whenever appropriate, individual members should seek and utilize peer review as well as provide critical review of the work of others.

2.5 Give comprehensive and thorough evaluations of computer systems and their impacts, including analysis of possible risks.

Computer professionals must strive to be perceptive, thorough, and objective when evaluating, recommending, and presenting system descriptions and alternatives. Computer professionals are in a position of special trust, and therefore have a special responsibility to provide objective, credible evaluations to employers, clients, users, and the public. When providing evaluations the professional must also identify any relevant conflicts of interest, as stated in imperative 1.3.

As noted in the discussion of principle 1.2 on avoiding harm, any signs of danger from systems must be reported to those who have opportunity and/or responsibility to resolve them. See the guidelines for imperative 1.2 for more details concerning harm, including the reporting of professional violations.

2.6 Honor contracts, agreements, and assigned responsibilities.

Honoring one's commitments is a matter of integrity and honesty. For the computer professional this includes ensuring that system elements perform as intended. Also, when one contracts for work with another party, one has an obligation to keep that party properly informed about progress toward completing that work.

A computing professional has a responsibility to request a change in any assignment that he or she feels cannot be completed as defined. Only after serious consideration and with full disclosure of risks and concerns to the employer or client, should one accept the assignment. The major underlying principle here is the obligation to accept personal accountability for professional work. On some occasions other ethical principles may take greater priority.

A judgment that a specific assignment should not be performed may not be accepted. Having clearly identified one's concerns and reasons for that judgment, but failing to procure a change in that assignment, one may yet be obligated, by contract or by law, to proceed as directed. The computing professional's ethical judgment should be the final guide in deciding whether or not to proceed. Regardless of the decision, one must accept the responsibility for the consequences.

However, performing assignments "against one's own judgment" does not relieve the professional of responsibility for any negative consequences.

2.7 Improve public understanding of computing and its consequences.

Computing professionals have a responsibility to share technical knowledge with the public by encouraging understanding of computing, including the impacts of computer systems and their limitations. This imperative implies an obligation to counter any false views related to computing.

2.8 Access computing and communication resources only when authorized to do so.

Theft or destruction of tangible and electronic property is prohibited by imperative 1.2 – "Avoid harm to others." Trespassing and unauthorized use of a computer or communication system is addressed by this imperative. Trespassing includes accessing communication networks and computer systems, or accounts and/or files associated with those systems, without explicit authorization to do so. Individuals and organizations have the right to restrict access to their systems so long as they do not violate the discrimination principle (see 1.4). No one should enter or use another's computer system, software, or data files without permission. One must always have appropriate approval before using system resources, including communication ports, file space, other system peripherals, and computer time.

3. ORGANIZATIONAL LEADERSHIP IMPERATIVES.

As an ACM member and an organizational leader, I will . . . .

BACKGROUND NOTE: This section draws extensively from the draft IFIP [International Federation for Information Processing] Code of Ethics, especially its sections on organizational ethics and international concerns. The ethical obligations of organizations tend to be neglected in most codes of professional conduct, perhaps because these codes are written from the perspective of the individual member. This dilemma is addressed by stating these imperatives from the perspective of the organizational leader. In this context "leader" is viewed as any organizational member who has leadership or educational responsibilities. These imperatives generally may apply to organizations as well as their leaders. In this context "organizations" are corporations, government agencies, and other "employers," as well as volunteer professional organizations.

3.1 Articulate social responsibilities of members of an organizational unit and encourage full acceptance of those responsibilities.

Because organizations of all kinds have impacts on the public, they must accept responsibilities to society. Organizational procedures and attitudes oriented toward quality and the welfare of society will reduce harm to members of the public, thereby serving public interest and fulfilling social responsibility. Therefore, organizational leaders must encourage full participation in meeting social responsibilities as well as quality performance.

3.2 Manage personnel and resources to design and build information systems that enhance the quality of working life.

Organizational leaders are responsible for ensuring that computer systems enhance, not degrade, the quality of working life. When implementing a computer system, organizations must consider the personal and professional development, physical safety, and human dignity of all workers. Appropriate human-computer ergonomic standards should be considered in system design and in the workplace.

3.3 Acknowledge and support proper and authorized uses of an organization's computing and communication resources.

Because computer systems can become tools to harm as well as to benefit an organization, the leadership has the responsibility to clearly define appropriate and inappropriate uses of organizational computing resources. While the number and scope of such rules should be minimal, they should be fully enforced when established.

3.4 Ensure that users and those who will be affected by a system have their needs clearly articulated during the assessment and design of requirements; later the system must be validated to meet requirements.

Current system users, potential users and other persons whose lives may be affected by a system must have their needs assessed and incorporated in the statement of requirements. System validation should ensure compliance with those requirements.

3.5 Articulate and support policies that protect the dignity of users and others affected by a computing system.

Designing or implementing systems that deliberately or inadvertently demean individuals or groups is ethically unacceptable. Computer professionals who are in decision making positions should verify that systems are designed and implemented to protect personal privacy and enhance personal dignity.

3.6 Create opportunities for members of the organization to learn the principles and limitations of computer systems.

This complements the imperative on public understanding (2.7). Educational opportunities are essential to facilitate optimal participation of all organizational members. Opportunities must be available to all members to help them improve their knowledge and skills in computing, including courses that familiarize them with the consequences and limitations of particular types of systems. In particular, professionals must be made aware of the dangers of building systems around oversimplified models, the improbability of anticipating and designing for every possible operating condition, and other issues related to the complexity of this profession.

4. COMPLIANCE WITH THE CODE.

As an ACM member I will . . . .

4.1 Uphold and promote the principles of this Code.

The future of the computing profession depends on both technical and ethical excellence. Not only is it important for ACM computing professionals to adhere to the principles expressed in this Code, each member should encourage and support adherence by other members.

4.2 Treat violations of this code as inconsistent with membership in the ACM.

Adherence of professionals to a code of ethics is largely a voluntary matter. However, if a member does not follow this code by engaging in gross misconduct, membership in ACM may be terminated.

This Code and the supplemental Guidelines were developed by the Task Force for the Revision of the ACM Code of Ethics and Professional Conduct: Ronald E. Anderson, Chair, Gerald Engel, Donald

Gotterbarn, Grace C. Hertlein, Alex Hoffman, Bruce Jawer, Deborah G. Johnson, Doris K. Lidtke, Joyce Currie Little, Dianne Martin, Donn B. Parker, Judith A. Perrolle, and Richard S. Rosenberg. The Task Force was organized by ACM/SIGCAS and funding was provided by the ACM SIG Discretionary Fund. This Code and the supplemental Guidelines were adopted by the ACM Council on October 16, 1992.

This Code may be published without permission as long as it is not changed in any way and it carries the copyright notice. Copyright ©1997, Association for Computing Machinery, Inc.

ACM/Code of Ethics. Last Update: 05/12/03[2]

9.2 Software Engineering Code of Ethics and Professional Practice

(Version 5.2) as recommended by the ACM/IEEE-CS Joint Task Force on Software Engineering Ethics and Professional Practices and jointly approved by the ACM and the IEEE-CS as the standard for teaching and practicing software engineering.

Software Engineering Code of Ethics and Professional Practice
ACM/IEEE-CS Joint Task Force on Software Engineering Ethics and Professional Practices
Short Version
PREAMBLE

The short version of the code summarizes aspirations at a high level of the abstraction; the clauses that are included in the full version give examples and details of how these aspirations change the way we act as software engineering professionals. Without the aspirations, the details can become legalistic and tedious; without the details, the aspirations can become high sounding but empty; together, the aspirations and the details form a cohesive code.

Software engineers shall commit themselves to making the analysis, specification, design, development, testing and maintenance of software a beneficial and respected profession. In accordance with their commitment to the health, safety and welfare of the public, software engineers shall adhere to the following Eight Principles:

1. PUBLIC – Software engineers shall act consistently with the public interest.
2. CLIENT AND EMPLOYER – Software engineers shall act in a manner that is in the best interests of their client and employer consistent with the public interest.
3. PRODUCT – Software engineers shall ensure that their products and related modifications meet the highest professional standards possible.
4. JUDGMENT – Software engineers shall maintain integrity and independence in their professional judgment.

5. MANAGEMENT – Software engineering managers and leaders shall subscribe to and promote an ethical approach to the management of software development and maintenance.
6. PROFESSION – Software engineers shall advance the integrity and reputation of the profession consistent with the public interest.
7. COLLEAGUES – Software engineers shall be fair to and supportive of their colleagues.
8. SELF – Software engineers shall participate in lifelong learning regarding the practice of their profession and shall promote an ethical approach to the practice of the profession.

Software Engineering Code of Ethics and Professional Practice
ACM/IEEE-CS Joint Task Force on Software Engineering Ethics and Professional Practices
Full Version
PREAMBLE

Computers have a central and growing role in commerce, industry, government, medicine, education, entertainment and society at large. Software engineers are those who contribute by direct participation or by teaching, to the analysis, specification, design, development, certification, maintenance and testing of software systems. Because of their roles in developing software systems, software engineers have significant opportunities to do good or cause harm, to enable others to do good or cause harm, or to influence others to do good or cause harm. To ensure, as much as possible, that their efforts will be used for good, software engineers must commit themselves to making software engineering a beneficial and respected profession. In accordance with that commitment, software engineers shall adhere to the following Code of Ethics and Professional Practice.

The Code contains eight Principles related to the behavior of and decisions made by professional software engineers, including practitioners, educators, managers, supervisors and policy makers, as well as trainees and students of the profession. The Principles identify the ethically responsible relationships in which individuals, groups, and organizations participate and the primary obligations within these relationships. The Clauses of each Principle are illustrations of some of the obligations included in these relationships. These obligations are founded in the software engineer's humanity, in special care owed to people affected by the work of software engineers, and the unique elements of the practice of software engineering. The Code prescribes these as obligations of anyone claiming to be or aspiring to be a software engineer.

It is not intended that the individual parts of the Code be used in isolation to justify errors of omission or commission. The list of Principles and Clauses is not exhaustive. The Clauses should not be read as separating the acceptable from the unacceptable in professional conduct in all practical situations. The Code is not a simple ethical algorithm that generates ethical decisions. In some situations standards may be in tension with each other or with standards from other sources. These situations require the software engineer to use ethical judgment to act in a manner which is most consistent with the spirit of the Code of Ethics and Professional Practice, given the circumstances.

Ethical tensions can best be addressed by thoughtful consideration of fundamental principles, rather than blind reliance on detailed regulations. These Principles should influence software engineers to consider broadly who is affected by their work; to examine if they and their colleagues are treating other human beings with due respect; to consider how the public, if reasonably well informed, would view their decisions; to analyze how the least empowered will be affected by their decisions; and to consider whether their acts would be judged worthy of the ideal professional working as a software engineer. In all these judgments concern for the health, safety and welfare of the public is primary; that is, the "Public Interest" is central to this Code.

The dynamic and demanding context of software engineering requires a code that is adaptable and relevant to new situations as they occur. However, even in this generality, the Code provides support for software engineers and managers of software engineers who need to take positive action in a specific case by documenting the ethical stance of the profession. The Code provides an ethical foundation to which individuals within teams and the team as a whole can appeal. The Code helps to define those actions that are ethically improper to request of a software engineer or teams of software engineers.

The Code is not simply for adjudicating the nature of questionable acts; it also has an important educational function. As this Code expresses the consensus of the profession on ethical issues, it is a means to educate both the public and aspiring professionals about the ethical obligations of all software engineers.

PRINCIPLES

Principle 1: PUBLIC

Software engineers shall act consistently with the public interest. In particular, software engineers shall, as appropriate:

1.01. Accept full responsibility for their own work.

1.02. Moderate the interests of the software engineer, the employer, the client and the users with the public good.

1.03. Approve software only if they have a well-founded belief that it is safe, meets specifications, passes appropriate tests, and does not diminish quality of life, diminish privacy or harm the environment. The ultimate effect of the work should be to the public good.

1.04. Disclose to appropriate persons or authorities any actual or potential danger to the user, the public, or the environment, that they reasonably believe to be associated with software or related documents.

1.05. Cooperate in efforts to address matters of grave public concern caused by software, its installation, maintenance, support or documentation.

1.06. Be fair and avoid deception in all statements, particularly public ones, concerning software or related documents, methods and tools.

1.07. Consider issues of physical disabilities, allocation of resources, economic disadvantage and other factors that can diminish access to the benefits of software.

1.08. Be encouraged to volunteer professional skills to good causes and contribute to public education concerning the discipline.

Principle 2: CLIENT AND EMPLOYER
Software engineers shall act in a manner that is in the best interests of their client and employer, consistent with the public interest. In particular, software engineers shall, as appropriate:

2.01. Provide service in their areas of competence, being honest and forthright about any limitations of their experience and education.
2.02. Not knowingly use software that is obtained or retained either illegally or unethically.
2.03. Use the property of a client or employer only in ways properly authorized, and with the client's or employer's knowledge and consent.
2.04. Ensure that any document upon which they rely has been approved, when required, by someone authorized to approve it.
2.05. Keep private any confidential information gained in their professional work, where such confidentiality is consistent with the public interest and consistent with the law.
2.06. Identify, document, collect evidence and report to the client or the employer promptly if, in their opinion, a project is likely to fail, to prove too expensive, to violate intellectual property law, or otherwise to be problematic.
2.07. Identify, document, and report significant issues of social concern, of which they are aware, in software or related documents, to the employer or the client.
2.08. Accept no outside work detrimental to the work they perform for their primary employer.
2.09. Promote no interest adverse to their employer or client, unless a higher ethical concern is being compromised; in that case, inform the employer or another appropriate authority of the ethical concern.

Principle 3: PRODUCT
Software engineers shall ensure that their products and related modifications meet the highest professional standards possible. In particular, software engineers shall, as appropriate:

3.01. Strive for high quality, acceptable cost and a reasonable schedule, ensuring significant tradeoffs are clear to and accepted by the employer and the client, and are available for consideration by the user and the public.
3.02. Ensure proper and achievable goals and objectives for any project on which they work or propose.
3.03. Identify, define and address ethical, economic, cultural, legal and environmental issues related to work projects.

3.04. Ensure that they are qualified for any project on which they work or propose to work by an appropriate combination of education and training, and experience.

3.05. Ensure an appropriate method is used for any project on which they work or propose to work.

3.06. Work to follow professional standards, when available, that are most appropriate for the task at hand, departing from these only when ethically or technically justified.

3.07. Strive to fully understand the specifications for software on which they work.

3.08. Ensure that specifications for software on which they work have been well documented, satisfy the users' requirements and have the appropriate approvals.

3.09. Ensure realistic quantitative estimates of cost, scheduling, personnel, quality and outcomes on any project on which they work or propose to work and provide an uncertainty assessment of these estimates.

3.10. Ensure adequate testing, debugging, and review of software and related documents on which they work.

3.11. Ensure adequate documentation, including significant problems discovered and solutions adopted, for any project on which they work.

3.12. Work to develop software and related documents that respect the privacy of those who will be affected by that software.

3.13. Be careful to use only accurate data derived by ethical and lawful means, and use it only in ways properly authorized.

3.14. Maintain the integrity of data, being sensitive to outdated or flawed occurrences.

3.15. Treat all forms of software maintenance with the same professionalism as new development.

Principle 4: JUDGMENT
Software engineers shall maintain integrity and independence in their professional judgment. In particular, software engineers shall, as appropriate:

4.01. Temper all technical judgments by the need to support and maintain human values.

4.02. Only endorse documents either prepared under their supervision or within their areas of competence and with which they are in agreement.

4.03. Maintain professional objectivity with respect to any software or related documents they are asked to evaluate.

4.04. Not engage in deceptive financial practices such as bribery, double billing, or other improper financial practices.

4.05. Disclose to all concerned parties those conflicts of interest that cannot reasonably be avoided or escaped.

4.06. Refuse to participate, as members or advisors, in a private, governmental or professional body concerned with software related issues, in which they, their employers or their clients have undisclosed potential conflicts of interest.

Principle 5: MANAGEMENT

Software engineering managers and leaders shall subscribe to and promote an ethical approach to the management of software development and maintenance. In particular, those managing or leading software engineers shall, as appropriate:

5.01. Ensure good management for any project on which they work, including effective procedures for promotion of quality and reduction of risk.

5.02. Ensure that software engineers are informed of standards before being held to them.

5.03. Ensure that software engineers know the employer's policies and procedures for protecting passwords, files and information that is confidential to the employer or confidential to others.

5.04. Assign work only after taking into account appropriate contributions of education and experience tempered with a desire to further that education and experience.

5.05. Ensure realistic quantitative estimates of cost, scheduling, personnel, quality and outcomes on any project on which they work or propose to work, and provide an uncertainty assessment of these estimates.

5.06. Attract potential software engineers only by full and accurate description of the conditions of employment.

5.07. Offer fair and just remuneration.

5.08. Not unjustly prevent someone from taking a position for which that person is suitably qualified.

5.09. Ensure that there is a fair agreement concerning ownership of any software, processes, research, writing, or other intellectual property to which a software engineer has contributed.

5.10. Provide for due process in hearing charges of violation of an employer's policy or of this Code.

5.11. Not ask a software engineer to do anything inconsistent with this Code.

5.12. Not punish anyone for expressing ethical concerns about a project.

Principle 6: PROFESSION

Software engineers shall advance the integrity and reputation of the profession consistent with the public interest. In particular, software engineers shall, as appropriate:

6.01. Help develop an organizational environment favorable to acting ethically.

6.02. Promote public knowledge of software engineering.

6.03. Extend software engineering knowledge by appropriate participation in professional organizations, meetings and publications.

6.04. Support, as members of a profession, other software engineers striving to follow this Code.

6.05. Not promote their own interest at the expense of the profession, client or employer.

6.06. Obey all laws governing their work, unless, in exceptional circumstances, such compliance is inconsistent with the public interest.

6.07. Be accurate in stating the characteristics of software on which they work, avoiding not only false claims but also claims that might reasonably be supposed to be speculative, vacuous, deceptive, misleading, or doubtful.

6.08. Take responsibility for detecting, correcting, and reporting errors in software and associated documents on which they work.

6.09. Ensure that clients, employers, and supervisors know of the software engineer's commitment to this Code of ethics, and the subsequent ramifications of such commitment.

6.10. Avoid associations with businesses and organizations which are in conflict with this Code.

6.11. Recognize that violations of this Code are inconsistent with being a professional software engineer.

6.12. Express concerns to the people involved when significant violations of this Code are detected unless this is impossible, counter-productive, or dangerous.

6.13. Report significant violations of this Code to appropriate authorities when it is clear that consultation with people involved in these significant violations is impossible, counter-productive or dangerous.

Principle 7: COLLEAGUES

Software engineers shall be fair to and supportive of their colleagues. In particular, software engineers shall, as appropriate:

7.01. Encourage colleagues to adhere to this Code.

7.02. Assist colleagues in professional development.

7.03. Credit fully the work of others and refrain from taking undue credit.

7.04. Review the work of others in an objective, candid, and properly documented way.

7.05. Give a fair hearing to the opinions, concerns, or complaints of a colleague.

7.06. Assist colleagues in being fully aware of current standard work practices including policies and procedures for protecting passwords, files and other confidential information, and security measures in general.

7.07. Not unfairly intervene in the career of any colleague; however, concern for the employer, the client or public interest may compel software engineers, in good faith, to question the competence of a colleague.

7.08. In situations outside of their own areas of competence, call upon the opinions of other professionals who have competence in that area.

Principle 8: SELF

Software engineers shall participate in lifelong learning regarding the practice of their profession and shall promote an ethical approach to the practice of the profession. In particular, software engineers shall continually endeavor to:

8.01. Further their knowledge of developments in the analysis, specification, design, development, maintenance and testing of software and related documents, together with the management of the development process.

8.02. Improve their ability to create safe, reliable, and useful quality software at reasonable cost and within a reasonable time.

8.03. Improve their ability to produce accurate, informative, and well-written documentation.

8.04. Improve their understanding of the software and related documents on which they work and of the environment in which they will be used.

8.05. Improve their knowledge of relevant standards and the law governing the software and related documents on which they work.

8.06. Improve their knowledge of this Code, its interpretation, and its application to their work.

8.07. Not give unfair treatment to anyone because of any irrelevant prejudices.

8.08. Not influence others to undertake any action that involves a breach of this Code.

8.09. Recognize that personal violations of this Code are inconsistent with being a professional software engineer.

This Code was developed by the ACM/IEEE-CS Joint Task Force on Software Engineering Ethics and Professional Practices (SEEPP):

Executive Committee: Donald Gotterbarn (Chair), Keith Miller and Simon Rogerson;

Members: Steve Barber, Peter Barnes, Ilene Burnstein, Michael Davis, Amr El-Kadi, N. Ben Fairweather, Milton Fulghum, N. Jayaram, Tom Jewett, Mark Kanko, Ernie Kallman, Duncan Langford, Joyce Currie Little, Ed Mechler, Manuel J. Norman, Douglas Phillips, Peter Ron Prinzivalli, Patrick Sullivan, John Weckert, Vivian Weil, S. Weisband and Laurie Honour Werth.

This Code may be published without permission as long as it is not changed in any way and it carries the copyright notice. Copyright © 1999 by the Association for Computing Machinery, Inc. and the Institute for Electrical and Electronics Engineers, Inc.[3]

9.3 The Ten Commandments of Computer Ethics

1. Thou shalt not use a computer to harm other people.

2. Thou shalt not interfere with other people's computer work.

3. Thou shalt not snoop around in other people's computer files.

4. Thou shalt not use a computer to steal.

5. Thou shalt not use a computer to bear false witness.

6. Thou shalt not copy or use proprietary software for which you have not paid.

7. Thou shalt not use other people's computer resources without authorization or proper compensation.

8. Thou shalt not appropriate other people's intellectual output.

9. Thou shalt think about the social consequences of the program you are writing or the system you are designing.

10. Thou shalt always use a computer in ways that ensure consideration and respect for your fellow humans.[4]

9.4 Chapter Summary

This chapter contains the ACM Code of Ethics and Professional Conduct, the Software Engineering Code of Ethics and Professional Practice, and the Ten Commandments of Computer Ethics.

9.5 Your Turn

Question 1. Although there is a good deal of overlap between the ACM Code and the Software Engineering Code, can you point out anything significant that appears in one code but not in the other?

Question 2. Name one advantage and one disadvantage of having a professional code of ethics.

Question 3. The ACM Code, in section 1.1, says that computer professionals should respect the diversity of all cultures. Why would this be a *professional* obligation?

Question 4. According to section 1.2 of the ACM Code, what things should be done before taking the step of "blowing the whistle"?

Question 5. Does section 1.4 of the ACM Code prohibit discrimination on the basis of sexual preference? Do you think a professional code should prohibit such discrimination? Why, or why not?

Question 6. The Ten Commandments of Computer Ethics has been criticized for being subject to too many exceptions and because some of the commandments are trivial in comparison to others on the list. In what ways do you find this criticism to be true and in what ways do you find it to be false?

TEN

Computer Ethics and International Development

10.1 Introduction

One of the areas in which the rapid growth of technology, especially digital technology, is having a huge impact is international development. It is causing a "digital divide," that is, a widening of the gulf between nations that have well-developed technologies and those that have little or none. To remedy this problem, the United Nations has organized a program called the World Summit on the Information Society (WSIS). A brief consideration of this Summit will identify some of the problems that a lack of technology, or an imbalance of technology, has caused in the area of international development and some suggestions for possible solutions to these problems.

10.2 The World Summit on the Information Society

The World Summit on the Information Society is a worldwide effort to improve and make more equitable the communication of information throughout the nations of the world. Specifically, WSIS defines itself in these words: "The digital revolution in information and communication technologies has created the platform for a free flow of information, ideas and knowledge across the globe. This revolution has made a profound impression on the way the world functions. The Internet has become an important global resource, a resource that is critical to both the developed world as a business and social tool and the developing world as a passport to equitable participation, as well as economic, social and educational development. The purpose of the World Summit on the Information Society is to ensure that these benefits are accessible to all while promoting specific advantages in areas such as e-strategies, e-commerce, e-governance, e-health, education, literacy, cultural diversity, gender equality, sustainable development and environmental protection."[1]

Planning for the Summit began in 1998. The Summit was held in two phases, the first in Geneva, Switzerland, in 2003, and the second in Tunis, Tunisia, in 2005. More than 11,000 participants from 175 countries attended the Geneva phase of WSIS and more than 19,000 participants from 174 countries attended the Tunis phase.

The two phases of WSIS produced large amounts of documentation. It would be impossible to survey all of it here. Sample selections from the Geneva Plan of Action, the Geneva Declaration of Principles, the Tunis Commitment, and the Tunis Agenda for the Information Society will be given here in order to provide WSIS views on the ethical dimensions of the Information Society and WSIS recommendations for the governance of the Internet.

10.3 Geneva Plan of Action (10–12 December 2003)

C7. ICT applications: benefits in all aspects of life

14. ICT applications can support sustainable development, in the fields of public administration, business, education and training, health, employment, environment, agriculture and science within the framework of national e-strategies. This would include actions within the following sectors:
15. E-government
    a. Implement e-government strategies focusing on applications aimed at innovating and promoting transparency in public administrations and democratic processes, improving efficiency and strengthening relations with citizens.
    b. Develop national e-government initiatives and services, at all levels, adapted to the needs of citizens and business, to achieve a more efficient allocation of resources and public goods.

c. Support international cooperation initiatives in the field of e-government, in order to enhance transparency, accountability and efficiency at all levels of government.

16. E-business

    a. Governments, international organizations and the private sector, are encouraged to promote the benefits of international trade and the use of e-business, and promote the use of e-business models in developing countries and countries with economies in transition.

    b. Through the adoption of an enabling environment, and based on widely available Internet access, governments should seek to stimulate private sector investment, foster new applications, content development and public/private partnerships.

    c. Government policies should favour assistance to, and growth of SMMEs, in the ICT industry, as well as their entry into e-business, to stimulate economic growth and job creation as an element of a strategy for poverty reduction through wealth creation.

17. E-learning (see section C4)

    a. Governments, international organizations and the private sector, are encouraged to promote the benefits of international trade and the use of e-business, and promote the use of e-business models in developing countries and countries with economies in transition.

    b. Through the adoption of an enabling environment, and based on widely available Internet access, governments should seek to stimulate private sector investment, foster new applications, content development and public/private partnerships.

    c. Government policies should favour assistance to, and growth of SMMEs, in the ICT industry, as well as their entry into e-business, to stimulate economic growth and job creation as an element of a strategy for poverty reduction through wealth creation.

18. E-health

    a. Promote collaborative efforts of governments, planners, health professionals, and other agencies along with the participation of international organizations for creating a [sic] reliable, timely, high quality and affordable health care and health information systems and for promoting continuous medical training, education, and research through the use of ICTs, while respecting and protecting citizens' right to privacy.

b. Facilitate access to the world's medical knowledge and locally-relevant content resources for strengthening public health research and prevention programmes and promoting women's and men's health, such as content on sexual and reproductive health and sexually transmitted infections, and for diseases that attract full attention of the world including HIV/AIDS, malaria and tuberculosis.

c. Alert, monitor and control the spread of communicable diseases, through the improvement of common information systems.

d. Promote the development of international standards for the exchange of health data, taking due account of privacy concerns.

e. Encourage the adoption of ICTs to improve and extend health care and health information systems to remote and underserved areas and vulnerable populations, recognising women's roles as health providers in their families and communities.

f. Strengthen and expand ICT-based initiatives for providing medical and humanitarian assistance in disasters and emergencies.

19. E-employment

a. Encourage the development of best practices for e-workers and e-employers built, at the national level, on principles of fairness and gender equality, respecting all relevant international norms.

b. Promote new ways of organizing work and business with the aim of raising productivity, growth and well-being through investment in ICTs and human resources.

c. Promote teleworking to allow citizens, particularly in the developing countries, LDCs, and small economies, to live in their societies and work anywhere, and to increase employment opportunities for women, and for those with disabilities. In promoting teleworking, special attention should be given to strategies promoting job creation and the retention of the skilled working force.

d. Promote early intervention programmes in science and technology that should target young girls to increase the number of women in ICT carriers.

20. E-environment

   a. Governments, in cooperation with other stakeholders are encouraged to use and promote ICTs as an instrument for environmental protection and the sustainable use of natural resources.

   b. Government, civil society and the private sector are encouraged to initiate actions and implement projects and programmes for sustainable production and consumption and the environmentally safe disposal and recycling of discarded hardware and components used in ICTs.

   c. Establish monitoring systems, using ICTs, to forecast and monitor the impact of natural and man-made disasters, particularly in developing countries, LDCs and small economies.

21. E-agriculture

   a. Ensure the systematic dissemination of information using ICTs on agriculture, animal husbandry, fisheries, forestry and food, in order to provide ready access to comprehensive, up-to-date and detailed knowledge and information, particularly in rural areas.

   b. Public-private partnerships should seek to maximize the use of ICTs as an instrument to improve production (quantity and quality).

22. E-science

   a. Promote affordable and reliable high-speed Internet connection for all universities and research institutions to support their critical role in information and knowledge production, education and training, and to support the establishment of partnerships, cooperation and networking between these institutions.

   b. Promote electronic publishing, differential pricing and open access initiatives to make scientific information affordable and accessible in all countries on an equitable basis.

   c. Promote the use of peer-to-peer technology to share scientific knowledge and pre-prints and reprints written by scientific authors who have waived their right to payment.

d. Promote the long-term systematic and efficient collection, dissemination and preservation of essential scientific digital data, for example, population and meteorological data in all countries.

e. Promote principles and metadata standards to facilitate cooperation and effective use of collected scientific information and data as appropriate to conduct scientific research.[2]

10.4 Geneva Declaration of Principles (13 December 2003)

A. Our Common Vision of the Information Society

1. We, the representatives of the peoples of the world, assembled in Geneva from 10–12 December 2003 for the first phase of the World Summit on the Information Society, declare our common desire and commitment to build a people-centred, inclusive and development-oriented Information Society, where everyone can create, access, utilize and share information and knowledge, enabling individuals, communities and peoples to achieve their full potential in promoting their sustainable development and improving their quality of life, premised on the purposes and principles of the Charter of the United Nations and respecting fully and upholding the Universal Declaration of Human Rights.

2. Our challenge is to harness the potential of information and communication technology to promote the development goals of the Millennium Declaration, namely the eradication of extreme poverty and hunger; achievement of universal primary education; promotion of gender equality and empowerment of women; reduction of child mortality; improvement of maternal health; to combat HIV/AIDS, malaria and other diseases; ensuring environmental sustainability; and development of global partnerships for development for the attainment of a more peaceful, just and prosperous world. We also reiterate our commitment to the achievement of sustainable development and agreed development goals, as contained in the Johannesburg Declaration and Plan of Implementation

and the Monterrey Consensus, and other outcomes of relevant United Nations Summits.

3. We reaffirm the universality, indivisibility, interdependence and interrelation of all human rights and fundamental freedoms, including the right to development, as enshrined in the Vienna Declaration. We also reaffirm that democracy, sustainable development, and respect for human rights and fundamental freedoms as well as good governance at all levels are interdependent and mutually reinforcing. We further resolve to strengthen respect for the rule of law in international as in national affairs.

4. We reaffirm, as an essential foundation of the Information Society, and as outlined in Article 19 of the Universal Declaration of Human Rights, that everyone has the right to freedom of opinion and expression; that this right includes freedom to hold opinions without interference and to seek, receive and impart information and ideas through any media and regardless of frontiers. Communication is a fundamental social process, a basic human need and the foundation of all social organization. It is central to the Information Society. Everyone, everywhere should have the opportunity to participate and no one should be excluded from the benefits the Information Society offers.

5. We further reaffirm our commitment to the provisions of Article 29 of the Universal Declaration of Human Rights, that everyone has duties to the community in which alone the free and full development of their personality is possible, and that, in the exercise of their rights and freedoms, everyone shall be subject only to such limitations as are determined by law solely for the purpose of securing due recognition and respect for the rights and freedoms of others and of meeting the just requirements of morality, public order and the general welfare in a democratic society. These rights and freedoms may in no case be exercised contrary to the purposes and principles of the United Nations. In this way, we shall promote an Information Society where human dignity is respected.

6. In keeping with the spirit of this declaration, we rededicate ourselves to upholding the principle of the sovereign equality of all States.

7. We recognize that science has a central role in the development of the Information Society. Many of the building blocks of the Information Society are the result of scientific and technical advances made possible by the sharing of research results.

8. We recognize that education, knowledge, information and communication are at the core of human progress, endeavour and well-being. Further, Information and Communication Technologies (ICTs) have an immense impact on virtually all aspects of our lives. The rapid progress of these technologies opens completely new opportunities to attain higher levels of development. The capacity of these technologies to reduce many traditional obstacles, especially those of time and distance, for the first time in history makes it possible to use the potential of these technologies for the benefit of millions of people in all corners of the world.

9. We are aware that ICTs should be regarded as tools and not as an end in themselves. Under favourable conditions, these technologies can be a powerful instrument, increasing productivity, generating economic growth, job creation and employability and improving the quality of life of all. They can also promote dialogue among people, nations and civilizations.

10. We are also fully aware that the benefits of the information technology revolution are today unevenly distributed between the developed and developing countries and within societies. We are fully committed to turning this digital divide into a digital opportunity for all, particularly for those who risk being left behind and being further marginalized.

11. We are committed to realizing our common vision of the Information Society for ourselves and for future generations. We recognize that young people are the future workforce and leading creators and earliest adopters of ICTs. They must

therefore be empowered as learners, developers, contributors, entrepreneurs and decision-makers. We must focus especially on young people who have not yet been able to benefit fully from the opportunities provided by ICTs. We are also committed to ensuring that the development of ICT applications and operation of services respects the rights of children as well as their protection and well-being.

12. We affirm that development of ICTs provides enormous opportunities for women, who should be an integral part of, and key actors in, the Information Society. We are committed to ensuring that the Information Society enables women's empowerment and their full participation on the basis on equality in all spheres of society and in all decision-making processes. To this end, we should mainstream a gender equality perspective and use ICTs as a tool to that end.

13. In building the Information Society, we shall pay particular attention to the special needs of marginalized and vulnerable groups of society, including migrants, internally displaced persons and refugees, unemployed and underprivileged people, minorities and nomadic people. We shall also recognize the special needs of older persons and persons with disabilities.

14. We are resolute to empower the poor, particularly those living in remote, rural and marginalized urban areas, to access information and to use ICTs as a tool to support their efforts to lift themselves out of poverty.

15. In the evolution of the Information Society, particular attention must be given to the special situation of indigenous peoples, as well as to the preservation of their heritage and their cultural legacy.

16. We continue to pay special attention to the particular needs of people of developing countries, countries with economies in transition, Least Developed Countries, Small Island Developing States, Landlocked Developing Countries, Highly Indebted Poor Countries, countries and territories under occupation, countries recovering from conflict and

countries and regions with special needs as well as to conditions that pose severe threats to development, such as natural disasters.

17. We recognize that building an inclusive Information Society requires new forms of solidarity, partnership and cooperation among governments and other stakeholders, i.e. the private sector, civil society and international organizations. Realizing that the ambitious goal of this Declaration – bridging the digital divide and ensuring harmonious, fair and equitable development for all – will require strong commitment by all stakeholders, we call for digital solidarity, both at national and international levels.

18. Nothing in this Declaration shall be construed as impairing, contradicting, restricting or derogating from the provisions of the Charter of the United Nations and the Universal Declaration of Human Rights, any other international instrument or national laws adopted in furtherance of these instruments.

B. An Information Society for All: Key Principles

19. We are resolute in our quest to ensure that everyone can benefit from the opportunities that ICTs can offer. We agree that to meet these challenges, all stakeholders should work together to: improve access to information and communication infrastructure and technologies as well as to information and knowledge; build capacity; increase confidence and security in the use of ICTs; create an enabling environment at all levels; develop and widen ICT applications; foster and respect cultural diversity; recognize the role of the media; address the ethical dimensions of the Information Society; and encourage international and regional cooperation. We agree that these are the key principles for building an inclusive Information Society.

B1) The role of governments and all stakeholders in the promotion of ICTs for development

20. Governments, as well as private sector, civil society and the United Nations and other international organizations have an important role and responsibility in the development of the

Information Society and, as appropriate, in decision-making processes. Building a people-centred Information Society is a joint effort which requires cooperation and partnership among all stakeholders.

B2) Information and communication infrastructure: an essential foundation for an inclusive information society

21. Connectivity is a central enabling agent in building the Information Society. Universal, ubiquitous, equitable and affordable access to ICT infrastructure and services, constitutes one of the challenges of the Information Society and should be an objective of all stakeholders involved in building it. Connectivity also involves access to energy and postal services, which should be assured in conformity with the domestic legislation of each country.

22. A well-developed information and communication network infrastructure and applications, adapted to regional, national and local conditions, easily-accessible and affordable, and making greater use of broadband and other innovative technologies where possible, can accelerate the social and economic progress of countries, and the well-being of all individuals, communities and peoples.

23. Policies that create a favourable climate for stability, predictability and fair competition at all levels should be developed and implemented in a manner that not only attracts more private investment for ICT infrastructure development but also enables universal service obligations to be met in areas where traditional market conditions fail to work. In disadvantaged areas, the establishment of ICT public access points in places such as post offices, schools, libraries and archives, can provide effective means for ensuring universal access to the infrastructure and services of the Information Society.

B3) Access to information and knowledge

24. The ability for all to access and contribute information, ideas and knowledge is essential in an inclusive Information Society.

25. The sharing and strengthening of global knowledge for development can be enhanced by removing barriers to equitable access to information for economic, social, political, health, cultural, educational, and scientific activities and by facilitating access to public domain information, including by universal design and the use of assistive technologies.

26. A rich public domain is an essential element for the growth of the Information Society, creating multiple benefits such as an educated public, new jobs, innovation, business opportunities, and the advancement of sciences. Information in the public domain should be easily accessible to support the Information Society, and protected from misappropriation. Public institutions such as libraries and archives, museums, cultural collections and other community-based access points should be strengthened so as to promote the preservation of documentary records and free and equitable access to information.

27. Access to information and knowledge can be promoted by increasing awareness among all stakeholders of the possibilities offered by different software models, including proprietary, open-source and free software, in order to increase competition, access by users, diversity of choice, and to enable all users to develop solutions which best meet their requirements. Affordable access to software should be considered as an important component of a truly inclusive Information Society.

28. We strive to promote universal access with equal opportunities for all to scientific knowledge and the creation and dissemination of scientific and technical information, including open access initiatives for scientific publishing.

B4) Capacity building

29. Each person should have the opportunity to acquire the necessary skills and knowledge in order to understand, participate actively in, and benefit fully from, the Information Society and the knowledge economy. Literacy and universal primary education are key factors for building a fully

inclusive information society, paying particular attention to the special needs of girls and women. Given the wide range of ICT and information specialists required at all levels, building institutional capacity deserves special attention.

30. The use of ICTs in all stages of education, training and human resource development should be promoted, taking into account the special needs of persons with disabilities and disadvantaged and vulnerable groups.

31. Continuous and adult education, re-training, life-long learning, distance-learning and other special services, such as telemedicine, can make an essential contribution to employability and help people benefit from the new opportunities offered by ICTs for traditional jobs, self-employment and new professions. Awareness and literacy in ICTs are an essential foundation in this regard.

32. Content creators, publishers, and producers, as well as teachers, trainers, archivists, librarians and learners, should play an active role in promoting the Information Society, particularly in the Least Developed Countries.

33. To achieve a sustainable development of the Information Society, national capability in ICT research and development should be enhanced. Furthermore, partnerships, in particular between and among developed and developing countries, including countries with economies in transition, in research and development, technology transfer, manufacturing and utilization of ICT products and services are crucial for promoting capacity building and global participation in the Information Society. The manufacture of ICTs presents a significant opportunity for creation of wealth.

34. The attainment of our shared aspirations, in particular for developing countries and countries with economies in transition, to become fully-fledged members of the Information Society, and their positive integration into the knowledge economy, depends largely on increased capacity building in the areas of education, technology know-how and access to

information, which are major factors in determining development and competitiveness.

B5) Building confidence and security in the use of ICTs

35. Strengthening the trust framework, including information security and network security, authentication, privacy and consumer protection, is a prerequisite for the development of the Information Society and for building confidence among users of ICTs. A global culture of cyber-security needs to be promoted, developed and implemented in cooperation with all stakeholders and international expert bodies. These efforts should be supported by increased international cooperation. Within this global culture of cyber-security, it is important to enhance security and to ensure the protection of data and privacy, while enhancing access and trade. In addition, it must take into account the level of social and economic development of each country and respect the development-oriented aspects of the Information Society.

36. While recognizing the principles of universal and non-discriminatory access to ICTs for all nations, we support the activities of the United Nations to prevent the potential use of ICTs for purposes that are inconsistent with the objectives of maintaining international stability and security, and may adversely affect the integrity of the infrastructure within States, to the detriment of their security. It is necessary to prevent the use of information resources and technologies for criminal and terrorist purposes, while respecting human rights.

37. Spam is a significant and growing problem for users, networks and the Internet as a whole. Spam and cyber-security should be dealt with at appropriate national and international levels.

B6) Enabling environment

38. An enabling environment at national and international levels is essential for the Information Society. ICTs should be used as an important tool for good governance.

39. The rule of law, accompanied by a supportive, transparent, pro-competitive, technologically neutral and predictable policy and regulatory framework reflecting national realities,

is essential for building a people-centred Information Society. Governments should intervene, as appropriate, to correct market failures, to maintain fair competition, to attract investment, to enhance the development of the ICT infrastructure and applications, to maximize economic and social benefits, and to serve national priorities.

40. A dynamic and enabling international environment, supportive of foreign direct investment, transfer of technology, and international cooperation, particularly in the areas of finance, debt and trade, as well as full and effective participation of developing countries in global decision-making, are vital complements to national development efforts related to ICTs. Improving global affordable connectivity would contribute significantly to the effectiveness of these development efforts.

41. ICTs are an important enabler of growth through efficiency gains and increased productivity, in particular by small and medium sized enterprises (SMEs). In this regard, the development of the Information Society is important for broadly-based economic growth in both developed and developing economies. ICT-supported productivity gains and applied innovations across economic sectors should be fostered. Equitable distribution of the benefits contributes to poverty eradication and social development. Policies that foster productive investment and enable firms, notably SMEs, to make the changes needed to seize the benefits from ICTs, are likely to be the most beneficial.

42. Intellectual Property protection is important to encourage innovation and creativity in the Information Society; similarly, the wide dissemination, diffusion, and sharing of knowledge is important to encourage innovation and creativity. Facilitating meaningful participation by all in intellectual property issues and knowledge sharing through full awareness and capacity building is a fundamental part of an inclusive Information Society.

43. Sustainable development can best be advanced in the Information Society when ICT-related efforts and programmes are

fully integrated in national and regional development strategies. We welcome the New Partnership for Africa's Development (NEPAD) and encourage the international community to support the ICT-related measures of this initiative as well as those belonging to similar efforts in other regions. Distribution of the benefits of ICT-driven growth contributes to poverty eradication and sustainable development.

44. Standardization is one of the essential building blocks of the Information Society. There should be particular emphasis on the development and adoption of international standards. The development and use of open, interoperable, non-discriminatory and demand-driven standards that take into account needs of users and consumers is a basic element for the development and greater diffusion of ICTs and more affordable access to them, particularly in developing countries. International standards aim to create an environment where consumers can access services worldwide regardless of underlying technology.

45. The radio frequency spectrum should be managed in the public interest and in accordance with principle of legality, with full observance of national laws and regulation as well as relevant international agreements.

46. In building the Information Society, States are strongly urged to take steps with a view to the avoidance of, and refrain from, any unilateral measure not in accordance with international law and the Charter of the United Nations that impedes the full achievement of economic and social development by the population of the affected countries, and that hinders the well-being of their population.

47. Recognizing that ICTs are progressively changing our working practices, the creation of a secure, safe and healthy working environment, appropriate to the utilisation of ICTs, respecting all relevant international norms, is fundamental.

48. The Internet has evolved into a global facility available to the public and its governance should constitute a core issue of the Information Society agenda. The international management

of the Internet should be multilateral, transparent and democratic, with the full involvement of governments, the private sector, civil society and international organizations. It should ensure an equitable distribution of resources, facilitate access for all and ensure a stable and secure functioning of the Internet, taking into account multilingualism.

49. The management of the Internet encompasses both technical and public policy issues and should involve all stakeholders and relevant intergovernmental and international organizations. In this respect it is recognized that:

   a. Policy authority for Internet-related public policy issues is the sovereign right of States. They have rights and responsibilities for international Internet-related public policy issues;

   b. The private sector has had and should continue to have an important role in the development of the Internet, both in the technical and economic fields;

   c. Civil society has also played an important role on Internet matters, especially at community level, and should continue to play such a role;

   d. Intergovernmental organizations have had and should continue to have a facilitating role in the coordination of Internet-related public policy issues;

   e. International organizations have also had and should continue to have an important role in the development of Internet-related technical standards and relevant policies.

50. International Internet governance issues should be addressed in a coordinated manner. We ask the Secretary-General of the United Nations to set up a working group on Internet governance, in an open and inclusive process that ensures a mechanism for the full and active participation of governments, the private sector and civil society from both developing and developed countries, involving relevant intergovernmental and international organizations and forums, to investigate and make proposals for action, as appropriate, on the governance of Internet by 2005.

B7) ICT applications: benefits in all aspects of life

    51. The usage and deployment of ICTs should seek to create benefits in all aspects of our daily life. ICT applications are potentially important in government operations and services, health care and health information, education and training, employment, job creation, business, agriculture, transport, protection of environment and management of natural resources, disaster prevention, and culture, and to promote eradication of poverty and other agreed development goals. ICTs should also contribute to sustainable production and consumption patterns and reduce traditional barriers, providing an opportunity for all to access local and global markets in a more equitable manner. Applications should be user-friendly, accessible to all, affordable, adapted to local needs in languages and cultures, and support sustainable development. To this effect, local authorities should play a major role in the provision of ICT services for the benefit of their populations.

B8) Cultural diversity and identity, linguistic diversity and local content

    52. Cultural diversity is the common heritage of humankind. The Information Society should be founded on and stimulate respect for cultural identity, cultural and linguistic diversity, traditions and religions, and foster dialogue among cultures and civilizations. The promotion, affirmation and preservation of diverse cultural identities and languages as reflected in relevant agreed United Nations documents including UNESCO's Universal Declaration on Cultural Diversity, will further enrich the Information Society.

    53. The creation, dissemination and preservation of content in diverse languages and formats must be accorded high priority in building an inclusive Information Society, paying particular attention to the diversity of supply of creative work and due recognition of the rights of authors and artists. It is essential to promote the production of and accessibility to all content – educational, scientific, cultural or recreational – in

diverse languages and formats. The development of local content suited to domestic or regional needs will encourage social and economic development and will stimulate participation of all stakeholders, including people living in rural, remote and marginal areas.

54. The preservation of cultural heritage is a crucial component of identity and self–understanding of individuals that links a community to its past. The Information Society should harness and preserve cultural heritage for the future by all appropriate methods, including digitisation.

B9) Media

55. We reaffirm our commitment to the principles of freedom of the press and freedom of information, as well as those of the independence, pluralism and diversity of media, which are essential to the Information Society. Freedom to seek, receive, impart and use information for the creation, accumulation and dissemination of knowledge are important to the Information Society. We call for the responsible use and treatment of information by the media in accordance with the highest ethical and professional standards. Traditional media in all their forms have an important role in the Information Society and ICTs should play a supportive role in this regard. Diversity of media ownership should be encouraged, in conformity with national law, and taking into account relevant international conventions. We reaffirm the necessity of reducing international imbalances affecting the media, particularly as regards infrastructure, technical resources and the development of human skills.

B10) Ethical dimensions of the Information Society

56. The Information Society should respect peace and uphold the fundamental values of freedom, equality, solidarity, tolerance, shared responsibility, and respect for nature.

57. We acknowledge the importance of ethics for the Information Society, which should foster justice, and the dignity and worth of the human person. The widest possible protection should

be accorded to the family and to enable it to play its crucial role in society.

58. The use of ICTs and content creation should respect human rights and fundamental freedoms of others, including personal privacy, and the right to freedom of thought, conscience, and religion in conformity with relevant international instruments.

59. All actors in the Information Society should take appropriate actions and preventive measures, as determined by law, against abusive uses of ICTs, such as illegal and other acts motivated by racism, racial discrimination, xenophobia, and related intolerance, hatred, violence, all forms of child abuse, including paedophilia and child pornography, and trafficking in, and exploitation of, human beings.

B11) International and regional cooperation

60. We aim at making full use of the opportunities offered by ICTs in our efforts to reach the internationally agreed development goals, including those contained in the Millennium Declaration, and to uphold the key principles set forth in this Declaration. The Information Society is intrinsically global in nature and national efforts need to be supported by effective international and regional cooperation among governments, the private sector, civil society and other stakeholders, including the international financial institutions.

61. In order to build an inclusive global Information Society, we will seek and effectively implement concrete international approaches and mechanisms, including financial and technical assistance. Therefore, while appreciating ongoing ICT cooperation through various mechanisms, we invite all stakeholders to commit to the "Digital Solidarity Agenda" set forth in the Plan of Action. We are convinced that the worldwide agreed objective is to contribute to bridge the digital divide, promote access to ICTs, create digital opportunities, and benefit from the potential offered by ICTs for development. We recognize the will expressed by some to create an

international voluntary "Digital Solidarity Fund," and by others to undertake studies concerning existing mechanisms and the efficiency and feasibility of such a Fund.

62. Regional integration contributes to the development of the global Information Society and makes strong cooperation within and among regions indispensable. Regional dialogue should contribute to national capacity building and to the alignment of national strategies with the goals of this Declaration of Principles in a compatible way, while respecting national and regional particularities. In this context, we welcome and encourage the international community to support the ICT-related measures of such initiatives.

63. We resolve to assist developing countries, LDCs and countries with economies in transition through the mobilization from all sources of financing, the provision of financial and technical assistance and by creating an environment conducive to technology transfer, consistent with the purposes of this Declaration and the Plan of Action.

64. The core competences of the International Telecommunication Union (ITU) in the fields of ICTs – assistance in bridging the digital divide, international and regional cooperation, radio spectrum management, standards development and the dissemination of information – are of crucial importance for building the Information Society.

C. Towards an Information Society for All Based on Shared Knowledge

65. We commit ourselves to strengthening cooperation to seek common responses to the challenges and to the implementation of the Plan of Action, which will realize the vision of an inclusive Information Society based on the Key Principles incorporated in this Declaration.

66. We further commit ourselves to evaluate and follow-up progress in bridging the digital divide, taking into account different levels of development, so as to reach internationally agreed development goals, including those contained in the

Millennium Declaration, and to assess the effectiveness of investment and international cooperation efforts in building the Information Society.

67. We are firmly convinced that we are collectively entering a new era of enormous potential, that of the Information Society and expanded human communication. In this emerging society, information and knowledge can be produced, exchanged, shared and communicated through all the networks of the world. All individuals can soon, if we take the necessary actions, together build a new Information Society based on shared knowledge and founded on global solidarity and a better mutual understanding between peoples and nations. We trust that these measures will open the way to the future development of a true knowledge society.[3]

10.5 Tunis Commitment (16–18 November 2005)

1. We, the representatives of the peoples of the world, have gathered in Tunis from 16–18 November 2005 for this second phase of the World Summit on the Information Society (WSIS) to reiterate our unequivocal support for the Geneva Declaration of Principles and Plan of Action adopted at the first phase of the World Summit on the Information Society in Geneva in December 2003.

2. We reaffirm our desire and commitment to build a people-centred, inclusive and development-oriented Information Society, premised on the purposes and principles of the Charter of the United Nations, international law and multilateralism, and respecting fully and upholding the Universal Declaration of Human Rights, so that people everywhere can create, access, utilize and share information and knowledge, to achieve their full potential and to attain the internationally agreed development goals and objectives, including the Millennium Development Goals.

3. We reaffirm the universality, indivisibility, interdependence and interrelation of all human rights and fundamental freedoms, including the right to development, as enshrined in the Vienna

Declaration. We also reaffirm that democracy, sustainable development, and respect for human rights and fundamental freedoms as well as good governance at all levels are interdependent and mutually reinforcing. We further resolve to strengthen respect for the rule of law in international as in national affairs.

4. We reaffirm paragraphs 4, 5 and 55 of the Geneva Declaration of Principles. We recognize that freedom of expression and the free flow of information, ideas, and knowledge, are essential for the Information Society and beneficial to development.

5. The Tunis Summit represents a unique opportunity to raise awareness of the benefits that Information and Communication Technologies (ICTs) can bring to humanity and the manner in which they can transform people's activities, interaction and lives, and thus increase confidence in the future.

6. This Summit is an important stepping-stone in the world's efforts to eradicate poverty and to attain the internationally agreed development goals and objectives, including the Millennium Development Goals. By the Geneva decisions, we established a coherent long-term link between the WSIS process, and other relevant major United Nations conferences and summits. We call upon governments, private sector, civil society and international organizations to join together to implement the commitments set forth in the Geneva Declaration of Principles and Plan of Action. In this context, the outcomes of the recently concluded 2005 World Summit on the review of the implementation of the Millennium Declaration are of special relevance.

7. We reaffirm the commitments made in Geneva and build on them in Tunis by focusing on financial mechanisms for bridging the digital divide, on Internet governance and related issues, as well as on follow-up and implementation of the Geneva and Tunis decisions, as referenced in the Tunis Agenda for the Information Society.

8. While reaffirming the important roles and responsibilities of all stakeholders as outlined in paragraph 3 of the Geneva Plan of Action, we acknowledge the key role and responsibilities of governments in the WSIS process.

9. We reaffirm our resolution in the quest to ensure that everyone can benefit from the opportunities that ICTs can offer, by recalling that governments, as well as private sector, civil society and the United Nations and other international organizations, should work together to: improve access to information and communication infrastructure and technologies as well as to information and knowledge; build capacity; increase confidence and security in the use of ICTs; create an enabling environment at all levels; develop and widen ICT applications; foster and respect cultural diversity; recognize the role of the media; address the ethical dimensions of the Information Society; and encourage international and regional cooperation. We confirm that these are the key principles for building an inclusive Information Society, the elaboration of which is found in the Geneva Declaration of Principles.

10. We recognize that access to information and sharing and creation of knowledge contributes significantly to strengthening economic, social and cultural development, thus helping all countries to reach the internationally agreed development goals and objectives, including the Millennium Development Goals. This process can be enhanced by removing barriers to universal, ubiquitous, equitable and affordable access to information. We underline the importance of removing barriers to bridging the digital divide, particularly those that hinder the full achievement of the economic, social and cultural development of countries and the welfare of their people, in particular, in developing countries.

11. Furthermore, ICTs are making it possible for a vastly larger population than at any time in the past to join in sharing and expanding the base of human knowledge, and contributing to its further growth in all spheres of human endeavour as well as its application to education, health and science. ICTs have enormous potential to expand access to quality education, to boost literacy and universal primary education, and to facilitate the learning process itself, thus laying the groundwork for the establishment of a fully inclusive and development-oriented Information Society and knowledge economy which respects cultural and linguistic diversity.

12. We emphasize that the adoption of ICTs by enterprises plays a fundamental role in economic growth. The growth and productivity enhancing effects of well-implemented investments in ICTs can lead to increased trade and to more and better employment. For this reason, both enterprise development and labour market policies play a fundamental role in the adoption of ICTs. We invite governments and the private sector to enhance the capacity of Small, Medium and Micro Enterprises (SMMEs), since they furnish the greatest number of jobs in most economies. We shall work together, with all stakeholders, to put in place the necessary policy, legal and regulatory frameworks that foster entrepreneurship, particularly for SMMEs.

13. We also recognize that the ICT revolution can have a tremendous positive impact as an instrument of sustainable development. In addition, an appropriate enabling environment at national and international levels could prevent increasing social and economic divisions, and the widening of the gap between rich and poor countries, regions, and individuals – including between men and women.

14. We also recognize that in addition to building ICT infrastructure, there should be adequate emphasis on developing human capacity and creating ICT applications and digital content in local language, where appropriate, so as to ensure a comprehensive approach to building a global Information Society.

15. Recognizing the principles of universal and non-discriminatory access to ICTs for all nations, the need to take into account the level of social and economic development of each country, and respecting the development-oriented aspects of the Information Society, we underscore that ICTs are effective tools to promote peace, security and stability, to enhance democracy, social cohesion, good governance and the rule of law, at national, regional and international levels. ICTs can be used to promote economic growth and enterprise development. Infrastructure development, human capacity building, information security and network security are critical to achieve these goals. We further recognize the need to

effectively confront challenges and threats resulting from use of ICTs for purposes that are inconsistent with objectives of maintaining international stability and security and may adversely affect the integrity of the infrastructure within States, to the detriment of their security. It is necessary to prevent the abuse of information resources and technologies for criminal and terrorist purposes, while respecting human rights.

16. We further commit ourselves to evaluate and follow up progress in bridging the digital divide, taking into account different levels of development, so as to reach internationally agreed development goals and objectives, including the Millennium Development Goals, and to assess the effectiveness of investment and international cooperation efforts in building the Information Society.

17. We urge governments, using the potential of ICTs, to create public systems of information on laws and regulations, envisaging a wider development of public access points and supporting the broad availability of this information.

18. We shall strive unremittingly, therefore, to promote universal, ubiquitous, equitable and affordable access to ICTs, including universal design and assistive technologies, for all people, especially those with disabilities, everywhere, to ensure that the benefits are more evenly distributed between and within societies, and to bridge the digital divide in order to create digital opportunities for all and benefit from the potential offered by ICTs for development.

19. The international community should take necessary measures to ensure that all countries of the world have equitable and affordable access to ICTs, so that their benefits in the fields of socio-economic development and bridging the digital divide are truly inclusive.

20. To that end, we shall pay particular attention to the special needs of marginalized and vulnerable groups of society including migrants, internally displaced persons and refugees, unemployed and underprivileged people, minorities and nomadic people, older persons and persons with disabilities.

21. To that end, we shall pay special attention to the particular needs of people of developing countries, countries with economies in transition, Least Developed Countries, Small Island Developing States,

Landlocked Developing Countries, Highly Indebted Poor Countries, countries and territories under occupation, and countries recovering from conflict or natural disasters.

22. In the evolution of the Information Society, particular attention must be given to the special situation of indigenous peoples, as well as to the preservation of their heritage and their cultural legacy.

23. We recognize that a gender divide exists as part of the digital divide in society and we reaffirm our commitment to women's empowerment and to a gender equality perspective, so that we can overcome this divide. We further acknowledge that the full participation of women in the Information Society is necessary to ensure the inclusiveness and respect for human rights within the Information Society. We encourage all stakeholders to support women's participation in decision-making processes and to contribute to shaping all spheres of the Information Society at international, regional and national levels.

24. We recognize the role of ICTs in the protection of children and in enhancing the development of children. We will strengthen action to protect children from abuse and defend their rights in the context of ICTs. In that context, we emphasize that the best interests of the child are a primary consideration.

25. We reaffirm our commitment to empowering young people as key contributors to building an inclusive Information Society. We will actively engage youth in innovative ICT-based development programmes and widen opportunities for youth to be involved in e-strategy processes.

26. We recognize the importance of creative content and applications to overcome the digital divide and to contribute to the achievement of the internationally agreed development goals and objectives, including the Millennium Development Goals.

27. We recognize that equitable and sustainable access to information requires the implementation of strategies for the long-term preservation of the digital information that is being created.

28. We reaffirm our desire to build ICT networks and develop applications, in partnership with the private sector, based on open or interoperable standards that are affordable and accessible to all,

available anywhere and anytime, to anyone and on any device, leading to a ubiquitous network.

29. Our conviction is that governments, the private sector, civil society, the scientific and academic community, and users can utilize various technologies and licensing models, including those developed under proprietary schemes and those developed under open-source and free modalities, in accordance with their interests and with the need to have reliable services and implement effective programmes for their people. Taking into account the importance of proprietary software in the markets of the countries, we reiterate the need to encourage and foster collaborative development, inter-operative platforms and free and open-source software, in ways that reflect the possibilities of different software models, notably for education, science and digital inclusion programmes.

30. Recognizing that disaster mitigation can significantly support efforts to bring about sustainable development and help in poverty reduction, we reaffirm our commitment to leveraging ICT capabilities and potential through fostering and strengthening cooperation at the national, regional, and international levels.

31. We commit ourselves to work together towards the implementation of the Digital Solidarity Agenda, as agreed in paragraph 27 of the Geneva Plan of Action. The full and quick implementation of that agenda, observing good governance at all levels, requires in particular a timely, effective, comprehensive and durable solution to the debt problems of developing countries where appropriate, a universal, rule-based, open, non-discriminatory and equitable multilateral trading system, that can also stimulate development worldwide, benefiting countries at all stages of development, as well as, [sic] to seek and effectively implement concrete international approaches and mechanisms to increase international cooperation and assistance to bridge the digital divide.

32. We further commit ourselves to promote the inclusion of all peoples in the Information Society through the development and use of local and/or indigenous languages in ICTs. We will continue our efforts to protect and promote cultural diversity, as well as cultural identities, within the Information Society.

33. We acknowledge that, while technical cooperation can help, capacity building at all levels is needed to ensure that the required institutional and individual expertise is available.

34. We recognize the need for, and strive to mobilize resources, both human and financial, in accordance with chapter two of the Tunis Agenda for the Information Society, to enable us to increase the use of ICT for development and realize the short-, medium- and long-term plans dedicated to building the Information Society as follow-up and implementation of the outcomes of WSIS.

35. We recognize the central role of public policy in setting the framework in which resource mobilization can take place.

36. We value the potential of ICTs to promote peace and to prevent conflict which, inter alia, negatively affects achieving development goals. ICTs can be used for identifying conflict situations through early-warning systems preventing conflicts, promoting their peaceful resolution, supporting humanitarian action, including protection of civilians in armed conflicts, facilitating peacekeeping missions, and assisting post conflict peace-building and reconstruction.

37. We are convinced that our goals can be accomplished through the involvement, cooperation and partnership of governments and other stakeholders, i.e. the private sector, civil society and international organizations, and that international cooperation and solidarity at all levels are indispensable if the fruits of the Information Society are to benefit all.

38. Our efforts should not stop with the conclusion of the Summit. The emergence of the global Information Society to which we all contribute provides increasing opportunities for all our peoples and for an inclusive global community that were unimaginable only a few years ago. We must harness these opportunities today and support their further development and progress.

39. We reaffirm our strong resolve to develop and implement an effective and sustainable response to the challenges and opportunities of building a truly global Information Society that benefits all our peoples.

40. We strongly believe in the full and timely implementation of the decisions we took in Geneva and Tunis, as outlined in the Tunis Agenda for the Information Society.[4]

10.6 Tunis Agenda for the Information Society (18 November 2005)

[Areas of omission of material presented in the Tunis Agenda are indicated by "...."]

INTERNET GOVERNANCE
29. We reaffirm the principles enunciated in the Geneva phase of the WSIS, in December 2003, that the Internet has evolved into a global facility available to the public and its governance should constitute a core issue of the Information Society agenda. The international management of the Internet should be multilateral, transparent and democratic, with the full involvement of governments, the private sector, civil society and international organizations. It should ensure an equitable distribution of resources, facilitate access for all and ensure a stable and secure functioning of the Internet, taking into account multilingualism.
30. We acknowledge that the Internet, a central element of the infrastructure of the Information Society, has evolved from a research and academic facility into a global facility available to the public.
31. We recognize that Internet governance, carried out according to the Geneva principles, is an essential element for a people-centred, inclusive, development-oriented and non-discriminatory Information Society. Furthermore, we commit ourselves to the stability and security of the Internet as a global facility and to ensuring the requisite legitimacy of its governance, based on the full participation of all stakeholders, from both developed and developing countries, within their respective roles and responsibilities. ...
34. A working definition of Internet governance is the development and application by governments, the private sector and civil society, in their respective roles, of shared principles, norms, rules, decision-making procedures, and programmes that shape the evolution and use of the Internet.
35. We reaffirm that the management of the Internet encompasses both technical and public policy issues and should involve all stakeholders and relevant intergovernmental and international organizations. In this respect it is recognized that:
    a. Policy authority for Internet-related public policy issues is the sovereign right of States. They have rights and responsibilities for international Internet-related public policy issues. ...
37. We seek to improve the coordination of the activities of international and intergovernmental organizations and other institutions concerned with

Internet governance and the exchange of information among themselves. A multi-stakeholder approach should be adopted, as far as possible, at all levels. . . .

40. We underline the importance of the prosecution of cybercrime, including cybercrime committed in one jurisdiction, but having effects in another. . . .

41. We resolve to deal effectively with the significant and growing problem posed by spam. We take note of current multilateral, multi-stakeholder frameworks for regional and international cooperation on spam, for example, the APEC Anti-Spam Strategy, the London Action Plan, the Seoul-Melbourne Anti–Spam Memorandum of Understanding and the relevant activities of OECD and ITU. We call upon all stakeholders to adopt a multi-pronged approach to counter spam that includes, inter alia, consumer and business education; appropriate legislation, law-enforcement authorities and tools; the continued development of technical and self-regulatory measures; best practices; and international cooperation.

42. We reaffirm our commitment to the freedom to seek, receive, impart and use information, in particular, for the creation, accumulation and dissemination of knowledge. We affirm that measures undertaken to ensure Internet stability and security, to fight cybercrime and to counter spam, must protect and respect the provisions for privacy and freedom of expression as contained in the relevant parts of the Universal Declaration of Human Rights and the Geneva Declaration of Principles. . . .

44. We also underline the importance of countering terrorism in all its forms and manifestations on the Internet, while respecting human rights and in compliance with other obligations under international law, as outlined in UNGA A/60/L.1 with reference to Article 85 of the 2005 World Summit Outcome. . . .

47. We recognize the increasing volume and value of all e-business, both within and across national boundaries. We call for the development of national consumer-protection laws and practices, and enforcement mechanisms where necessary, to protect the right of consumers who purchase goods and services online, and for enhanced international cooperation to facilitate a further expansion, in a non-discriminatory way, under applicable national laws, of e-business as well as consumer confidence in it. . . .

49. We reaffirm our commitment to turning the digital divide into digital opportunity, and we commit to ensuring harmonious and equitable development for all. We commit to foster and provide guidance on development areas in the broader Internet governance arrangements, and to include, amongst other issues, international interconnection costs, capacity building and technology/know-how transfer. We encourage the realization of multilingualism in the Internet development environment, and we support the development of software that renders itself easily to localization, and enables users to choose appropriate solutions from different software models including open-source, free and proprietary software. . . .

53. We commit to working earnestly towards multilingualization of the Internet, as part of a multilateral, transparent and democratic process, involving governments and all stakeholders, in their respective roles. In this context, we also support local content development, translation and adaptation, digital archives, and diverse forms of digital and traditional media, and recognize that these activities can also strengthen local and indigenous communities. We would therefore underline the need to:
    a. Advance the process for the introduction of multilingualism in a number of areas including domain names, e-mail addresses and keyword look-up;
    b. Implement programmes that allow for the presence of multilingual domain names and content on the Internet and the use of various software models in order to fight against the linguistic digital divide and to ensure the participation of all in the emerging new society;. . . .
    c. Strengthen cooperation between relevant bodies for the further development of technical standards and to foster their global deployment. . . .
55. We recognize that the existing arrangements for Internet governance have worked effectively to make the Internet the highly robust, dynamic and geographically diverse medium that it is today, with the private sector taking the lead in day-to-day operations, and with innovation and value creation at the edges.
56. The Internet remains a highly dynamic medium and therefore any framework and mechanisms designed to deal with Internet governance should be inclusive and responsive to the exponential growth and fast evolution of the Internet as a common platform for the development of multiple applications.
57. The security and stability of the Internet must be maintained.
58. We recognize that Internet governance includes more than Internet naming and addressing. It also includes other significant public policy issues such as, inter alia, critical Internet resources, the security and safety of the Internet, and developmental aspects and issues pertaining to the use of the Internet.
59. We recognize that Internet governance includes social, economic and technical issues including affordability, reliability and quality of service.
60. We further recognize that there are many cross-cutting international public policy issues that require attention and are not adequately addressed by the current mechanisms.
61. We are convinced that there is a need to initiate, and reinforce, as appropriate, a transparent, democratic, and multilateral process, with the participation of governments, private sector, civil society and international organizations, in their respective roles. This process could envisage creation of a suitable framework or mechanisms, where justified, thus spurring the ongoing and active evolution of the current arrangements in order to synergize the efforts in this regard.

62. We emphasize that any Internet governance approach should be inclusive and responsive and should continue to promote an enabling environment for innovation, competition and investment.
63. Countries should not be involved in decisions regarding another country's country-code Top-Level Domain (ccTLD). Their legitimate interests, as expressed and defined by each country, in diverse ways, regarding decisions affecting their ccTLDs, need to be respected, upheld and addressed via a flexible and improved framework and mechanisms.
64. We recognize the need for further development of, and strengthened cooperation among, stakeholders for public policies for generic Top-Level Domain names (gTLDs).
65. We underline the need to maximize the participation of developing countries in decisions regarding Internet governance, which should reflect their interests, as well as in development and capacity building.
69. We further recognize the need for enhanced cooperation in the future, to enable governments, on an equal footing, to carry out their roles and responsibilities, in international public policy issues pertaining to the Internet, but not in the day-to-day technical and operational matters, that do not impact on international public policy issues. . . .[5]

10.7 Chapter Summary

This chapter has provided an introduction to WSIS and its work. In particular it has provided selections from the Geneva Declaration of Principles, the Geneva Plan of Action, the Tunis Agenda for the Information Society, and the Tunis Commitment, which pertain to technical/political/ethical issues.

10.8 Your Turn

Question 1. Which items in the Ethical Dimensions of the Information Society (Geneva Declaration of Principles, B10) deal with what might be considered virtues and which deal with items that might be considered vices?

Question 2. In WSIS's statements about Internet Governance, does WSIS seem to have a concern about the policies and activities of particular countries? If so, which countries do you think these would be?

ELEVEN

Robotics and Ethics

11.1 Introduction

You may be wondering what a chapter on robotics and ethics is doing in a book on computer ethics. Simply put, robotics today is heavily dependent upon artificial intelligence, and artificial intelligence is a branch of computer science. I would feel I was short-changing the reader if I had not included this chapter.

The Roboethics Roadmap, a product of the European Robotics Research Network (EURON), begins with the following statement: "We can forecast that in the XXI century humanity will coexist with the first alien intelligence we have ever come into contact with – robots." EURON is a group that aims to promote excellence in robotics by creating resources and exchanging knowledge, as well as looking to the future. Its objectives are research coordination, a joint program of research, education and training, industrial links, and dissemination.[1] It is clear from the quoted statement that EURON is serious about looking to the future through a multinational approach that will prepare for the advent of the relationship between humans and intelligent robots.

A major product of EURON is a robotics research roadmap that is meant to investigate opportunities for developing and employing robot technology over the next twenty years. The first release of this roadmap took place in July of 2006. More than fifty people who produced it had participated in previous activities on robotics, possessed a cross-cultural attitude, and were interested in applied ethics. The cross-cultural attitude is an important consideration here because EURON is aware that various cultures, religions, and societies have differing concepts of ethics.

EURON is well aware that robotics is a new science still in its formative stages. For this reason it takes a cautious view of the future and only hints at problems inherent in the possible emergence of human functions in the robot, such as consciousness, free will, self-consciousness, a sense of dignity, emotions, and so on. It has also decided to limit its focus to the human ethics of robot designers, manufacturers, and users – not the artificial ethics of the robots themselves. EURON expects that the different elements in society working in robotics, along with the stakeholders in robotics, will eventually join the process of building a Roboethics Roadmap. EURON envisions that these participants will include parliaments, academic institutions, research labs, public ethics committees, professions, industry, educational systems, and the mass media.[2]

Future developments about the ethical issues relating to robotics have been discussed at previous gatherings of robotics professionals. For example, in February of 2004 the Fukuoka World Robot Declaration was issued in Fukuoka, Japan. It states the following expectations for next-generation robots: "a) next generation robots will be partners that coexist with human beings; b) next generation robots will assist human beings both physically and psychologically; c) next-generation robots will contribute to the realization of a safe and peaceful society."

11.2 What Is Roboethics?

Roboethics is a term that was first used in 2002 by Gianmarco Veruggio, a robotics engineer who is based in Genoa, Italy. He has had a leading role in the development of EURON and in its concern that, as the scope, scale, and speed of robotics development increases, thought must be given to the ethical aspects of the human/robotics relationship before a crisis occurs.

The name *roboethics* works well for referring to the intersection of robotics and ethics for several reasons:

- Naming *things* gives them reality (nomina sunt consequentia rerum – names are the consequence of things)

- People more readily pay attention to a concept that is linked to "the inherent nature of the material"
- It recalls the well-known word *bioethics*[3]

11.3 Ethical Issues in Robotics

EURON has identified some ethical issues that relate to roboethics. As noted, these can differ in their definition and application according to various cultures, religions, and societies. The issues that EURON has identified are:

- Concepts of immanentism and transcendentalism
- What is human? Post-human? Cyborg?
- Human life/artificial life
- Human intelligence/artificial intelligence
- Privacy versus traceability of actions
- Integrity of the person/perception of the human being
- Diversity (gender, ethnicity, minority)
- Freedom
- Human enhancement (physical, cognitive, nanotechnology)
- What is science/knowledge?
- Animal welfare

EURON has further specified ethical issues as they bear upon a society that is immersed in Information and Communication Technology (ICT):

- Dual-use technology (every technology can be used or misused)
- Anthropomorphization of machines
- Humanization of the human/machine relationship (cognitive and affective bonds toward machines)
- Technology addiction
- Digital divide, socio-technological gap (age, social layers, world areas)
- Fair access to technological resources
- Effects of technology on the global distribution of wealth and power
- Environmental impact of technology

EURON has also articulated a number of principles to be followed in roboethics:

- Respect for human dignity and human rights
- Equality, justice, and equity
- Benefit/harm analysis
- Respect for cultural diversity and pluralism
- Nondiscrimination and nonstigmatization
- Autonomy and individual responsibility
- Informed consent
- Privacy
- Confidentiality
- Solidarity and cooperation
- Social responsibility
- Sharing of benefits
- Responsibility toward the biosphere[4]

11.4 Disciplines Involved in Robotics

Robotics is a new science, some might say an application of engineering, that involves several disciplines, to wit:

- Mechanics
- Physics/mathematics
- Automation and control
- Electronics
- Computer science/artificial intelligence
- Cybernetics[5]

11.5 The Roboethics Roadmap in EURON's Own Words

The Roboethics Roadmap, being a product of professionals interested in robotics and roboethics, provides a great deal of specificity about EURON's planning with regard to robots. The following extended quotation concerning this is made with the permission of EURON:

Specificity of robotics:
   It is the first time in history that humanity is approaching the threshold of replicating an intelligent and autonomous entity. This compels the scientific

community to examine closely the very concept of intelligence – in humans, animals, and machines – from a cybernetic standpoint.

In fact, complex concepts like autonomy, learning, consciousness, evaluation, free will, decision making, freedom, emotions, and many others shall be analysed, taking into account that the same concept shall not have, in humans, animals, and machines, the same semantic meaning.

From this standpoint, it can be seen as natural and necessary that robotics draws on several other disciplines:

Logic/Linguistics
Neuroscience/Psychology
Biology/Physiology
Philosophy/Literature
Natural History/Anthropology
Art/Design

Roboethics *de facto* unifies the so called *two cultures*, Science and Humanities.

The effort to design roboethics should make the unity of these two cultures a primary assumption. This means that experts shall view robotics as a whole – in spite of the current early stage that recalls a *melting pot*– so they can achieve the *vision* of robotics' future.

About robotics:

In 1942, novelist Isaac Asimov formulated the Three Laws of Robotics in the short story *Runaround*:[6]

1. *A robot may not injure a human being, or through inaction, allow a human being to come to harm.*
2. *A robot must obey the orders given it by human beings except where such orders would conflict with the First Law.*
3. *A robot must protect its own existence as long as such protection does not conflict with the First or Second Law.*

Later on Asimov added the Fourth Law (known as Law Zero):

4. *No robot may harm humanity or, through inaction, allow humanity to come to harm.*

The theme of the relationship between humankind and *autonomous* machines – or, automata – appeared early in world literature, developed firstly through legends and myths, more recently by scientific and moral essays.

The topic of the rebellions of automata recurs in the classic European literature, as well as the misuse or the evil use of the product of ingenuity. It is not so in all the world cultures: for instance, the mythology of the Japanese cultures does not include such paradigms. On the contrary, machines (and, in general, human products) are always beneficial and friendly to humanity.

These cultural differences in attitudes toward machines are a subject the Roboethics Roadmap should take into account and analyse.

Questions:

- Although farsighted and forewarning, could Asimov's Three Laws become really the *Ethics of Robots*?
- Is roboethics the ethics of robots or the ethics of robotic scientists?
- How far can we go in embodying ethics in a robot? And, which kind of "ethics" is the correct one for Robotics?
- How contradictory is, on the one hand, the need to implement roboethics in robots, and, on the other, the development of robot autonomy?
- Is it right that robots can exhibit a "personality"?
- Is it right that robots can express "emotion"?

1. What is a robot:

Robotics scientists, researchers, and the general public have different evaluations about robots, which should be taken into account in the Roboethics Roadmap.

a) Robots are nothing but machines:

Many consider robots as mere machines – very sophisticated and helpful ones – but always machines. According to this view, robots do not have any hierarchically higher characteristics, nor will they be provided with consciousness, free will, or with the level of autonomy superior to that embodied by the designer. In this frame, roboethics can be compared to an Engineering Applied Ethics.

b) Robots have ethical dimensions:

In this view, an ethical dimension is intrinsic within robots. This derives from a conception according to which technology *is not an addition to man but is, in fact, one of the ways in which mankind distinguishes itself from animals.* So that, like language and computers but even more, humanoid robots are symbolic devices designed by humanity to extend, enhance, and improve our innate powers, and to act with charity and good intentions. (J. M. Galvan)

c) Robots as moral agents:

Artificial agents, particularly but not only those in Cyberspace, extend the class of entities that can be involved in moral situations. For they can be conceived as moral patients (as entities that can be acted upon for good or evil) and also as moral agents (not necessarily exhibiting free will, mental states or responsibility, but as entities that can perform actions, again for good or evil). This complements the more traditional approach, common at least since Montaigne and Descartes, which considers whether or not (artificial) agents have mental states, feelings, emotions and so on. By focusing directly on 'mind-less morality' we are able to avoid that question and also many of the concerns of Artificial Intelligence. (L. Floridi)

d) Robots, evolution of a new species:

According to this point of view, not only will our robotics machines have autonomy and consciences, but humanity will create machines that *exceed us in the moral as well as the intellectual dimensions*. Robots, with their rational mind and unshaken morality, will be the new species: Our machines will be better than we are, and we will be better for having created them. (J. Storrs Hall)

e) Main positions on robotics:

Since the First International Symposium on Roboethics, three main ethical positions emerged from the robotics community (D. Cerqui):

1. Not interested in ethics:

This is the attitude of those who consider that their actions are strictly technical and do not think they have a social or moral responsibility for their work.

2. Interested in short-term ethical questions:

This is the attitude of those who express their ethical concern in terms of "good" or "bad," and who refer to some cultural values and social conventions. This attitude includes respecting and helping humans in diverse areas, such as implementing laws or in helping elderly people.

3. Interested in long-term ethical concerns:

This is the attitude of those who express their ethical concern in terms of global, long-term questions: for instance, the "Digital divide" between South and North; or young and elderly. They are aware of the gap between industrialized and poor countries, and wonder whether the former should not change their way of developing robotics in order to be more useful to the latter.

Other disciplines involved in roboethics:

The design of roboethics will require the combined commitment of experts of several disciplines, who, working in transnational projects, committees, and commissions, will have to adjust laws and regulations to the problems resulting from the scientific and technological achievements in robotics.

In all likelihood we will witness the birth of a new *curricula studiorum* [course of studies] and specialties necessary to manage a subject so complex, just as has happened with Forensic Medicine.

In particular, we mention the following fields as the main ones to be involved in roboethics:

- Robotics
- Computer Science
- Artificial Intelligence
- Philosophy
- Ethics
- Theology
- Biology/Physiology

- Cognitive Sciences
- Neurosciences
- Law
- Sociology
- Psychology
- Industrial Design

Humanoids:

One of the most ambitious aims of robotics is to design an autonomous robot that could reach – and even surpass – human intelligence and even performance in partially unknown, changing, and unpredictable environments.

"Essentially, it is expected that a robot will provide assistance in housework, for aged people and for entertainment to keep up the amenity of life and human environment in the next century. A type of human robot, a Humanoid, is expected to work together with human partners in our living environment, and it will share the same working space and will experience the same thinking and behaviour patterns as a human being. The robot will integrate information from sensors and show coordinated actions which realize a high level of communication with a human without any special training using multimedia such as speech, facial expression and body movement."[7]

Artificial Mind:

We shall introduce here, in summary, the concept of intelligence. In this Roadmap, we limit ourselves to defining intelligence from an engineering point of view, that is, an operational intelligence – although we are aware of the fact that our terminology regarding robots' functions is often taken from the language used for human beings.

Artificial Intelligence shall be able to lead the robot to fulfill the missions required by the endusers. To achieve this goal, in recent years scientists have been working on AI techniques in many fields. Among them:

a) Artificial vision
b) Perception and analysis of the environment
c) Natural language processing
d) Human interaction
e) Cognitive systems
f) Machine learning, behaviors
g) Neural networks

From our point of view, one of the fundamental aspects of robots is their capability to learn: to learn the characteristics of the surrounding environment, that is, a) the physical environment, but also, b) the living beings who inhabit it. This means that robots working in a given environment have to recognize [distinguish] human beings from other *objects.*

In addition to learning about the environment, robots have to learn about their own behaviour, through a self reflective process. They have to learn from experience, replicating somehow the natural processes of the evolution of intelligence in living beings (synthesis procedures, trial-and-error, learning by doing, and so on).

It is almost inevitable that human designers are inclined to replicate their own conception of intelligence in the intelligence of robots. In turn, the former gets incorporated into the control algorithm of the robots. Robotics intelligence is a learned intelligence, fed by the world's models uploaded by the designers. It is a self-developed intelligence, evolved through the experience robots have achieved and through the learned effects of their actions. Robotics intelligence comprises also the ability to evaluate; to attribute a judgment to the actions carried out.

All these processes embodied in robots produce a kind of intelligent machine endowed with the capability to express a certain degree of autonomy. It follows that a robot can behave, in some situations, in a way which is unpredictable for their human designers.

Basically, the increasing autonomy of the robots could give rise to unpredictable and non-predictable behaviours.

So without necessarily imagining some Sci-Fi scenarios where robots are provided with consciousness, free will and emotions, in a few years we are going to cohabit with robots endowed with self knowledge and autonomy – in the engineering meaning of these words.

Artificial Body:

Humanoids are robots whose body structure resembles the human one.

They answer to an old dream of humanity, and certainly do not spring only from rational, engineering, or utilitarian motivations, but also from psycho-anthropological ones.

Humanoids are the expression of one of the demands of our European culture, which is that humankind should create some mechanical being in the shape of a human. In the Japanese culture, the demand is to carefully replicate nature in all its forms.

It is a very difficult and demanding enterprise, a project on the level of the *Mission to the Moon*. But, precisely because of its characteristic of being one of humanity's dreams, the investments are high and the speed of progress very quick.

It has been forecasted that it will be possible, in certain situations, to confuse humanoids with humans. Humanoids will assist human operators in human environments, will replace human beings, and will cooperate with human beings in many ways.

Given the high cost and the delicacy of the humanoids, they will probably be employed in tasks and in environments where the human shape would really be needed, that is, in all these situations where the human-robot interaction is primary, compared to any other mission – human-robot interactions in health care, children/disabled people/elderly assistance, baby sitting, office clerks, museum guides, entertainers, sexual robots, and so on. They will also be employed in testimonials for commercial products.

In the frame of this Roadmap, there is no need to closely examine the techno-logical aspects of humanoids (actuators, artificial muscles, robot path planning, visual aspect and the realization of emotion in humanoid robots, expressions of verbal and non-verbal information in robots, environment and human recog-nition of human faces, human-machine communication interface, and so on). Many of these technologies come from biorobotics, and many, born in the humanoids lab, are and will be applied to biorobotics.

Benefits:

- Intelligent machines can assist humans to perform very difficult tasks, and behave like true and reliable companions in many ways.
- Humanoids are robots so adaptable and flexible that they will be rapidly used in many situations and circumstances.
- Their shape, and the sophisticated human-robot interaction, will be very useful for those situations where a human shape is needed.
- Faced with an aging population, the Japanese society foresees humanoid robots as one way to enable people to continue to lead an active and productive life in their old age, without being a burden to other people.
- Research carried out in humanoid laboratories over the world will have as a side effect the development of platforms to study the human body, for training, haptic tests and training, with extraordinary outcomes for health care, education, edutainment, and so on.

Problems:

- Reliability of the internal evaluation systems of robots
- Unpredictability of robots' behaviour
- Traceability of evaluation/actions procedures
- Identification of robots
- Safety – wrong action can lead to dangerous situations for living beings and the environment
- Security – in cases where the autonomy of the robot is controlled by wrong intentioned people who can modify the robot's behaviour in dangerous and fraudulent ways

Because humanoids incorporate almost all the characteristics of the whole spectrum of robots, their use implies the emergence of nearly all the problems we are examining below. In particular, their introduction in human environments, workplaces, homes, schools, hospitals, public places, offices, and so on, will deeply and dramatically change our society.

We have forecasted problems connected to:

- Replacement of human beings (economic problems, human unemploy-ment, reliability, dependability, and so on)
- Psychological problems (deviations in human emotions, problems of attachment, disorganization in children, fears, panic, confusion between real and artificial, feelings of subordination toward robots)

- Well before evolving to become conscious agents, humanoids can be an extraordinary tool used to control human beings

Recommendations:
Activate working groups inside Standards Committees to study the possibility to define international technical/legal rules for commercial robots regarding:

- Safety: We should provide for systems for the control of robots' autonomy. Operators should be able to limit robots' autonomy when the correct robot behaviour is not guaranteed
- Security: Hardware and software keys to avoid inappropriate or illegal use of the robot
- Traceability: As in the case of sensitive systems, we should provide for systems like the aircraft's black box to be able to register and document robots' behaviours
- Identifiability: Like cars and other vehicles, robots too should have identification numbers and serial numbers
- Privacy: Hardware and software systems to encrypt and password-protect sensitive data needed by the robot to perform its tasks or acquired during its activity

Promote cross-cultural updates for engineering scientists that allow them to monitor the medium and long term effects of applied robotics technologies.

Promote among robotics scientists the spirit of the Fukuoka World Robot Declaration (2004):

1. Next-generation robots will be partners that coexist with human beings
2. Next-generation robots will assist human beings both physically and psychologically
3. Next-generation robots will contribute to the realization of a safe and peaceful society[8]

[In addition to considering humanoids, the Roadmap also goes on to cover advanced production systems, adaptive robot servants and intelligent homes, network robotics, outdoor robotics, health care and life quality, military robotics, and edutainment].

11.6 Difficulties of Programming Robots for Ethics

Much has been said about future developments in robotics. One possibility is that robots will have an ethical dimension. As we will see, this does not necessarily involve free will or conscience in the robots.

An interesting description of how ethics might be programmed into robots has been given in an article entitled "Towards Machine Ethics" written by Michael Anderson, Susan Leigh Anderson, and Chris Armen in 2004. They write that, "In contrast to computer hacking, software property issues, privacy issues and other topics normally ascribed to *computer* ethics, *machine* ethics is concerned with the consequences of behavior of machines towards human users and other machines."[9]

They argue that as machines are given more responsibility, it is appropriate that an equal measure of accountability be asked of them. This, of course, requires that they have a process by which they can make ethical decisions for which they may be held accountable. Using examples of two ethical theories, the authors show how such a process might be programmed into robots.

The first example is Act Utilitarianism, a theory formulated by Jeremy Bentham in the late 1700s. This theory holds that what is ethical is that which promotes happiness. Bentham considered happiness to be the surplus of pleasure over pain for those affected by any given action (see Chapter 3).

The authors decided to formulate an algorithm that computes which action, from among all alternatives, produces the greatest net pleasure. They write that this "requires as input the number of peoples affected, and for each person, the intensity of the pleasure/displeasure (e.g., on a scale of 2 to −2), the duration of the pleasure (e.g., in days), and the probability that this pleasure/displeasure will occur for each possible action. For each person, the algorithm simply computes the product of the intensity, the duration, and the probability, to obtain the net pleasure for each person. It then adds the individual net pleasure to obtain the Total Net Pleasure . . . This computation would be performed for each alternative action. The action with the highest Total Net Pleasure is the right action."[10]

The authors point out that Act Utilitarianism has been criticized because it can violate a person's rights by sacrificing one person for the greater good. So they give another example to show how this shortcoming can be corrected by using the theories of W. D. Ross and John Rawls.

Ross' theory is duty-based rather than following Bentham's orientation toward consequences. Ross proposes seven *prima facie* duties: fidelity, reparation, gratitude, justice, beneficence, non-maleficence, and self-improvement. Unfortunately, Ross provides no way to determine which duty is the strongest. At this point the authors suggest Rawls' "reflective equilibrium" approach.[11] This involves considering the possible weightings of all the pertinent duties and then testing them by our intuitions concerning particular cases, then revising the weightings to reflect our intuitions and testing them again. In sum, the authors say "instead of computing a single value based only on pleasure/displeasure, we must compute the sum of up to seven values, depending on the number of Ross' duties relevant to the particular action. The value for each such duty could be computed as with Hedonistic Act Utilitarianism, as the product of Intensity, Duration, and Probability.[12]

The process described sounds exhausting if done by a human being, but it would be well suited to machine computation. Of course the algorithm and the programming would be contributed by human programmers and the old rule would still stand that no program can be better than its programmer.

So we are left with the question: Although it would seem possible to program a machine for ethical decision making, could such decision making be described as autonomous?

11.7 Chapter Summary

The chapter began with an introduction that spoke of the relationship of robotics to computer ethics. Then EURON's Roadmap project was described. This was followed by a definition of "roboethics" and a listing of ethical issues in the field of robotics. Next, the disciplines involved in robotics and roboethics were examined. This was followed by an extended quotation from the EURON Roadmap that covered the specifics of robotics (including Asimov's Three Laws of Robotics). The final section of the Roadmap covered the topic of humanoids under the headings of artificial mind, artificial body, benefits, problems, and recommendations. The chapter concluded with a section on the difficulties of programming robots with ethics, using the research of Michael Anderson, Susan Leigh Anderson, and Chris Armen.

11.8 Your Turn

Question 1. Respond to this statement from Section 11.5: How contradictory is, on the one hand, the need to implement ethics in robots, and, on the other, the development of robot autonomy?

Question 2. It has been predicted that robots will be used as sexual partners. Would this be ethical if the purpose were therapy? If robots were used for prostitution in places where prostitution is legal, would this be ethical if the aim of the use was to reduce the sexual exploitation of women and children and the spread of venereal disease?

Question 3. Section 11.6 of this chapter ends with a question: "So we are left with the question: Although it would seem possible to program a machine for ethical decision making, could such decision making be described as autonomous?" Describe how you would answer this question.

TWELVE

Theft and Piracy Concerns

12.1 Introduction

"Theft" is used here in the sense of the second meaning defined in *Webster's Third New International Dictionary,* which states, "the taking of property unlawfully." "Piracy" is used here in the sense of the third meaning defined in *Webster's Third New International Dictionary,* which states, "an unauthorized appropriation and reproduction of another's production, invention, or conception, esp. in infringement of a copyright."

The computer has made possible new forms of stealing and unauthorized appropriation of property. We will consider a number of them in this chapter. There is no claim that this is an exclusive list of such forms, but hopefully enough will be included here to provide a sense of how the Internet has changed things in regard to theft and piracy.

12.2 Cybersquatting

Not the most transparent of all technical terms, "cybersquatting" means the acquiring of a domain name on the Internet with the hope of selling it, in turn, to a business or individual who might be desirous of using it. The closer such a domain name is related to the name of a business or individual who is its prospective buyer, the better the chance the cybersquatter will have of selling it to such an entity and the higher the price the cybersquatter might be able to get for it. The relationship of the name to the potential buyer might be that the domain name is just one letter off from the business name of the potential buyer or it might be that the domain name incorporates a phrase that is associated with the business or professional activity of the potential buyer. Sometimes the seller does not even own the name to be sold but simply reserves it and defers paying for it as long as possible, thus encumbering the name and making it essentially unavailable to anyone else who is seeking to purchase it.

It might be objected at this point that such behavior is just good business practice and that it is not unethical. The problem is that many people do not just simply register a particular domain name and then hope to sell it for a higher price. They sometimes use the domain to put up information – sometimes false information – which will embarrass the potential buyer or put the potential buyer at a business disadvantage. Then they offer to sell the domain name at a high price to the targeted individual or business so that the individual or business can remove the embarrassing information. Leaving aside such legal questions as fraud, extortion, and blackmail, this latter kind of cybersquatting is clearly not ethical behavior. Congress has acted on this subject by outlawing bad faith cybersquatting as a violation of trademark law.[1]

12.3 Fake IDs

Computers can be used to make fake identification cards that are used for purposes of misrepresentation. One of the most common fake identification cards is a state driver's license. The reason that it is the most common is that a driver's license is most often used as a means to verify the ID cardholder's age for purposes of sale of liquor. One can find hundreds of listings on the Web where one can order fake IDs, often with "next day delivery" guaranteed. Your author even found one of these sites that claimed: "I am offering you the TRUTH on where to buy fake id!"[2] My guess is that the writer of this statement did not appreciate its irony.

Sometimes fake ID businesses try to claim that they are not acting illegally, but are just selling "novelty" ID cards. However, many states have made the sale of such "novelty" cards illegal.

12.4 Identity Theft

To begin this topic, let me give you an account of something that happened to me personally. Recently I took a trip by car to a city a hundred or so miles from my home. As I was preparing to return home, I took the car to a gas station and tried to fill it with gas. I say "tried," because my credit card was refused when I inserted it at the pump. I took the card inside the station and the attendant tried to process it there. It didn't work. I called the "customer service" number on the back of my credit card and was told that my card was "suspended." I asked why. The customer service representative said it was because of some suspicious activity that had recently taken place involving my credit card number. It seems that someone had made a long distance phone call and used my credit card number to pay for the call. That call was made without challenge by the phone company involved. The caller tried to place another call a couple of days later and was challenged at that time. Since the caller did not know the authenticating information to answer the challenge, the card was suspended. I asked why I had not been notified and was told that the customer service had tried to call me – but I was out of town. Fortunately, I did have enough cash with me to buy enough gasoline to make it back to my home.

Actually, my experience was not a full-blown case of identity theft. The thief had not yet had the billing information for my card transferred to his or her mailing address so that – when the bill was sent, including charges that I did not make – I would not see it. Nor had the thief opened an account using my name and information related to my identity. After I called the customer service department of my credit card provider and verified that I had not made the phone call charges in question, they cancelled my card number and provided me with a new one – which took several days to arrive. But this was nothing compared to what people who experience full-scale identity theft have to go through to recover their credit and straighten out their credit history. The Federal Trade Commission estimates that as many as nine million Americans annually have their identity stolen.[3]

Where does the computer fit into this? Believe it or not, much personal information – such as passwords, social security numbers, driver's license numbers, and even credit card numbers, are available on the Web. These can be bought and used by thieves to provide authentication for criminal transactions. Sometimes personal information is obtained by "phishing" (see Section 12.8) and sometimes, of course, the information is simply discovered off-line.

12.5 Intellectual Property

Intellectual property is something produced by using one's mind, such as an invention, a literary work, a work of art, a piece of music, a photograph, or a computer program. In regard to computer programs, the most common way to protect intellectual property is by copyright or patent. Trademarks, service marks, and trade secrets are other forms of protection, but since they are not often applied to computer programs they will not be discussed here.

With regard to copyright, an idea cannot be copyrighted but its expression can. The length of copyright protection can change due to revision of laws and can vary from country to country. Obtaining permission for the use of copyrighted photographs can be most difficult. I can personally testify to this from my experience in writing this book. Often the biggest problem is finding out who owns the photograph's copyright.

A patent covers an invented process or thing and so can include an idea as well as its expression. For example, my grandfather, Robert Newton Barger I, M.D., registered a patent with the Canadian Intellectual Property Office in 1892 for a "Combined folding bed, billiard table rack, and settee."[4] A bed, a billiard table rack, and a settee (sofa) had all previously existed as items of furniture, but nobody had thought to combine them into one item before!

In the computing field, software has been protected as intellectual property by both copyrights and patents. Hardware has generally been protected only by patents.

All of the protections for intellectual property are not so much intended to be monopolies for the benefit of their owners as they are to be encouragements for invention. As the U.S. Constitution states: "Congress shall have power ... To promote the Progress of Science and useful Arts, by securing for limited Times to Authors and Inventors the exclusive Right to their respective Writings and Discoveries;"[5]

12.6 Peer-to-Peer Music Sharing

Peer-to-peer music sharing is properly a problem related to intellectual property. However, it has occupied so much attention and caused such widespread litigation in American society in recent years that it deserves separate consideration here.

Let's face it. One of the things that makes unethical music sharing so tempting is the ease of acquiring music off the Web. It requires little more than a simple download operation on the computer. The assumption would seem to be, "How could anything this easy to do be wrong?" Most people who would not go into a music store and shoplift a CD would seem to have no inhibitions about taking music off the Web.

Napster was one of the first, and probably the most well-known, of companies that facilitated peer-to-peer music sharing on the Internet. It did this by using files that have an MP3 format. This format makes possible the compression of sound so that audio files can be easily shared across the Internet. Problems arose when the Recording Industry Association of America (RIAA) sued Napster for facilitating the acquisition of copyrighted music without payment of compensation. After years of litigation, Napster was forced to cease the facilitation of music file sharing for which copyright fees were not paid. Napster currently operates as an online fee-based music subscription service.

The legal victory of RIAA over Napster did not solve the basic problem, however. College students continue to exchange music files, even without the facilitation of companies such as the original Napster. On February 28, 2007, the RIAA issued the following report: "The Recording Industry Association of America (RIAA), on behalf of the major record companies, today sent 400 prelitigation settlement letters to 13 different universities. Each letter informs the school of a forthcoming copyright infringement lawsuit against one of its students or personnel. The RIAA will request that universities forward those letters to the appropriate network user. Under this new approach, a student (or other network user) can settle the record company claims against him or her at a discounted rate before a lawsuit is ever filed."[6]

So it appears that the RIAA strategy is to pursue litigation against individual students. Will it be successful? It is hard to foresee a win-win solution to this problem.

12.7 Open-Source Software

The following definition of open-source software has been offered by the Open Source Initiative: "Open source is a development method for software that harnesses the power of distributed peer review and transparency of process. The promise of open source is better quality, higher reliability, more flexibility, lower cost, and an end to predatory vendor lock-in."[7] An example of an open-source operating system in widespread use today is Linux, created by Linus Torvalds at the University of Helsinki in Finland. It has become the main alternative for Unix and Microsoft operating systems.[8]

One of the foremost advocates of open-source software has been Richard Stallman, the force behind the GNU (which stands for "GNU's not Unix") operating system. When asked the question, "Shouldn't a programmer be able to ask for a reward for his creativity?" Stallman essentially expanded on the definition of open-source software given in the preceding paragraph by replying:

There is nothing wrong with wanting pay for work, or seeking to maximize one's income, as long as one does not use means that are destructive. But the means customary in the field of software today are based on destruction.

Extracting money from users of a program by restricting their use of it is destructive because the restrictions reduce the amount and the ways that the program can be used. This reduces the amount of wealth that humanity derives from the program. When there is a deliberate choice to restrict, the harmful consequences are deliberate destruction.

The reason a good citizen does not use such destructive means to become wealthier is that, if everybody did so, we would all become poorer from the mutual destructiveness. This is Kantian ethics; or, the Golden Rule. Since I do not like consequences that result if everyone hoards information, I am required to consider it wrong for one to do so. Specifically, the desire to be rewarded for one's creativity does not justify depriving the world in general of all or part of that creativity.[9]

The boss in the "Dilbert" comic strip tells his employees: "From now on, I want you to use open source software for everything we do. It's free."[10] True, even The Boss is in favor of the concept of open source, but not for Stallman's altruistic reasons.

The opposite of open-source software is proprietary software. Literally, it is software that is owned. Its owners usually put limitations on its use, such as prohibitions concerning redistribution, modification, and the ability to view its source code. I suspect that the debate between open-source and proprietary software is a long way from being resolved.

12.8 Phishing

"Phishing" is an activity where the phisher sends spam e-mail or pop-up messages to multiple addresses, disguising his/her identity as a legitimate entity (such as a bank). The object of the phisher is to lure recipients into revealing personal data that may then be used by the phisher for identity theft. Phishing and a related activity called pharming, to be discussed next, get their names from slang speech that started with the term "phreaking." Phreaking was used to denote the gaining of illegal access to a telephone system in order to make free calls.[11]

The U.S. Federal Trade Commission offers these tips regarding phishing:

- If you get an e-mail or pop-up message that asks for personal or financial information, do not reply. And don't click on the link in the message, either. Legitimate companies don't ask for this information via e-mail. If you are concerned about your account, contact the organization mentioned in the e-mail using a telephone number you know to be genuine, or open a new Internet browser session and type in the company's correct Web address yourself. In any case, don't cut and paste the link from the message into your Internet browser – phishers can make links look like they go to one place, but that actually send you to a different site.
- Area codes can mislead. Some scammers send an e-mail that appears to be from a legitimate business and ask you to call a phone number to update your account or access a "refund." Because they use Voice over Internet Protocol technology, the area code you call does not reflect where the scammers really are. If you need to reach an organization you do business with, call the number on your financial statements or on the back of your

credit card. In any case, delete random e-mails that ask you to confirm or divulge your financial information.

- Use anti-virus and anti-spyware software, as well as a firewall, and update them all regularly. Some phishing e-mails contain software that can harm your computer or track your activities on the Internet without your knowledge. Anti-virus software and a firewall can protect you from inadvertently accepting such unwanted files. Anti-virus software scans incoming communications for troublesome files. Look for anti-virus software that recognizes current viruses as well as older ones; that can effectively reverse the damage; and that updates automatically.

  A firewall helps make you invisible on the Internet and blocks all communications from unauthorized sources. It's especially important to run a firewall if you have a broadband connection. Operating systems (like Windows or Linux) or browsers (like Internet Explorer or Netscape) also may offer free software "patches" to close holes in the system that hackers or phishers could exploit.

- Don't e-mail personal or financial information. E-mail is not a secure method of transmitting personal information. If you initiate a transaction and want to provide your personal or financial information through an organization's website, look for indicators that the site is secure, like a lock icon on the browser's status bar or a URL for a website that begins "https:" (the "s" stands for "secure"). Unfortunately, no indicator is foolproof; some phishers have forged security icons.

- Review credit card and bank account statements as soon as you receive them to check for unauthorized charges. If your statement is late by more than a couple of days, call your credit card company or bank to confirm your billing address and account balances.

- Be cautious about opening any attachment or downloading any files from e-mails you receive, regardless of who sent them. These files can contain viruses or other software that can weaken your computer's security.

- Forward spam that is phishing for information to spam@uce.gov and to the company, bank, or organization impersonated in the phishing e-mail. Most organizations have information on their websites about where to report problems. You also may report phishing e-mail to reportphishing@antiphishing.org. The Anti-Phishing Working Group, a consortium of ISPs, security vendors, financial institutions and law enforcement agencies, uses these reports to fight phishing.

- If you believe you've been scammed, file your complaint at ftc.gov, and then visit the FTC's Identity Theft website at www.consumer.gov/idtheft. Victims of phishing can become victims of identity theft. While you can't entirely control whether you will become a victim of identity theft, you can take some steps to minimize your risk. If an identity thief is opening credit accounts in your name, these new accounts are likely to show up on your credit report. You may catch an incident early if you order a free copy of your credit report periodically from any of the three major credit bureaus. See www.annualcreditreport.com for details on ordering a free annual credit report.[12]

12.9 Pharming

Ironically, the following paragraph defining "pharming" appears on the Web site of Farmers Bank and Trust: "In pharming, thieves redirect a consumer to an imposter Web page even when the individual types the correct address into his browser. They can do this by changing – or 'poisoning' – some of the address information that Internet service providers store to speed up Web browsing. Some ISPs and companies have a software bug on their computer servers that lets fraudsters hack in and change those addresses."[13]

It is not as easy to avoid pharming attacks as it is to avoid phishing attacks. This is because phishing attacks simply try to entice you to send in personal information by disguising their e-mail as coming from a legitimate institution, such as a bank. With pharming, there is technologically based deception that is much more difficult to identify and avoid. The best way to avoid being pharmed is to use a secure hypertext transfer connection to a Web site. A secure connection uses the abbreviation https, instead of http, to open the connection.

Finally, you may hear the word "vishing" used in connection with Internet scams. Vishing is a scam that uses Voice-over-Internet Protocol phones instead of redirected links to steal your information.

12.10 Software Bombs

A software bomb is code inserted into a program to cause the program, and/or data associated with it, to be destroyed when a particular condition occurs. Take, for example, the case of a software program that allows a trial period of thirty days before it must be purchased. After the trial period starts, the program tests for the passage of this time. If a registration number (to be supplied to the purchaser upon receipt of payment) has not been entered into the computer by the end of the trial period, the program will erase itself and possibly other data created by the program during the trial period.

12.11 Sale of Term Papers Online

If you use a search engine to search for term papers available for sale or for free online, you will find that the search will turn up literally hundreds of such sites. What is the morality of this activity?

Actually, there are several questions that need to be addressed in this regard. With regard to the company, is this ethical? Some companies would contend that they are simply performing an educational service by providing *examples* of well-written term papers that students can study to improve their writing styles. This seems to me to be similar to the argument that fake ID cards are just *novelty* cards and that there is little chance that they would actually be used for misrepresentation. What the term-paper mills are in fact doing is supporting and encouraging plagiarism. That is to say, they are providing the means for students to pass off writing that was done by other people as their own. By any philosophical view, this is unethical. I would argue that most laws are made to enforce ethical views. Another way of putting this is: laws are made for people who wouldn't do the right thing unless they were under external pressure to do so. On this view, it is interesting to note that many states have passed laws making the sale of term papers by term-paper mills illegal.

Another question concerns the student who is buying or using the paper. Not only is this person guilty of plagiarism, but they are missing the opportunity to research and write about a subject which a term-paper assignment would provide. Besides cheating on the assignment, they are cheating themselves.

Some universities and colleges are dealing with this problem by submitting papers, or parts of papers, turned in by students to online checking systems to see if the papers contain uncited copied material. Also, some instructors require a special type of approach to the topic, or the inclusion of several different introductions or conclusions in a paper. Certainly the online world has increased the opportunities for learning, but this term paper mill topic indicates that it has also provided the means to abuse these opportunities.

12.12 Sale of Academic Degrees Online

The sale of academic degrees online raises issues similar to the sale of term papers online. In both cases, the "product" being offered enables the recipients to avoid the education that – if they had actually gone to college, studied, researched, and did the academic work – they would have genuinely acquired.

What the diploma mills offer is a degree that says that the recipient is certified as a bachelor of arts or science, a master of arts or science, or a doctor of philosophy. This degree is acquired without any time being spent on a campus and, in many cases, without any study or academic work being done. How can this happen? Do the words "life experience" mean anything to you? They apparently mean something to the diploma mills, because the mills will give people academic credit for certain types of "life experience" that they have had in return for the payment of large amounts of money. Usually "life experience" means a number of years spent in some job.

Many of the diploma mills advertise that their school is "accredited." But as a *CBS News 60 Minutes* segment about Hamilton University – which at the time operated out of Evanston, Wyoming – reported, the accreditation board that accredited Hamilton was "set up by Hamilton, for Hamilton." Hamilton was even able to operate tax-free because it built a little church (without pews) on the parking lot of its "campus," which was an old Motel 6.[14]

I can't deal with this topic without recalling the story of Aspen State Teachers College, supposedly located in Aspen, Colorado. It was "founded" by some ski bums in the 1970s who wrote home asking for money while supposedly attending the nonexistent Aspen State Teachers College. Aspen business people good-naturedly took advantage of this spoof and started issuing Aspen State Teachers College ID cards. Although these truly were "novelty" cards, one person was reported to have used his card to purchase a Eurail pass in Europe.[15] The College's tongue-in-cheek motto was: "To educate through the observation of real life experience."[16] Even though Aspen State Teachers College was a myth-ical institution, as far as I know nobody ever used its name to sell a bogus college degree.

12.13 Web Spoofing

There are a number of forms of Web spoofing. They are briefly explained in a press release from the Federal Bureau of Investigation that is excerpted here:

"Spoofing," or "phishing," frauds attempt to make Internet users believe that they are receiving e-mail from a specific, trusted source, or that they are securely connected to a trusted web site, when that is not the case. Spoofing is gener-ally used as a means to convince individuals to provide personal or financial information that enables the perpetrators to commit credit card/bank fraud or other forms of identity theft. Spoofing also often involves trademark and other intellectual property violations.

In "E-mail spoofing" the header of an e-mail appears to have originated from someone or somewhere other than the actual source. Spam distributors and criminals often use spoofing in an attempt to get recipients to open and possibly even respond to their solicitations.

"IP Spoofing" is a technique used to gain unauthorized access to computers, whereby the intruder sends a message to a computer with an IP address indicating that the message is coming from a trusted port.

"Link alteration" involves altering the return address in a web page sent to a consumer to make it go to the hacker's site rather than the legitimate site. This is accomplished by adding the hacker's address before the actual address in any e-mail, or page that has a request going back to the original site. If an individual unsuspectingly receives a spoofed e-mail requesting him/her to "click here to update" their [sic] account information, and then are [sic] redirected to a site that looks exactly like their [sic] Internet Service Provider, or a commercial site like EBay or PayPal, there is an increasing chance that the individual will follow through in submitting their personal and/or credit information.[17]

12.14 Chapter Summary

This chapter dealt with theft and piracy concerns that are summarized here. Cybersquatting is the acquiring of a domain name on the Internet with the hope of selling it, in turn, to a business or individual who might be desirous of using it. Fake IDs are sold on the Internet mostly for purposes of misrepresentation. For example, they are used by underage people in order to buy liquor. Identity theft is achieved by stealing personal information about an individual and using it to appear to be that person in order to charge purchases to that person's credit card account. Intellectual property is something produced by the mental activity of a person. It is protected by such means as copyrights and patents. Music sharing by computer can involve a violation of copyright. Open-source software allows anyone to use it without restriction. It is the opposite of proprietary software. Phishing and pharming are attempts to deceive users into providing others with their personal information that can then be used to steal from them. Software bombs are pieces of code in software that can activate and cause the software or other data to be erased. Term papers and academic degrees are sold on the Internet and used by buyers to make it appear that they have engaged in research, writing, and formal academic study. Web spoofing is creating the appearance that a criminal's Web site actually is the Web site of a legitimate institution in order to steal information or money from someone.

12.15 Your Turn

Question 1. In Section 12.6 concerning peer-to-peer music sharing, it was noted that the Recording Industry Association of America's (RIAA) latest strategy to stop illegal peer-to-peer music sharing is to send prelitigation settlement offers to students by way of the administrators of their universities. Presumably the settlement offers are sent by way of university administrators because students are using the university's network to share music. Do you think it is appropriate for the RIAA to involve the university administration in this way? Why or why not?

Question 2. Richard Stallman is quoted in Section 12.7 of this chapter. Which of the four basic philosophic views you studied in Chapter 3 do his comments represent? Which of his comments would you use to support your identification of his philosophic view?

Question 3. Software bombs are described in Section 12.10. Do you think it is ethical for a company to market software with this kind of protection built into it? Why or why not? What about the ethicalness of destroying data that was created by the program during the trial period? What would be the company's responsibility if still other data, completely unrelated to the program in question, were also destroyed by the software? [Question 3 and the idea for the software bomb case were originally framed by John Murray, an electrical engineer who worked with our Computer Ethics class in the 1990s.]

THIRTEEN

Cases Concerning Theft and Piracy

In this chapter a number of cases will be presented that involve forms of piracy. By piracy is meant the taking of something, or the attempt to take something, which a person is not entitled to take.

13.1 Internet Fraud Case

An e-mail message with no "Subject" line received on January 19, 1999, by Robert Newton Barger from a person using a fictitious name.

ATTN: ROBERT
DATE: January 19, 1999
CC: FRIENDS CLUB
EXTREMELY URGENT AND HIGHLY CONFIDENTIAL
I am [fictitious name] the President of 'FRIENDS CLUB,' a charity organiza-
tion. The club inherited and was disbursed the heavy fortune through revenue
allocation from the Funds and Properties Inheritance Board by the Federal Gov-
ernment of Zaire Central Africa.

I got your contact as a reliable, competent and trustworthy person that has
a good name. The friends club was disbursed on Friday, January 15, 1999 at
10.35am by the financial controller of the Funds and Properties Inheritance
Board, Dr K. S. Chaka, the sum of One Hundred and Thirty One Million USD
($131,000,000.00) to organise charity, promote scholarship programmes and aid
the less privileged. This fund is an inheritance contained in the Federal Revenue
Allocation for 1999 to charity.

The friends club pledged to ascertain a programme of excellence ever lasting
and wishes to invest in a steady lucrative business in Europe or America to achieve
its goal. It is my duty to safeguard, persist, and ensure a successful programme
for the club. We have started by flying the funds through a security company as
trustee to Abidjan, Ivory Coast, a free and safe African country practising [sic]

first class democracy to ensure the safety of the funds from theft and also avoid new generation banking fraud affecting the world banking system today which is why you have been contacted.

The friends club wishes to safeguard the inherited funds from several failing banks especially here in Africa that has [sic] either been defrauded or mismanaged making it unreliable and unsecure. There has [sic] also been several theft cases of funds publicised [sic] through the media (television, radio, newspaper, etc.) in the past. In effect, the club has advised the Federal Government of Zaire through the Funds and Properties Inheritance Board, not to publicise [sic] the inheritance until the funds are successfully moved into a reliable and secure overseas account for safety and investing.

I would have loved to negotiate your offer, but due to the urgency, I am making a straight offer of Six Million Five Hundred and Fifty Thousand (US$6,550,000.00) to you if you accept to be employed by the club for a few days as a custodian to claim the money from the security company here in Africa before it is made public. You would be required to make a trip to Abidjan, Ivory Coast, provide a personal bank account of at least US$10,000 in Abidjan for the deposit of the funds by the security firm and retransfer our balance to our recommended account thereafter. Below is an agreement draft to be signed between you and the club in Abidjan and the security company as witness.

I urge you not to discuss this with anyone to handle this business with the high confidentiality it requires. Below are my credentials. I look forward to receiving your telephone numbers now through e-mail.

Yours truly,

[fictitious name]

NOTE: I AM COMMUNICATING YOU [sic] FROM A LIBRARY VIA THE INTERNET AND WOULD WAIT BETWEEN NOW TILL THURSDAY, 21 JANUARY 1999 TO RECEIVE YOUR TELEPHONE NUMBER TO COMMUNICATE YOU APPROPRIATELY SINCE THERE IS NO SUCH THING AS SECURE E-MAIL. I WON'T COMMUNICATE YOU AGAIN THROUGH E-MAIL. PLEASE.... MAKE SURE YOU SEND YOUR TELEPHONE NUMBERS.... TO THIS E-MAIL ADDRESS NOW.

13.2 Free Software Case

(© 2000 by John Halleck, used with permission)

In the early days of the Macintosh, the "point and click" interface was a wonderful "new" idea (actually most of the idea comes from Xerox . . .). Now one can buy a "head mounted mouse" that moves the mouse on the screen based on the movements of your head. With a little thought you can see that this could be a boon for quadriplegics. It was not long before people thought of combining the "point and click" with the head mounted mouse.

There were, however, several problems that made this combination a non-trivial challenge. I was assigned the task of writing a program that would use this combination of "point and click" with the head mounted mouse to support the occupational rehabilitation program at this University. There were also other efforts at other places, and unknown to us, at least one commercial effort. I wrote a program called KeyMouse (called, in house, the Mac Key Mouse) After the program was written, the University agreed to distribute the program without cost to anyone who could make use of it. Some time after that we received a letter from the lawyers for a company demanding that we cease doing so. For the sake of this discussion we'll call the company "Screen Keyboards Inc." (SKI) and we'll call their program "ScreenMouse." There was an initial round where they claimed trademark infringement because the program here "looked the same" as their program. But since they both looked just like the original Macintosh utility, that issue was dropped. There are, however, several ethical (rather than legal) issues that remained.

Background on the company side: SKI is a company that was started to create products like ScreenMouse. It was their main product and possibly their only commercial success. They priced the program rather high ($7000 a copy) to recover their costs. They sold their program to those who had insurance that could cover the cost. Those people bought it because the cost was worth it because of the improvement in quality of life that computer access gave them. There were even cases where it meant the person could become employed. Arguments the company could make (I hasten to add that nobody at the company made these. These are just those that the company COULD have made): We've invested many staff-months in the product and in marketing. We have a right to recover our costs, and a publicly funded organization like a university has no right to compete with us. Selling ScreenMouse allows us to fund the writing of further programs that will benefit the handicapped community for years to come. By killing the market for the program you are killing future programs, and since the University is not planning any follow-on programs you are doing a disservice to the community.

Background on the University side: The program was produced in response to an internal need, so the cost of producing it was already covered. The program only took a few staff-weeks to write. Since the program was distributed mostly over the network (by ftp in those days and not the web) the distribution costs were trivial. Most of the people whose lives could be improved by the program were poor, and couldn't afford high cost programs. The University felt it worthwhile just to allow those people to have a copy. Arguments the University could make (I hasten to add that nobody at the University made these, these are those that the University COULD have made): If you spent staff months writing a program we wrote in staff-weeks, that is your internal problem. If the University stops distribution of the program now, it causes many people to have a much worse quality of life than they would otherwise have. Most (but admittedly not all) of the people we distribute the program to would be unable to afford the company program to begin with.

Conclusion: Why is this a COMPUTER ethics problem and not just a common ethics problem? Computer Science is one of the few areas where things can actually be distributed for free. Outside of computing, no company can afford to give its products away for free and therefore it doesn't have to worry about its market "going away" because someone gives the product away.

In the field of computing it is still possible to find areas where there is a single commercial product and destroy its market by distributing a free product. I hasten to add that this is not easy, but it can often be done by someone who wants to spend some time on it. Sometimes it takes only a few weeks.

Free software raises many issues with which other fields have not had to deal. There are laws in the commercial arena that prevent the killing of competitors by selling below cost. But there are no laws that prevent the distribution of products for free if the distribution costs are free.

This case deals with public institutions vs. commercial companies, and raises emotional issues of the quality of life of the handicapped, but there are still ethical issues that remain about the social responsibilities that go with free software. There are even specialty areas that will NEVER have a commercial product because there are free programs there. Whether this is good or bad depends a lot on what your ethical views of companies happen to be.

13.3 Finals Week Case

(© 1996 by John Halleck, used with permission)

A professor who had a final to give on Tuesday, received an electronic mail message Monday afternoon. The "From:" address on the message was a student in his class. The message stated that if the final was too hard, the student was going to "end it all." The student had been depressed all quarter and had an electronic mail signature all quarter that implied that it might be better to end it all.

The professor happened to run into the student that evening by sheer luck. The professor confronted the student about the message. The student disclaimed any knowledge whatsoever of the message and denied sending it. Of course, the student ended up even more depressed after this.

The professor asked the local systems group about this, and they tracked the message down to another student (who happened to be a grad student employed by the professor!). This student had forged the mail message with the name of the depressed student.

This is an ugly situation in any case, with or without computers. With computers, however, it is even uglier, since the message that the professor received had NO clues in it that would have implied that the student had not sent it. There is nothing that the student could have done to prove that he did not send it.

How should the University treat this? How should the Professor treat this? Since this required special knowledge on the part of the guilty party, should this be treated as more serious than the equivalent non-computer offense? Should the guilty party be charged for the six staff-hours used to track him down?

When confronted, the graduate student confessed. If he had not, the only thing that could be proved is that his account sent the message. In that case what, if anything, should be done? If he said, "But I gave the password to my roommate," does that change anything?

13.4 Software Licensing: Stuck in the Middle Case

(© 1998 by Thomas Lapp, used with permission)

These days many companies have decided that it is cheaper to hire other companies to do computer work for them rather than hire their own computer staff. In this case study, you are working for SciTech Contracting Services, which is one of those companies that does computer work. Your company has been hired by Lakeside Industries to install the Netscape Navigator software on all of their PCs. In the agreement, Lakeside will obviously be responsible for paying the licensing fee that is required for all PCs running Netscape.

After getting part way through your contract with Lakeside, you discover that Lakeside is not paying Netscape for the copies that your company is installing for them. Yet Lakeside expects you to continue to install the software, since that is your contract with them.

So there is an apparent situation in which your company, in effect, is helping to violate the Netscape licensing agreement with Lakeside. You notify your Lakeside contact repeatedly that Lakeside is out of compliance with the licensing requirements for Netscape, but get no response from your calls and e-mail. What do you do, and how far do you take this information?

Some options to consider:

Do you go "up the chain" in Lakeside's management, since your contact doesn't seem to be doing anything with this knowledge? If so, describe who or which department in Lakeside you would talk to (i.e., CEO, Lakeside's legal, marketing, purchasing, or other departments).

Do you notify Netscape that Lakeside isn't paying for their software (the concept of "Whistleblowing")? If so, whom in Netscape do you notify and describe in detail who or what department in Netscape you would contact. If you are not familiar with business structures, possible options would be the Marketing representative, the Account representative, Netscape legal dept, or perhaps even an anonymous e-mail to Netscape.com. You may be able to think of other possible contacts as well.

As a complication, you discover while working in Lakeside's facilities that they have a strict policy that no software gets installed unless it is licensed from the vendor. Obviously, since you are installing Netscape and Lakeside isn't paying for it, Lakeside appears to be breaking its own internal policy. Using the same ethical perspective, does this change your action and if so, how? If not, why not?

13.5 Borrowed Hardware Case

(© 1996 by Thomas Lapp, used with permission)

You have been working at a small insurance company for the past year. The insurance company uses a LAN (local area network) to connect the desktop PCs to a server (a larger, more expensive PC) where all of the insurance software runs (this software comes from the Unique Corporation).

You've been told that the Unique Corporation's software that is being used is not working very well, and are asked to look into alternatives for the company. You've already been working with Unique Corporation support people on the problems, and they suggest that you upgrade to version 2.0 software, which they say will solve all of your present problems.

Unfortunately, the server that you have is not big enough to run both the existing software and the new version 2.0 software. So the Unique Corporation is willing to loan you a server to test it on. This is all very fine, and you get the test server installed and running.

Since you've been looking into alternatives, you also have received a copy of the new MicroSquish software to evaluate. But alas, MicroSquish cannot provide a server for you to test on. Your original plan was to rent a separate server for a few weeks to test the MicroSquish software, but that would cost money out of your already slim budget. One way out of this would be to use the server that you borrowed from Unique Corporation and install and test the MicroSquish software on that machine, saving you the cost of renting your own.

So you are left with a dilemma: Do you install the MicroSquish software on the server provided by Unique Corporation even though these are competing firms? After all, Unique Corporation provided the hardware to let you test Unique software, not MicroSquish software. Do you test the MicroSquish stuff, but just not tell Unique? Do you ask Unique Corporation if you can test the MicroSquish software on their machine? If you decide to test on the Unique Corporation's hardware, do you tell MicroSquish (after all, if any MicroSquish software were left on it when it went back to Unique Corporation, they might be able to figure out MicroSquish coding secrets)? Does your answer change if you find out that your users have to have a new program in four weeks, which isn't long enough to rent a machine and test the MicroSquish software? If so, in what way does your answer change?

13.6 Risks of Academic Cheating by Computer Case

This case is by Prentiss Riddle, ACM Forum on Risks to the Public in Computers and Related Systems. Reused without explicit authorization under blanket permission granted for all ACM Risks Forum Digest materials. The author, the RISKS moderator, and the ACM have no connection with this reuse.

RISKS-LIST: RISKS-FORUM Digest Thursday, 9 April 1992, Volume 13: Issue 37

Committee on Computers and Public Policy, Peter G. Neumann, moderator

Date: Thu, 9 Apr 92 9:21:08 CDT > From: [e-mail address deleted] (Prentiss Riddle)

   Subject: Risks of academic cheating by computer
   There is an academic cheating brouhaha this semester at the university where I work which is brimming over with computer risks. I am not privy to the details of the case, but here is a summary from the published accounts. This university has an Honor Code governing student cheating which is a source of much school pride. Students agree not to give or receive aid on schoolwork and as a result the university can function without the burden of proctored exams. Alleged violations of the Honor Code are taken before the Honor Council, an elected student body which has the authority to dole out substantial punishments. Honor Council cases are publicized in the form of anonymous abstracts which mask the identities of all parties. Enter the computer: Earlier this semester, two students were accused of colluding on a homework assignment which was done and handed in via one of the university's academic computer networks. Their TA noticed that portions of the two students' homework were identical, down to the initials of one of the students. Network officials were asked to examine backup tapes for the period of time in question and produced evidence which supported the theory that "Student B" had sent homework to "Student A" by electronic mail immediately before Student A turned it in. The students argued that they were innocent and were the victims of a frame-up by an unknown "User X" who they alleged had gained access to their accounts. The Honor Council refused to accept the "User X" theory and convicted both students. Student B's conviction was later overturned partly on the basis of further evidence supplied by network officials which suggested that Student A committed the acts of cheating alone by logging in to Student B's account. Although officially the case is closed, it is the subject of much heated debate in the student newspaper and local Usenet newsgroups at the university. Both students continue to maintain their innocence and their supporters have rallied around the slogan "Free Student A." Computer risks seem to surround this case on all sides. A few which come to mind:

- The risk of cheating by computer in the first place. While academic cheating is as old as academia, the computer can make it, like so many other things, easier than ever before.
- The risk of frame-ups. While the Honor Council appears to be satisfied that the computer evidence substantiates real cheating in this case, it is

clear that a person with access to one or more users' accounts could at least cause them a major nuisance and possibly succeed in framing them of [sic] cheating. With the penalties involved going as high as academic suspension from a school which costs thousands of dollars per semester, this is no light matter.

- The complexity of evidence in cases of computer cheating. Honor council members were quoted in the student paper as complaining about the new and bewildering kinds of evidence they are asked to consider in computer cheating cases, and critics of the Honor Council have complained about the dangers of being judged by people who are not users of the systems involved and don't thoroughly understand them.

- The burden on system administrators. The network official who provided the bulk of the evidence estimated that he spent a full week gathering and analyzing it. Since the case came up, the local academic network has extended the period of time it keeps daily backups before recycling them. How much data is it reasonable to keep, and to pore over, in order to provide evidence in cases like this? I don't know of a way to determine a firm answer.

- The danger to trust and to openness. Both the university's Honor Code and the tradition of open exchange of information within the computing community are threatened by cases like this. Must students be kept in a "padded shell" [sic] to prevent computerized cheating?

13.7 Chapter Summary

In the first case in this chapter (Internet Fraud case), a purported resident of Zaire wants the recipient of an e-mail message to safeguard US$131,000,000. For this trouble the e-mail recipient will be paid $6,550,000, but first the recipient must go to the Ivory Coast and open a bank account with at least $10,000 in it "for the deposit of the funds by the security firm" that is holding the $131,000,000. The second case (Free Software case) dealt with the social responsibilities associated with "free" software. The third case (Finals Week case) involved a graduate student who had forged an e-mail message with an undergraduate's name to make it appear that the undergraduate was about to commit suicide. The fourth case (Software Licensing: Stuck in the Middle case) involved a company hiring a contractor to install software and the contractor subsequently finding out that the company had not paid for the software. The fifth case (Borrowed Hardware case) considered using a loaned server for unauthorized purposes. The sixth case (Risks of Academic Cheating by Computer Case) dealt with two students who had apparently colluded on a homework assignment by using a computer.

13.8 Your Turn

Question 1. Use the ethical decision-making process described in Chapter 6 to solve the cases in this chapter, as directed by your instructor. Answer any additional questions contained in the cases.

FOURTEEN

Privacy Concerns

14.1 Introduction

There is sometimes a relationship between theft and privacy. Theft and related crimes, such as fraud, often occur after one's personal information has been compromised. In fact, compromised personal information can be the very means used to commit the crimes.

It used to be said that you need not be concerned about privacy unless you have something to hide. Now, most people understand that everyone should have something to hide, that is, personal information that can be used for identity theft or other kinds of fraud. In this chapter we will be talking about matters related to the privacy of information – information that can be used for good, or for bad, purposes.

14.2 Cookies

Something as yummy as a cookie doesn't sound like it could be a bad thing, does it? Usually it's not. We're talking here about *electronic* cookies, of course. They are bits of information sent to a browser by a Web server when contact is first made with it. Some servers place cookies on browsers that contact them, but not all of them do. If placed, the cookie is stored on the browser's computer and the information on it can be accessed the next time the browser is used to visit the Web server that placed the cookie. For instance, have you ever revisited a server and had the server call you by name. How could it do that? It must have been because you gave it your name on a previous visit and it was stored in a cookie.

Cookies are helpful in saving you from continuously having to supply the same information each time you return to a site. They can also remember a string of things you want to purchase on a site by using the "shopping cart" technique – keeping all the things you have selected to buy in a cookie memory until you are ready to check out. But cookies can also be dangerous. Cookies can record a lot of information about you and this information can theoretically be sold to people who might use it to send you offers of other things for sale, or for other purposes with which you may want nothing to do. If you want to see if a site has placed a cookie on your computer, go to the site. Erase the site's URL in the address locator box of your browser. Then replace it with the following:

javascript:alert(document.cookie);

This will display a pop-up box showing the contents of current cookies from the site.[1]

14.3 Data Mining

Data mining involves using computer algorithms to shift through large databases in order to glean personal information about potential buyers. This information might then be useful to sellers for marketing purposes. Often this data is scanned for correlations. The social networking Web site *Facebook* uses this kind of technology. "*Facebook* wants to combine information points about you as a person, and your network of friends, to create a more complete profile of you as a consumer," says Paul Gillin, author of *The New Influencers: Marketer's Guide to New Social Media*. "If you join a photography group [on *Facebook*], for instance, they can then target camera ads to you," he says. "This drives even more value out of its database."[2]

Data mining may be done without the knowledge of the customer and so a privacy issue arises. Further, data may be sold by one company to another and – while the customer might not mind the first company having the data – there may be an objection to the sale and resale of this information without restriction. Many companies now provide their customers with privacy policies about how customer information will be used and how a customer might take action to restrict the use of information.

14.4 Denial-of-Service Attacks

Here is how the U.S. Computer Emergency Readiness Team (US–CERT) describes denial-of-service attacks:

In a denial-of-service (DoS) attack, an attacker attempts to prevent legitimate users from accessing information or services. By targeting your computer and its network connection, or the computers and network of the sites you are trying to use, an attacker may be able to prevent you from accessing e-mail, web sites, online accounts (banking, etc.), or other services that rely on the affected computer.

The most common and obvious type of DoS attack occurs when an attacker "floods" a network with information. When you type a URL for a particular web site into your browser, you are sending a request to that site's computer server to view the page. The server can only process a certain number of requests at once, so if an attacker overloads the server with requests, it can't process your request. This is a "denial of service" because you can't access that site.

An attacker can use spam e-mail messages to launch a similar attack on your e-mail account. Whether you have an e-mail account supplied by your employer or one available through a free service such as Yahoo! or Hotmail, you are assigned a specific quota, which limits the amount of data you can have in your account at any given time. By sending many, or large, e-mail messages to the account, an attacker can consume your quota, preventing you from receiving legitimate messages.[3]

14.5 Employee Monitoring

The monitoring of employees by their employers, including the monitoring of employees' use of computers at work, is both legal and ethical as long as certain procedures are observed. The employer should first tell the employees that they should have no expectation of privacy since they are using computer equipment owned by the company, or at least computer connections provided by the company. Ethics would dictate, of course, that the monitoring of employees should not be carried beyond what is necessary for the purposes of company security or quality control.

14.6 Government Surveillance

The topic of government surveillance of citizens is quite different from the topic of employers' monitoring their employees. In a democracy, citizens are not related to the government in the same way that employees are related to their employer. Still, in the years following the 9/11 terrorist attacks in the United States, citizens have found that they must give up some of their privacy in order to prevent threats to homeland security. Even before 9/11, the government was empowered to apply for a court order that would allow for infringement on privacy in order to gather evidence of a crime.

There is an inherent tension between national security, on one hand, and personal privacy, on the other. Thus, there will always be discussion of the wisdom of this particular law or that particular regulation when it comes to the proper status of this tension. Some pertinent organizations are listed here where you may wish to consult the current state of this debate from time to time. Their Web site URLs are given in the respective notes: Center for Democracy & Technology,[4] Department of Homeland Security | Preserving our Freedoms, Protecting America,[5] Electronic Frontier Foundation,[6] Electronic Privacy Information Center.[7]

14.7 Hackers

Hackers are referred to by the U.S. Computer Emergency Readiness Team (US–CERT) in these words:

Hackers break into networks for the thrill of the challenge or for bragging rights in the hacker community. While remote cracking once required a fair amount of skill or computer knowledge, hackers can now download attack scripts and protocols from the Internet and launch them against victim sites. Thus while attack tools have become more sophisticated, they have also become easier to use. According to the Central Intelligence Agency, the large majority of hackers do not have the requisite expertise to threaten difficult targets such as critical U.S. networks. Nevertheless, the worldwide population of hackers poses a relatively high threat of an isolated or brief disruption causing serious damage.[8]

The classic set of responses to hacker arguments that maintain that computer break-ins are ethical has been given by Professor Eugene H. Spafford of Purdue University.[9] Spafford first addresses the contention – which he calls the "hacker ethic" – that information should be free, that it belongs to everyone, and that there should be no restraint against its retrieval and use. He argues that, if true, this concept would do away with the right of privacy and the dependability of information (that is, the ability to be sure that information is accurate).

A second reason that Spafford says hackers use as an excuse for computer break-ins is to expose security problems. Some hackers suggest that they ought to be thanked for their efforts because they are performing a public service. Spafford suggests that this is like breaking into homes in order to show that they are susceptible to burglars.

A third reason is what Spafford calls the "idle system argument." This is the notion that if a system is not being used at the moment by its owner, it is alright for someone else to use it. You will see a form of this argument made by the parasitic computing researchers in Chapter 19. Against this argument Spafford says that just because a system is not currently being used, someone is not thereby given the right to make use of it. It is the private property of its owner and only the owner can give permission to use it.

A fourth reason cited by Spafford is the "student hacker argument." Here the argument is that the hacker was just trying to find out how computer systems operate. Spafford does not accept this argument. Among other things, he points out that unintended damage may be caused by such a "learning" intrusion.

A last argument, the "social protector argument," is that hackers are just checking our computers to protect us against misuse of our data by the government or big corporations. Spafford responds that the end doesn't justify the means here. Furthermore, he says, what makes hackers think they would be the people that we would choose to be our protectors?

Spafford concludes by saying: "I have argued here that computer break-ins, even when no obvious damage results, are unethical. This must be the considered conclusion even if the result is an improvement in security, because the activity itself is disruptive and immoral."

"Of course, I have not discussed every possible reason for a break-in. There might well be an instance where a break-in might be necessary to save a life or to preserve national security. In such cases to perform one wrong act to prevent a greater wrong may be the right thing to do."[10]

Traditionally, hackers have been associated with color-coded hacker hats just as were the Western cowboys of old. There are white hat hackers, black hat hackers, and grey hat hackers.

White hat hackers are "the good guys." They don't really fit the US–CERT definition of hackers. They are people who work as consultants or employees for a company and who try to break into the company's computer system in order to test its security. Black hat hackers, on the other hand, are people who break into a computer system without authorization and intentionally cause harm to the system or the data stored on it. A third category, grey hat hackers, is – as the name might suggest – harder to define. A grey hat hacker might break into a system without authorization, but just for the fun of it without the intention of causing any damage.

14.8 Viruses and Worms

The topics of viruses and worms are well covered in these frequently asked questions published by the U.S. Computer Emergency Readiness Team:

What is a virus?

A computer virus is a program that spreads by first infecting files or the system areas of a computer or network router's hard drive and then making copies of itself. Some viruses are harmless, others may damage data files, and some may destroy files. Viruses used to be spread when people shared floppy disks and other portable media, now viruses are primarily spread through e-mail messages.

Unlike worms, viruses often require some sort of user action (e.g., opening an e-mail attachment or visiting a malicious web page) to spread.

What do viruses do?

A virus is simply a computer program – it can do anything that any other program you run on your computer can do. Some viruses are designed to deliberately damage files, and others may just spread to other computers.

What is a worm?

A worm is a type of virus that can spread without human interaction. Worms often spread from computer to computer and take up valuable memory and network bandwidth, which can cause a computer to stop responding. Worms can also allow attackers to gain access to your computer remotely.

What is a Trojan horse?

A Trojan horse is a computer program that is hiding a virus or other potentially damaging program. A Trojan horse can be a program that purports to do one action, when in fact, it is performing a malicious action on your computer. Trojan horses can be included in software that you download for free or as attachments in e-mail messages.[11]

Having just spoken about hackers, viruses, and worms, an appropriate way to close this chapter would be to tell the stories of two noted hackers. The first story is about Craig Neidorf. Neidorf was one of the founders of an electronic magazine named *Phrack*. In 1989 he published a story in *Phrack* about an enhanced 911-system (E911) that had been developed by Bell South Phone Company. He believed he had done nothing wrong and cooperated with a federal investigation that developed in regard to the publication of the story. He was eventually charged by the federal government with wire fraud, computer fraud, and interstate transportation of stolen property valued at $5,000 or more. The charges were later revised so that the computer fraud charge was dropped, but he was still charged with ten felonies that could have resulted in a maximum sentence of sixty-five years in prison. The government claimed that the E911 document was stolen and contained sensitive material and that anyone possessing it could disrupt 911 service. It turned out during Neidorf's trial that these latter claims were largely untrue and four days into the prosecution of its case the government dropped all charges against Neidorf.[12]

The second story is about Robert Tappan Morris. On November 2, 1988, while he was a graduate student at Cornell University he released the first worm to infect the Internet. It replicated much more quickly than he had estimated and soon was out of control. The Internet was brought to its knees with approximately 6,000 computers shutting down, including ones at NASA, some military facilities, and a few major universities. Morris' attorney, Thomas Guidoboni, said that Morris never intended to prevent authorized access, but that he had made a programming error that caused the spread of the worm. Evidence showed, however, that he programmed the worm to guess at passwords so that the worm could break into as many machines as possible. He also took steps to make the worm difficult to detect and eliminate. He released the worm from the Massachusetts Institute of Technology and made it appear that it had originated from the University of California–Berkeley so that the origin of the program could not be traced back to him at Cornell.[13] Paradoxically, Morris' father was a computer security expert at the National Security Agency. Morris was indicted under the Computer Fraud and Abuse Act of 1986. He received a sentence of 400 hours of community service and a $10,000 fine.[14]

14.9 Chapter Summary

This chapter dealt with privacy concerns. Privacy and theft/piracy are sometimes related in that loss of private information can facilitate theft/piracy.

The first topic in this chapter was cookies. Cookies are bits of information placed on a user's computer by a server that the user has visited. They are retrieved by the server and used to supply information about the user when the user next visits the server.

The next topic was data mining. Data mining involves using computer algorithms to shift through large databases in order to find personal information about potential buyers. This information might then be used by sellers for marketing purposes.

Consideration of data mining was followed by a treatment of denial-of-service (DoS) attacks. These attacks overload a server with requests and use up its resources, thus depriving it of the opportunity to communicate with other servers.

The next topics considered were employee monitoring and government surveillance. The first may be ethically permitted for purposes of security and quality control. The second is more problematic, involving a delicate balance between the prevention of terrorism or the gathering of criminal evidence and the preservation of privacy.

The last topics covered in the chapter were hackers, viruses, and worms.

Hackers are people who break into computer systems. They are known as white hat hackers, black hat hackers, or grey hat hackers: White hat if they are hired to check out a company's computer security, black hat if they intend to do harm by their system intrusion, and grey hat if they break in but intend no harm in so doing. The U.S. Computer Emergency Readiness Team describes a computer virus as a program that spreads by first infecting files or the system areas of a computer or network router's hard drive and then making copies of itself. Some viruses are harmless, others may damage data files, and some may destroy files. It describes a worm as a type of virus that can spread without human interaction. Worms often spread from computer to computer and take up valuable memory and network bandwidth, which can cause a computer to stop responding. Worms can also allow attackers to gain access to a computer remotely. The chapter ended with descriptions of the lawsuit against Craig Neidorf and of Robert Tappan Morris' release of the Internet Worm.

14.10 Your Turn

Question 1. Section 14.7 features some arguments against hackers by Professor Eugene H. Spafford. Would you characterize his philosophy as Idealist, Realist, Pragmatist, or Existentialist? What quotes from him would you use to support this characterization of his philosophy?

Question 2. What color hacker hat would you give Craig Neidorf?

Question 3. What color hacker hat would you give Robert Tappan Morris?

FIFTEEN

Cases Concerning Privacy

In this chapter a number of cases will be presented that involve violations of privacy.

15.1 Fingering Case

(© 2007 by John Halleck, used with permission)

The case concerns a student who used a computer to monitor his ex-girlfriend by checking how often she logged on, from what terminal she logged on, and with whom she communicated. First, here is a bit of background on this case. Most computer systems have a "finger" command of some sort. This command tells if a given user is on the system or not, information about when that person was last on, and, often, information as to the location where the person logged in. The finger command on a system at a fictitious university that will be known as Desert State University also says whether the person has new mail (and when it was last read). Some finger commands even tell from whom the person last received mail. This "feature" would no doubt have been disabled on machines at the University in the years after this case was originally written. Most people at the University would agree that this information is more or less "public."

Here is the substance of the case. Administrators discovered that one of their student machines was severely bogged down in a manner that made it painful for the average student to use. It was discovered that a particular student's script was eating up all the available resources of the machine. Contrary to stated policy, it was a background script that continued running twenty-four hours a day, whether or not the student who had written the script was logged on. This script had large amounts of network bandwidth communicating with other machines and used large amounts of central processing unit time. Since this was a student who had been the source of prior problems, the administrators were very curious as to what the student was doing. They were afraid he was trying to crack other systems using the University's system. It was discovered that the student was doing the finger command on his ex-girlfriend on every machine she had access to, several times a second. The result of these "fingers" was being compiled by the script to form a profile of when and where she was logging in, reading mail, and so forth. The script was gathering statistics on which labs she used, and how often she used them. The student thus had statistics on the labs where she read mail and what hours she kept. At the time this incident happened, the system mail logs were readable by users. So the student was searching the mail logs regularly (every sixty seconds) to see what mail had been delivered to her. He was collecting lists of the people with whom she corresponded, and how often she corresponded with them. The student's account was terminated on grounds that he violated the policy against background processes. The person being fingered (the ex-girlfriend) was also informed of what was happening.

There are a number of very serious ethical issues here concerning what the limits should be in investigating the student, what the student was doing, and what the administration's response should be. The student argued that the information was "public" and there was nothing wrong with what he was doing (except for the background process issue). By the student's argument, what he was doing would be acceptable if he were actually at the terminal doing it. The student also argued that the administration went too far in investigating what he was doing and that it should have just terminated the account when the problem was traced back to him. He argued that anything further that the administration did was just prying into his private life. The student argued that the administration violated his privacy by informing his ex-girlfriend of what he had been doing. The administration, on the other hand, argued that what he was doing was an invasion of the privacy of his ex-girlfriend. It argued that what he was doing was an excessive waste of computer resources. It argued that his history with the University meant that the administration didn't have to give him the benefit of the doubt on anything he was up to, and that meant that he would be investigated more than other students who might arouse suspicion. It argued that his behavior was such that his ex-girlfriend had a right to know what he had done. Any of these points could, in good faith, be argued either way. The issues here are serious, involving policy, ethics, social norms, and even the responsibilities of administrators who go beyond the written rules.

Here are the subsequent developments in the case. The ex-girlfriend regarded the student's actions as frightening, and these actions were added to the stalking complaint that she had already filed with the local police. Some things have changed since this case was first written a number of years ago. There are still vendors whose finger command gives out full information, but it would now be rare for administrators to allow that to happen. Having the system logs readable (so that one can see what mail went through) is also less common. However many vendors still set that level of readability as the default.

15.2 E-mail Addresses Case

(© 2000 by John Halleck, used with permission)

Various computer systems handle assignment of e-mail addresses in different manners. In the early days of computing they were handled by account name. Nowadays they are usually driven out of a table. Many sites use things like Joe.Blowtowski@foo.bar, while some use things that are more cryptic such as abc134@foo.bar. Some sites even do both, with higher-ups getting their names and peons getting the cryptic stuff.

The choice of what sort of addresses a site uses are determined by the administrators. The fancier addresses are more work to install and more work to keep current. For example, they have to be updated every time someone's name changes. For a university, where there are lots of people of an age likely to marry, this can happen a lot. Normally one would consider the choice truly an administrative one, but there can be some ethical side effects of the choices.

Full name issues: Multiple people can have the same name. (This university, for example, at one time had an EE class that had THREE people with exactly the same name.) This brings up the issues of who gets their name, and causes problems for the person that doesn't get their name.

People out on the net note that a site has, for example, names of the form Firstname.Lastname@foo.bar. Therefore if they know their friend's name, they will assume that the friend has an address built in that manner. Given the unbelievable tendency of people to send amazingly personal stuff to an address that they don't know works, this means that the wrong person (with the intended name) learns all kinds of interesting things about the intended person. They also inherit the stalkers, bill collectors, and other fun baggage of that other person. This same sort of problem exists with telephone books, but if someone calls up the wrong person they rapidly notice the error (for example, by hearing the wrong voice), so the process doesn't continue to the point of mistakenly sharing intimacies. With computers, on the other hand, one can progress to the point of mistakenly sharing information before any feedback is received.

Cryptic name issues: Cryptic names that one sees as e-mail addresses are usually generated by some mechanical algorithm. For example, a person's initials plus a number to make it unique is popular. So the first person with the initials JB gets JB1 and the second gets JB2, etc. This scheme makes it easy to generate the ID's for students before they even show up if you have the records. Unfortunately, this means that addresses that are "close" to a given address don't fail, they just go to someone else. So if I mistype (or misread) the address jb7 as jb2, I don't get an error when I send, but someone else gets the mail. If the address is part of a CC (carbon copy) list, I might not even notice a problem since the person that it is really sent to would reply and I wouldn't expect people CC'd to reply.

The situation in the previous paragraph may sound artificial, but it actually happens with more frequency than one might expect. We had a case at this university where the police got involved in a problem involving arguably illegal mail, because of exactly this issue. The sender was sending to a student at this university, and was CC'ing what he thought was the student's account here. But in reality the address was that of a faculty member who was on leave. When the faculty member finally got around to reading his/her mail, the faculty member discovered a large collection of e-mail with the complete history of what was going on. The faculty member brought this to the attention of the local administrators, and the administrators had little choice but to turn it over to the police. It became a rather ugly scene all around.

While the problem above was something that involved the police, much subtler privacy issues are not hard to imagine. Everyone from lovers to businessmen tends to have information in their letters that would at least make them feel bad if released to some random individuals.

The Correct Choice? There really is no "correct" choice. Some have suggested letting people pick their own e-mail name, but this doesn't really solve the problem either. "I've used that nickname on IRC for years, but it is already assigned to someone else." The collision problem with "self chosen" names tends to be greater than with people's actual names, and the name collision issues are actually worse. For example "Mycroft" – the first name of Sherlock Holmes' older brother – is almost unknown in real names, but is commonly picked by people for themselves. One could choose randomly generated e-mail addresses <we38j2423@foo.bar>, chosen by a program so as not to be "close" to the spelling of any other name. But those are practically impossible for most people to remember and it makes it horrendously difficult for people elsewhere to find, much less type, the address of the user here.

15.3 Deceased Student Case

(© 1998 by John Halleck, used with permission)

Any company that provides computer services is likely to have files belonging to many different people on its system. The more people you have, the more likely it is that you will eventually have files for people no longer able to take care of their own affairs. Such problems can occur with customers, or with one's own employees, or even one's administrators.

Here at Desert State University, we've had all these issues come up. Many of the ethical decisions are already made for us here by University policy, and many of the decisions get bumped up to University Legal to make. In an organization that doesn't have its own legal department, such decisions have to be made by the computer administrators themselves.

Many of the issues below are (in real life) decided by people attempting to apply their ethical experience in life to new situations. Since such items come up unexpectedly, administrators often make decisions that their hindsight tells them were not the right ones. Maybe a little discussion now will make it easier for someone to make the "right" decision later. The issues below are all taken from our experience. The names have been changed to avoid complications. Some supporting facts have been changed slightly to make the issues clearer.

Deceased Student Issues: Sally Forth walks in and informs us that –

- Her cousin Joseph Blowtowski (a student here) has died.
- She is here representing Joseph's mother, Jane Blowtowski.
- She would like to pick up all of Joe's electronic mail and computer files.
- Since the mother is computer illiterate, she'd like to get hard copies of the files.

This poses a number of problems, some of them ethical. For example, this might be a scam to get Joe's files. What should you take as acceptable evidence for the claims? (In real life, the University here has a policy that says that we turn the entire issue over to University Legal, which is what we did.)

If we assume that you have to make the decisions yourself, then there are plenty of issues to deal with. If you give the files to her, you could be directly contradicting Joe Blow's wishes in his will. He might have wanted them destroyed. . . .

- Do you give them up?
- Do you demand to see the will first? (What is acceptable evidence that there is no will?)
- Do you just give them to anyone that can show they are family?

On the other hand Joe might not have left a will. How does that change things?

Do you give up the files if you know they are of a nature that nobody's mother is likely to want to know about their son? If they show illegal activity? If they show that his accidental death is suicide? (For which of these items would you involve the police?)

Should you even be looking to see what the files are? Is it even practical to print them out for her without noticing what they are?

You notice that one file is clearly the finished assignment in a course he was taking. Do you turn it in for him?

Is it obvious why we decided to turn this over to the lawyers instead of deciding ourselves? We knew in advance that University Legal won't turn over anything to anybody without a court order. Does this change your opinion of whether or not we did the right thing? Would it be the right choice if we know that the only things in Joe's directory are school assignments? Would it be right to give that information to Sally? Is it acceptable to just claim that nothing is there in order to save Sally from having to deal with the courts?

There are files (such as programs) that can't be printed out. Do you just dump them on a disk and give it to them knowing they probably won't be able to do anything? Or just tell them that what printed was all there was? Or try to explain why programs aren't printable?

How long do you wait before trashing the files? Is there a "Statute of Limitations" for electronic files?

What if a will is one of the files?

The following are actual comments of local administrators trying to bring prior experience to the problem: (These comments in turn all bring up other issues. . . .)

"In the [U.S.] army when we had to send someone's effects back we opened his locker and threw away the drugs and dirty magazines, and sent the rest to the family."

"I can't be expected to know the legal [stuff], if they want the files they can show a court order."

"If the files were unimportant, I'd just tell them that we deleted them when we closed the account."

"I can't see how a dead guy cares about the files, I'd just delete them."

"The messages are between him and the person writing to him. I won't release them for anybody but the two of them."

"The dorms just box it up and send it to the parents, I think we should do the same."

"If they had moved their mail to a floppy, we would have given it to the parents with the rest of the stuff they might have left here. So . . . I think we should give it to them even if they didn't move the mail."

15.4 Incapacitated Administrator Case

(© 1998 by John Halleck, used with permission)

The following is really a conglomeration of three incidents. An administrator here (we'll call him Nick Klaws) had a sports accident that involved major head trauma. He was totally out of action for a month, and pretty much useless for another three months. He, like many folk, used his account for both personal and professional uses. Do we have the right to check his mail to see what problems were in progress? Should one person do this to minimize the spread of personal information or should it be done by a committee to insure that things are being done openly and above board?

The systems group volunteered to his supervisor that they could easily make a list of everyone sending him mail, so that those people sending University problems to him directly could be contacted. Should this list be obtained? Some companies have a strict "No personal stuff on your work account" policy. Some people ignore such a policy or bend it. If the company had such a policy would it change your answers? The courts have repeatedly ruled that one's employer owns the files you have on the employer's system (absent prior agreement). This changes the legal issues, but does it change the ethical issues?

Actual comments of local administrators trying to bring prior experience to the problem:

"I turned down the list of the people he was getting mail from. If it's a real problem they'll finally get mad enough to contact someone else here."

"I didn't want to contact the people that were sending him mail. If they were sending him personal mail I'd be in the position of having to give them the bad news, and I don't have the [courage] to notify all of them of what happened."

"He's working on many projects, both assigned and on his own. There is no way to know what we needed of his stuff without looking through all of it."

15.5 Chain Letter Case

(© 1996 by John Halleck, used with permission)

Part I – Background: The attorneys general for the state of Deseret and its neighbors are out to fight chain letters and pyramid schemes. They have suggested legislation outlawing them and have provided for stiff penalties. It seems obvious that a person who sent chain letters to five friends is less of a criminal than someone who sent out thousands of such letters. The penalties are therefore much higher if the number of letters or communications is higher, and penalties are especially severe for "mass operators" who mail out more than a thousand letters.

Here are the views of Joseph Blow, a chain-letter recipient who re-mailed his letter. "I got this chain letter from a friend. It said that it was legal since it was not being sent by the U.S. postal service and was not 'really' a chain letter. All I did was post ONE copy to a bulletin board. I didn't know that it was illegal. When you sign up for the bulletin board, they don't tell you that chain letters are illegal. Besides, I'm not even located in the state of Deseret. How am I supposed to know that my posting from East Dakota would violate the law in some other state?"

Here are the views of the State of Deseret Attorney General. "When he signed up for the bulletin board, they didn't tell him fraud, extortion, and murder were illegal either. It isn't their job to tell him such facts. Mr. Blow distributed a chain letter to 29,000 machines, with heaven only knows how many total readers. He knew that the mailing list had readers in other states (and even other countries) because he had seen postings (messages) from them. Pyramid schemes are a threat to society at large, and massive schemes clearly cause much more damage. The fact that he used a computer to mail thousands of copies does not change the fact that he admits to having mailed them. We recommend that he be extradited and tried on the offense, and – if found guilty – be given 10 years in prison."

Why is this a COMPUTER ethics problem and not just a common ethics problem? In the "noncomputer" world, it is on the order of 10 times as much work to mail out 10 items as it is to mail out one. A mailing of thousands of anything is a major undertaking, and a person doing this for illegal purposes is a mass operator. With computers, it is often nearly as easy to mail to thousands of places as it is to mail to one.

An argument of intent based on actions becomes a lot less clear. There are even cases where someone has, in fact, sent items to a national news-feed inadvertently. Should one's feeling of "right and wrong" about the issue be based on intent or on the amount of damage done? The technology makes it just as easy to get the message to other countries as it does to other states. This often makes it hard to remember that you are often operating nationally or internationally. Some forms of communication are actually illegal (chain letters and death threats, for example) but the rules vary from place to place. With noncomputer communications it is usually clear that you are mailing to another state or country, but with computer news-feeds you may not be able to tell without a lot of work. While it is not reasonable to most people that you should know the rules in every conceivable jurisdiction, it is equally unreasonable to assume that you don't need to know about any of them.

Part II – Why weren't there thousands of replies to Mr. Blow's re-posting of the chain letter?

System administrators tend to get angry about things like chain letters on their system. Whenever somebody in authority saw Mr. Blow's letter, they simply deleted it.

Computer Administrator View: Letters like this are a waste of everyone's time. They cause a flood of letters that interferes with normal usage of the system. We just delete them every time we see them. Why not? They are illegal anyway, and besides, they are being sent over MY system, using MY disks, and over network connections that I pay for. I have every right to keep this sort of stuff off of my system.

No, we don't keep a record of each nuisance of this sort. It would involve too much paperwork.

Civil Libertarian View: Even though each individual node (mainframe computer) in the network is privately owned, USENET news is treated by everyone as a public forum. If an administrator censors a message on his/her machine he/she has also censored it on the machines that depend on his/her machine for news.

A system administrator has no right to censor anybody's mail on sites other than his/her own, and clearly has no right to practice censorship of a public forum without giving people some way to protest the action. This censorship is being done anonymously, without records, without recourse, based on the personal standards of the site administrator. In this case it was an arguably illegal message, but the site administrator could just as easily be deleting messages that did not agree with his/her political or religious views, and nobody would be the wiser.

15.6 Administrator vs. Student Case

(© 1996 by John Halleck, used with permission)

Part I – Background: In order to insure normal service operations, the site administrator and the operators of a computer system have access to the entire system.

This means that there is not really ANYTHING on a computer that is truly private (files are usually protected from other users, but not from the system folks). The upshot of this is that computer sites have to trust the people in charge. These people can do anything on the system, including delete or create or read files, reroute mail, edit the log files, etc.

Many network programs (mail, for example) pass off to people things with which they can't deal. So, if somebody mis-types an address badly enough, the postmaster of the machine gets a copy of the headers of the message (and possibly the message itself).

The upshot of this is that all kinds of "funniness" tends to get dumped in the postmaster's lap regularly, and the postmaster sometimes ends up knowing all kinds of little facts about some of the system's users. The postmaster's system privileges allow him or her to investigate further if there appears to be need.

Most sites are VERY careful about who receives system privileges. Many sites will go so far as to pull system privileges away from anybody they suspect of wrongdoing, even without proof. Other sites just assume that this risk is a necessary evil, and don't worry about the people in charge.

The views of Nick Klaws (Site administrator for machine Mega.Pseumata at Desert State University): "We get a lot of students cheating here, so we keep close tabs on what they do. When we saw that Joe's account had a usage pattern much different than everyone else in his class, we went in to see what he was up to.

We found that he was (take your pick . . .)

- Doing accounting for a private company
- Keeping records on every Zork game ever played
- Editing a paper for the Bestiality study group
- Writing love letters to his girlfriend
- Writing love letters to his dog
- Using the machine for other than class-of-your-choice

We deleted the files and tossed him off of our machine. It's our machine, and we can do what we want with it. There is no law against what we did. If you stored your papers in a bin on my desk, and I looked into them because I thought there might be a problem, nobody would think it odd. Well, that machine is on my desk, I thought there might be a problem, and I looked through the files."

The views of Joseph Blow (the student who was tossed off the machine): "If you wanted to search my locker or room, you'd have to get a search warrant. Just because there is no specific law that says you have to get a warrant for the computer files does not make it right. There is an expectation of privacy when we put things into our private files."

Why is this a COMPUTER ethics problem and not just a common ethics problem? The handling of most computer actions is far ahead of any laws on the subject. It is only very recently that any laws have covered how people handle files on their own systems. As late as the early 1990's administrators could read anyone's mail for any reason (even entertainment) without breaking any law whatsoever. There have been a number of laws passed recently that cover parts of the issue, but many situations are still unclear, or the laws concerning them are still untested. For people working for commercial companies there are still very few legal privacy protections.

Part II – Joseph Blow: "Without a computer account, I can't pass my computer classes, and I can't graduate. Your actions effectively toss me out of the university without a hearing, and without recourse. They claimed there was no law against what they did. But by the same token, there is no law against what I did. In any noncomputer activity, the university has to abide by due process. There have to be hearings. There is always review before action is taken. Who elected you folks God, that you are not bound by the kinds of restraints that everyone else is?"

Nick Klaws: "If you are not going to follow the rules on our machine, you don't get to use our machine. It is not our fault if this causes you problems with your classes. Having a computer down for even a few hours causes serious problems. Having to wait for days before taking action could often mean that we would have to work months cleaning up the mess. The normal university procedures CAN'T be completed in less than a week. Even if they could, the university administrators don't understand the issues and we spend days getting the ideas across. In cases such as chain letters, for example, we might have to act immediately to prevent the system from becoming totally unusable."

Blow's Lawyer (hereafter B): "Do you have any proof that Mr. Blow caused the problems that caused him to be denied computer access?"

Desert State University's Lawyer (hereafter U): "We have the logs of the usage, copies of the files involved, and even a copy of the electronic mail Mr. Blow sent admitting the violation before he knew how much trouble he was in."

Lawyer vs. Lawyer: B: "These are all printouts of files on the computer?" U: "Yes." B: "Doesn't Mr. Klaus have the ability to read and write EVERY file on the system, including the files that you brought as evidence?" U: "Yes, but he did not alter those files." B: "How do you know?"

U: "The log file shows no such tampering." B: "Isn't that log file itself one to which he has access?" U: "Yes."

The problem here is that EVERY file on the system is accessible to the site administrator, and they generally leave no tracks when they change a file. ("What, the 'last written' date shows I edited it? No problem, I'll just set that date back...")

Even electronic mail to other sites is not tamper-proof. Any good postmaster can forge mail from anybody to anybody. With care the forgery is totally undetectable.

If you always believe the administrator, you will effectively concede to him or her the ability to take advantage of anybody at any time for any reason. But if you always believe the student, you will effectively give the student the ability to get away with anything he or she wishes to do, including violation of serious laws. Anything on the system can be faked (often the student also can fake items . . .), and there is no evidence of it, on or off the system.

15.7 Chapter Summary

This chapter contains a number of cases from real-life experience in the area of privacy. The first (Fingering case) deals with a stalking incident where a university student used the university's computer system to stalk his ex-girlfriend. The second (E-mail Addresses case) contains a discussion of issues regarding the assigning of e-mail addresses. The third (Deceased Student case) deals with issues involved in turning a deceased student's computer records over to his relatives. The fourth (Incapacitated Administrator case) deals with balancing the need to find out if the e-mail of a seriously injured university administrator contains unfinished university business, while still respecting that administrator's privacy. The fifth (Chain Letter case) deals with opposing views in a chain letter scheme. The sixth (Administrator vs. Student case) deals with opposing views on misuse of computers by an administrator and by a student.

15.8 Your Turn

Question 1. Use the ethical decision-making process described in Chapter 6 to solve the cases in this chapter, as directed by your instructor. Answer any additional questions contained in the cases.

SIXTEEN

Power Concerns

16.1 Introduction

Having spoken in Chapter 12 about theft and piracy concerns and in Chapter 14 about privacy concerns, it will be the task of this chapter to cover power concerns. "Power concerns" might sound like a catchall for any issues left over after those covered in Chapters 12 and 14. In a sense, this is the case. However, the choice of the term "power" is meant to focus more specifically upon ethical dilemmas involving the use of power or involving subjection to power.

16.2 Accountability of Bloggers

The *Merriam-Webster Online Dictionary* defines "blog" as "a Web site that contains an online personal journal with reflections, comments, and sometimes hyperlinks provided by the writer." The question of accountability has been raised in regard to blogging in as much as blogs are essentially public materials, intended for all to see, and meant as media to publicize the thoughts, feelings, and opinions of the blogger. If the press is to be held accountable for its reporting, should not bloggers also be held accountable for what they publish?

In 2005, a blogger was given press credentials for admission to the White House briefing room. The same *New York Times* story that reported this event continued by saying: "Increasingly, bloggers are penetrating the preserves of the mainstream news media. They have secured seats on campaign planes, at political conventions and in presidential debates, and have become a driving force in news events themselves."[1]

The growing influence of bloggers, especially in the fields of politics and the news, has led to the suggestion that bloggers should do their blogging in keeping with a code of ethics. As early as April of 2003 there was the suggestion made online that a code of ethics for bloggers should include such things as the requirement to be honest and fair, the requirement to minimize harm, and the requirement to be accountable.[2] The more that blogging activity increases, the more it would seem that calls will continue to be raised for some kind of accountability for bloggers.

16.3 Censorship/Free Speech

The words "censorship/free speech" present us with the horns of a dilemma. For example, on the one hand there is the need to protect children from viewing pornography on the Web. On the other there is the right of people to express their opinions as they see fit. Actually, this dilemma is more complicated than just an either/or situation. There may be other interested parties besides those concerned to censor pornography or to preserve free speech, for instance Internet service providers who may incur liability for hosting pornographers on their Web sites. There are also other issues in addition to pornography involved in the censorship/free speech debate. For instance, there are questions involving political censorship. How then is such a complex dilemma to be resolved?

As with most dilemmas where the rights and responsibilities of the interested parties seem to clash in an irreconcilable manner, grounds for compromise must be found. For instance, anyone should be permitted to say what she or he wishes as long as it does not constitute a physical threat or calumny against someone, but it would be wrong for a person claiming exercise of free expression to shout "Fire" in a crowded theatre (assuming, of course, that there was no fire). One might think that this is a far-fetched example, but in reality it is taken from a decision of the Supreme Court of the United States.[3]

I will briefly address the question of how a compromise might be reached in the two situations mentioned, namely, pornography and political censorship. In the case of pornography, compromise is usually found through law. Legislation has been passed in federal and state jurisdictions to ensure that children are protected against pornography and this legislation is usually written carefully enough to ensure that the guarantees of the First Amendment of the Constitution protecting free speech are not violated. If the Supreme Court finds that this legislation is unconstitutional, the legislature can try to pass other legislation that remedies the situation. With regard to political censorship, taking the case of the People's Republic of China and its relationship with Google as an example (see "Google and Chinese Censorship case" in Chapter 17), the compromise is again found through law. China can stipulate what it thinks should not be allowed on the Internet in terms of its national interest and Google is obligated to respect this stipulation if it wants to do business in China. As an American company, Google can say (as it did in fact say) that it would prefer that more access to information were allowed in China, but that it must respect the laws of a country in which it is doing business. Google has said that censoring search results clearly compromises its mission, but that failing to offer the Google search engine in China, which holds a fifth of the world's population, would be even worse than censoring search results.

A final case might be mentioned that involves free speech. This is the case of anti-abortion groups posting "wanted" posters (much as were used to alert people to watch for criminals in the Old West) on the Internet. The abortion doctors were sometimes referred to as baby-butchers in the posters. An abortion doctor was killed by a sniper in his home in 1998 and, in 1999, a federal judge said that some of the posters were "true threats to kill."[4]

16.4 Cyberchondria

The *Merriam-Webster Online Dictionary* defines hypochondria as "extreme depression of mind or spirits often centered on imaginary physical ailments." A new twist to this illness is called cyberchondria, which is hypochondria further aggravated by reading about these imaginary ailments on the Internet.

An ABC News report has stated, "With Internet access at nearly everyone's fingertips, trying to find the cause of a headache or muscle pain can be just a few keystrokes away. According to a Pew Internet study, more than 7 million Americans go online every day to research health or medical information."[5]

The ABC News report quotes Dr. Brian Fallon of Columbia University who says that ninety percent of hypochondriacs with Internet access become cyberchondriacs. He said it's a natural progression. "Cyberchondria can be a terrible, devastating disease in the sense that the individual focuses on nothing other than checking their symptoms on the Internet and it destroys their lives," he said.[6]

The Internet may be providing "too much of a good thing" as far as information about diseases goes. People who are hypochondriacs previously could read about symptoms in magazines and imagine that they had those symptoms, but with the Internet they now have access to thousands of descriptions of diseases with just the click of a mouse. There is the further problem that all of these sites are not equally authoritative. Cyberchondriacs may, in effect, end up letting these sites do a diagnosis for them rather than visiting their personal physician.

16.5 Internet Addiction

It has been jokingly said that there is a similarity between computer technologists and drug peddlers in that they both refer to their customers as "users." Many would contend that Internet addiction is not truly an addiction like drug addiction. But whether it is or not, most people would find that spending inordinate amounts of time on the Internet is, at the very least, an obsessive/compulsive activity.

The original reference to an addiction to the Internet was made by a New York City psychiatrist named Ivan Goldberg. In 1995 he posted a spoof about something he called "IAD" (Internet Addiction Disorder) in order to make fun of the American Psychiatric Association's (APA) method of expressing diagnoses of mental disorders in its *Diagnostic and Statistical Manual of Mental Disorders*. A surprising result of this joke was that many people recognized that they were afflicted by the "addiction" that Dr. Goldberg had described and responded by subscribing to his "Internet Addiction Support Group." Goldberg's 1995 posting may still be found in a couple of places on the Web. The copy in this chapter is from *The RISKS Digest*, Vol. 17, Issue 12. I have kept Goldberg's original indentation in order to preserve his parody of the APA's method of expressing a diagnosis:

ACM FORUM ON RISKS TO THE PUBLIC IN COMPUTERS AND RELATED SYSTEMS.
Reused without explicit authorization under blanket permission granted for all ACM Risks-Forum Digest materials. The author(s), the RISKS moderator, and the ACM have no connection with this reuse.

Internet Addiction by Ivan Goldberg

[Posted on Thu, 11 May 1995 12:14:59 GMT]

As the incidence and prevalence of Internet Addiction Disorder (IAD) has been increasing exponentially, a support group, The Internet Addiction Support Group (IASG) has been established. Below are the official criteria for the diagnosis of IAD and subscription information for the IASG.

Internet Addiction Disorder (IAD) – Diagnostic Criteria

A maladaptive pattern of Internet use, leading to clinically significant impairment or distress as manifested by three (or more) of the following, occurring at any time in the same 12-month period:

(I)   Tolerance, as defined by either of the following:
    (A) A need for markedly increased amounts of time on Internet to achieve satisfaction
    (B) Markedly diminished effect with continued use of the same amount of time on Internet
(II) Withdrawal, as manifested by either of the following:
    (A)   The characteristic withdrawal syndrome
        (1) Cessation of (or reduction) in Internet use that has been heavy and prolonged
        (2) Two (or more) of the following, developing within several days to a month after Criterion 1:
            (a) psychomotor agitation
            (b) anxiety
            (c) obsessive thinking about what is happening on Internet
            (d) fantasies or dreams about Internet
            (e) voluntary or involuntary typing movements of the fingers
        (3) The symptoms in Criterion 2 cause distress or impairment in social, occupational or another important area of functioning
    (B)   Use of Internet or a similar on-line service is engaged in to relieve or avoid withdrawal symptoms
(III) Internet is often accessed more often or for longer periods of time than was intended

(IV) There is a persistent desire or unsuccessful efforts to cut down or control Internet use

(V) A great deal of time is spent in activities related to Internet use (e.g., buying Internet books, trying out new WWW browsers, researching Internet vendors, organizing files of downloaded materials)

(VI) Important social, occupational, or recreational activities are given up or reduced because of Internet use.

(VII) Internet use is continued despite knowledge of having a persistent or recurrent physical, social, occupational, or psychological problem that is likely to have been caused or exacerbated by Internet use (sleep deprivation, marital difficulties, lateness for early morning appointments, neglect of occupational duties, or feelings of abandonment in significant others)

Subscribe to the Internet Addiction Support Group by e-mail:
Address: listserv@netcom.com
Subject: (leave blank)
Message: Subscribe i-a-s-g[7]

Dr. Goldberg still does not really believe that there is such a thing as an "addiction" to the Internet. He prefers to call it "pathological Internet-use disorder."[8]

16.6 Online Voting

The basic ethical concern that presents itself in considering the question of online voting is security. The various issues under this heading would involve insuring the identity of the voter, safeguarding the "one person, one vote" rule, the ability to preserve electronic "ballots" in tamper-free condition, and the handling of absentee ballots. By and large, these issues are not essentially different than those presently being handled in connection with the use of voting machines. A move to online voting – at least if it would still involve the requirement of coming to a polling place on election day (except in the case of absentee voting) – should not involve any insuperable problems.

16.7 Whistle-Blowing

A situation that occasionally faces computer professionals is what to do when a project with which they are associated goes wrong and the people who are in charge of the project refuse to acknowledge the problem or do anything about it. What should the computer professionals do in this case? If (especially if there is a risk to life or health and especially after trying to get those in authority to correct the situation) they decide to go public with what they know, this is known as whistle-blowing.

One of the classic cases of whistle-blowing occurred after the explosion of the Space Shuttle Challenger in 1986. The explosion was caused by the failure of "O-rings" that connected segments of Morton-Thiokol's Solid Rocket Booster that was to put the Shuttle in orbit. An engineer named Roger Boisjoly, together with other engineers who had worked on the O-rings, recommended postponing Challenger's launch, knowing that cold weather might cause the O-rings to fail. But a group of vice-presidents of Morton-Thiokol decided to recommend the launch, apparently knowing that conditions were unsafe.

Boisjoly was advised by Morton-Thiokol lawyers to just answer questions with a "yes" or a "no" when he was called before Congress to answer questions about the Challenger disaster. Instead, he blew the whistle. He was frozen out of his job at Morton-Thiokol, but eventually was awarded the Prize for Scientific Freedom and Responsibility from the American Association for the Advancement of Science.[9]

The following is a posting to *The RISKS Digest* that occurred in 1988 in response to a posting that was critical of whistle-blowing. The points it makes regarding ethical considerations are worth pondering.

ACM FORUM ON RISKS TO THE PUBLIC IN COMPUTERS AND RELATED SYSTEMS.

Reused without explicit authorization under blanket permission granted for all ACM Risks-Forum Digest materials. The author(s), the RISKS moderator, and the ACM have no connection with this reuse.

Whistle Blowing by Ronni Rosenberg

Tue, 2 Feb 88 15:02:27 EST

In response to the recent RISKS article that bashes whistle-blowing (Guthery, "Blowing Whistles or Blowing Smoke?", RISKS 6.19), I again want to defend whistle blowing as an ethically responsible – sometimes ethically required – action for some engineers in some circumstances.

Guthery writes: "the very last thing a whistle blower is interested in is accepting responsibility," a claim that is not supported by the literature on whistle blowing.

Whistle-blowing engineers typically are responsible for some aspect of a system's current use, not it's [sic] original engineering. In this sense, they are concerned about problems that others caused; e.g., Roger Boisjoly did not design the original shuttle O-rings, but he was responsible to some degree for their effectiveness. Complex systems are worked on by so many people, for so long, that the original engineers are likely to be gone by the time the system begins to be used and a problem arises – assuming one can even determine who was responsible for the original work. Is pointing out a critical problem in one's area of responsibility, when one becomes aware of it, really just "pointing my finger at everybody else in sight"?

Guthery's other main point, that "most whistle blowing has to do with how the papers were shuffled and the most predictable aftereffect of whistle blowing is still more bureaucracy," also is not supported by the literature. The whistle-blowing case studies that I've seen had to do with conscious decision-making to reject the concerns raised by engineers (as in the Boisjoly case, where Morton-Thiokol managers appear to have knowingly decided to launch with unsafe O-rings). Entrenched bureaucracy clearly is a problem, and most of the cases I've read about took place in very large organizations, and it is hard to get things done via bureaucracy. But like it or not, most engineers work in large organizations with a lot of money at stake, and you cannot enact major changes any other way. The results of whistle-blowing often are not just paper shuffling; sometimes they are saved lives or safer systems. Is the assumption that only papers will be shuffled just a rationalization for remaining silent when you should speak out?

I couldn't agree more with Guthery's statement that "I don't think we know enough about building computer systems to build good systems without making mistakes," but I disagree with his conclusion that we should just be allowed to make our mistakes, without the annoyance of whistle blowers pointing them out. We have the right to make mistakes only if we (1) acknowledge up front that this is the way we have to work, and (2) do not put a system into use, particularly in a critical application, if we are not sure that it works.

(1) Although the RISKS community seems to agree that many mistakes are made in any large system, for the most part, the computing "profession" does not admit this. The for-profit part of the industry claims – through ads, sales people, grant proposals – to deliver systems that work, period. But new products/systems are routinely delivered with many important bugs. Funders and customers get upset when they see what they really have to go through and spend to get a system that works reasonably well. Sometimes, as in the recent bank case, the customer abandons the whole project; you can be sure that time for "making mistakes" was not adequately built into the bank project.

(2) Whistle blowers usually act in situations where critical systems are in use, don't appear to be working safely, but are alleged to be working fine. What gives us the "right" to make mistakes in such situations? All the literature on professional ethics agrees that people with special expertise, such as engineers, have a special OBLIGATION to inform and educate others,

including the general public, about the limits and risks of the systems they build.

I am upset to see in the RISKS Forum the standard technological enthusiast's argument, that people who criticize technology are just Luddites. Some critics are more concerned about the uses of technology than engineers, who as we know can get so wrapped up in the technology that they fail to consider the people whom the system will affect. Most whistle-blowers come from inside the system, are not normally inclined to get involved in nontechnical issues, and try every internal channel before going public. We owe them special attention when they raise problems.

Before condemning whistle blowers because they've criticized a neat system, I encourage you to read about their cases and view the Boisjoly videotape (available for rent from CPSR/Boston). When you read about what they've suffered as a result of their complaints, and when you hear the anguish in Boisjoly's words, you may change your mind. For a good, readable discussion of engineering ethics, including several case studies of whistle-blowing, read Stephen H. Unger, *Controlling Technology: Ethics and the Responsible Engineer* (New York: Holt, Rinehart and Winston, 1982).[10]

16.8 Chapter Summary

Following an introduction in Section 16.1, Section 16.2 of this chapter considered the question of whether bloggers should be held accountable for what they publish. Section 16.3 considered the dilemmas involved in solving conflicts between censorship and free speech. Section 16.4 considered cyberchondria, a form of hypochondria further aggravated by reading about one's imagined illnesses on the Internet. Section 16.5 followed up with a consideration of Internet addiction – a condition that many would agree is a problem, but is not technically an addiction. Section 16.6 considered online voting. It was judged that – as long as presence at the polling place would still be required – this would not present any more problems than does machine voting currently. Section 16.7 considered the topic of whistle-blowing, using the case of the NASA Challenger disaster as an example.

16.9 Your Turn

Question 1. Section 16.2 considered the topic of accountability of bloggers. Do you think bloggers should be accountable to the public for what they write? Why or why not? Don't they have as much right as the next person to express themselves in any way they wish? Why or why not? Do you think there should be a code of ethics for bloggers? Why or why not?

Question 2. What is the ethical issue with cyberchondria? How would you recommend that it be handled?

Question 3. What is the ethical issue with Internet addiction (or obsessive/compulsive disorder)?

SEVENTEEN

Cases Concerning Power

17.1 Google and Chinese Censorship Case

(© 2007 by Robert Newton Barger)

Google, Inc., opened its doors in 1998 in Menlo Park, California. It was founded by two graduate students from Stanford University, Larry Page and Sergey Brin. In less than ten years it has become arguably the largest information retriever in the world and has established an international presence. This case will deal with the ethics of Google's cooperation with the government of the People's Republic of China in practicing censorship.

Google's presence in China began in 2005 when it opened a research and development center there. In 2006 it began a localized domain in China. The name of the domain is Google.cn. People in China could make a search on Google.com before 2006, but it was only available to about half of China's users. If those users entered search terms that were censored by the Chinese government, such as "Tiananmen Square," the site would immediately become unreachable for several hours.[1] A Chinese government directive issued in September, 2000, says that Internet content providers must restrict information that may harm the dignity and interests of the state or that foster evil cults or that damage social stability.[2] The Chinese government is said to have an extensive Internet filtering process in place that controls which overseas Web sites its citizens can access. With that filtering as a guide, foreign companies are expected to build their own lists of Web sites that would be deleted from Web search results.[3]

With regard to Google's stance on censorship, Google says, "It is Google's policy not to censor search results. However, in response to local laws, regulations, or policies, we may do so. When we remove search results for these reasons, we display a notice on our search results pages."[4] Other Chinese search engines, such as MSN, also give explicit notice when they censor results. Google has argued that censoring search results clearly compromises its mission, but that failing to offer the Google search engine in China, which holds a fifth of the world's population, would be even worse. It is worth noting that Google does not censor only in China. Google censors certain Nazi websites in Germany and it censors child pornography websites in the United States. It is not known exactly how Google censors, but its filtering process appears to be based on domains, sub-domains, URLs and keywords.[5]

Some of the questions to be considered in addressing the ethics of Google's censorship activities in China are the following: 1. Are Americans biased in their analysis of censorship issues by their long national tradition of First Amendment rights? 2. Is China justified in using censorship to enforce a puritanical form of morality and to prevent social and political instability in its rapidly developing country? 3. Is Google justified in going along with China's censorship policy in order to prevent an even worse suppression of information by the government, or is Google's motivation to cooperate with the government simply so it can make money in this largest of all markets?

17.2 Demon Worship Case

(© 1996 by John Halleck, used with permission)

In order to justify the funding for electronic mail and news, you are asked to compile a list of how many users use each of the newsgroups and on what machines you receive and send mail. You compile this list. Your company bigwigs notice that 350 users at your site read the "alt.demons" newsgroup. Since there is a company policy against demon worship, they are concerned.

- Should you comply with a request to give a list of those people that read the newsgroup?
- Do you give a list if you know that they intend to fire anybody on the list? Does this answer change if you once read the newsgroup to see what it was like?
- Do your answers change if the newsgroup is "alt.homosexual," "alt.vandalism," "misc.legal," "alt.sex.kiddyporn"?

17.3 System Privileges Case

(© 1996 by John Halleck, used with permission)

Most operating systems give the privilege of reading and writing any user's files as part of the normal "system" privileges. This means that on many machines, all of the system people can gain access (without leaving any traces) to everybody's personal files and mail. Normally the system people are a surprisingly ethical bunch, but there is the possibility for abuse.

You are given "system" privileges. Should you use them to read files in the following cases:

- You suspect a user of illegal or unethical activities and checking the user's files would establish this for sure.
- Your boss suspects a user of illegal activities, and wants you to check.
- You suspect SOMEBODY is doing illegal activities on the machine and you want to find out who it is.
- You suspect somebody MIGHT be doing illegal activities on the machine, and you want to find out for sure.
- You want to find out (by checking what newsgroups they read) if anybody else on the machine is into [perversion of your choice] as you happen to be.
- You hear a user saying how his/her data is "so much safer from prying eyes" now that it is on the computer. Do you burst their bubble by pointing out that system folk have access? What if the data affect you?
- Your company does not have the vaguest idea of how to manage a machine, and offer you system privileges when they are not needed.
  - Do you refuse them because you don't need them?
  - Do you accept them because they might come in handy later?
  - Do you accept them because everyone else did, and you don't want to be at a disadvantage?

17.4 The Computer Goes to Court Case

(© 2007 by Thomas Lapp, used with permission)

The liberal state of Calidonia, because of the increase in crime in the state, has found itself with the problem of having many more criminals to try in the courts than it has time to try them. In an attempt to decrease the length of time it takes to hear a case, as well as to attempt to hold "fair" trials, the state of Calidonia has recently revamped its judicial system in a radical new way.

Normally, one would say that the best way to judge someone accurately would be to have as much information about the case as possible. However, in court-rooms, not all of the information about a case is admissible as evidence. Of course, this does not stop a fast-talking lawyer from saying something, having it objected to, and struck. The result is that the jury hears something that they are told that they should disregard. This is naturally going to influence what they know, even if they cannot use it directly in making their decision.

We now introduce Calidonia's effort at a better judicial system. In courtrooms in the state, the jury box now is empty because the jurors are no longer anywhere near the courtroom. They are often in their homes, connected to the Judicial Computer System (JCS) through either their home computer or a terminal which is loaned to them during the period in which they serve as a juror. All of the evidence in the case is sent to them through a filter, and all information sent to the jury is approved by the judge so that everything the juror gets is "admissible to the record."

Do you think this would result in fair case hearings in Calidonia? Why or why not? What are the implications of someone getting into the files of a case and presenting evidence to a jury that they were not supposed to see? What about the situation in which an electronic mail message fails to be received by a few of the members and it is a key piece of information in the case? What other things must the state of Calidonia think about if it uses this system?

17.5 The Computer Becomes the Court Case

(© 2007 by Thomas Lapp, used with permission)

Lemon County of Calidonia is facing a problem of trial backlog even worse than the state in general. In order to move cases through the system even faster (yet with the same or better level of justice), the county is proposing replacing the people in the jury box with a single computer system that has been programmed with all pertinent legal precedents and has software that allows it to make decisions based on the facts given to it and its database of precedents.

Do you think that Lemon County should start to use this system? Why or why not? What advantages would there be to this? What disadvantages? If you were involved in a crime in Lemon County, Calidonia, would you want to be tried by this system? Why or why not?

17.6 File Transfer Case

(© 1996 by Thomas Lapp, used with permission)

Here's a problem for you to solve. It is based on the "who is responsible" idea.

I work with many computer programs that are related to moving data from one place to another. We'll call this program UUCP for the purposes of this example. I take care of the UUCP program, but I have no control over what the other people in the company put into the UUCP program for transmission to other computers.

I got a call from someone at another company saying that they had not received their file from our computer. I checked and indeed we had transmitted the file, and our side said it was successful. Therefore, we assume that the file was "lost" once it got to the other company.

Our policy would say that the person within my company who originated the file should resend the file to the other company. However, since I work with the UUCP program, I can mark files as being "transmitted" or "not transmitted" in order to cause them to be sent again.

Now, since it is after hours, and it may be hard to locate the person who created the file in the first place, should I:

- Mark the file as unsent and resend it again?
- Tell the other company that we sent the file okay and that it is "their problem"?
- Send an e-mail note to the person creating the file telling them that we sent okay, but that they didn't receive it, and they'll have to do something about it?
- A variation of 1, 2, and/or 3?

What would you do and why?

17.7 Fix Bug Case

(© 1996 by John Halleck, used with permission)

You've just discovered that there is a bug in code you wrote. It is a stupid error (we all make them) that will cost a lot of time to fix. There is a good chance that the code with the bug will never be run by an average user. Do you:

- Fix it on general principles? Even if you are behind on other projects?
- Report it to your boss? Even if it makes you look careless?
- Wait and see if the user notices it? ("If it's not broke don't fix it.")
- Check your other projects for the same error? Even if you are behind?
- Add a note to the manual stating that it is supposed to work that way?
- Send a warning to the user? (Even though this might cause them to demand that you fix it?)
- Send a note to your customer support group so that they can help if a user stumbles over the bug? (Even if this means that your competitor can now show you shipped the program knowing it had problems?)

17.8 Life-and-Death Computer Case

The three pieces in this case are used with blanket permission from:

ACM Forum on Risks to the Public in Computers and Related Systems. Reused without explicit authorization under blanket permission granted for all ACM RISKS-Forum Digest materials. The author(s), the RISKS moderator, and the ACM have no connection with this reuse.

Life-and-Death Computer by Warren M. McLaughlin

Sun, 5 Jan 92 13:21 EST

The Washington Post, 5 Jan 1992, page C6:

As technologies become more powerful, the distinction between a helping tool and a decision-making tool keeps gaining importance. Nowhere is this clearer than in the case of the new diagnosis-aiding computers, which offer doctors the benefit of a gigantic data base – far larger than their own experience could be – compiled from the results of many thousands of cases nationwide. By conglomerating and analyzing the results of these cases, the computer can read out a series of alternative treatments, a probability rating on the success of a given procedure or – most controversially – the statistical risk of a patient's dying upon arrival in an intensive care unit in a given condition. Physicians with access to such a machine now bear a responsibility at least as weighty as that of diagnosis itself: that of balancing the computer's seemingly precise numbers and instant certainties with the knowledge that its results are dependent upon human judgment.

According to the staff in a Michigan hospital using a program of this type called APACHE, the computer's predictions of a patient's statistical probability of dying – calculated to two decimal points – are used strictly as tools, rather as any doctor might estimate, say, a 10 percent chance of survival from a given operation. A better description of risk, in that scenario, need not govern the doctor's (or the family's) decision as to whether the risk should be taken, only inform it better than individual experience ever can. But the incomplete results of a different study performed in France suggested that doctors with access to that kind of risk data were more likely than others to terminate care. The fear among practitioners is that hospital administrators or health bureaucrats, all increasingly beleaguered and pushed by public pressure toward cost cutting, might see computer-confirmed statistics on death risk as a road to easier triage.

Given the capability for vastly enhanced diagnosis by means of computers, the medical profession will be stuck with the same responsibility – also vastly enhanced – as before: first, to recognize that a computer can serve the cause of accurate diagnosis only on the basis of properly entered information by the physician using his or her senses; second, to keep in mind a fact much of the general public has trouble with, which is that a statistic about the probability of an event bears no causal relationship to that event. A person with a 95 percent chance of dying under a procedure is not the same thing as a person whom that procedure cannot help, or a person from whom care can be withheld with no compunctions. Obscure that distinction, and you take a step toward making the computer the master – a bad one.[6]

Re: Life-and-Death Computer by Tom Perrine
Tue, 7 Jan 92 11:03:13 PST

The Washington Post editorial in Risks 13.01 (Subject: Life-and-Death Computer) overlooked one other problem with the APACHE software: it has the potential to generate self-fulfilling prophecies.

It appears that APACHE is really reporting on patient "profiles": age, weight, general medical condition, cross-referenced with specific complaints or injuries and treatments and survival rates.

Since APACHE reduces people to profiles, we might as well use that term in discussion.

Let's say that a "profile" is not treated with a given procedure, in part due to the "advice" of APACHE, and then dies. If the information concerning this "profile" is then fed back into the APACHE database, this will decrease the "survivability" quotient for subsequent "profiles" with the same initial set of problems. Each time a patient (oops, "profile") with a given complaint is not treated (and dies), the survival quotient decreases again.

Each time APACHE (indirectly) advises a doctor to withhold treatment for a condition, it increases the probability that it will "advise" withholding treatment for the next patient (oops, "profile") with the same basic complaint/injury, leading to another death, leading to another survival quotient decrease.

The editorial remarks that "a computer can serve the cause of accurate diagnosis only on the basis of properly entered information by the physician using his or her senses." Even if data is 100% correct, it still leads to positive feedback, which will further skew the output data.[7]

Life-and-death computer: Numbers lie, by anonymous
Wed, 8 Jan 92 06:12:15 -0500

In RISKS 13.01, Warren McLaughlin cites a Washington Post article about programs which give highly-precise probabilities on medical treatment outcomes, and how this can lead to doctors relinquishing their proper decision-making responsibility.

It seems clear to me that the problem here isn't that the doctor is relinquishing his responsibility by being too trusting of the software, so much as it is the programmer is relinquishing the responsibility to the doctor by presenting bad information.

The problems inherent in encoding weights for different courses of action (or any other "non-monotonic" comparison) is [sic] very familiar to anyone familiar with expert systems. In addition to the illusion of accuracy illustrated in the article, there are numerous other kinds of error introduced at every step, from the initial assignment of weights for the raw data (what is a "favorable outcome" in treatments to prolong life in a terminal disease), observed situation (what is "slight swelling of the lymph nodes"), anomalies when these are reasoned on in conjunction with each other (often you can prove $a>b>c>a$), and then, finally, in the way they are reported.

Assuming that these problems are dealt with in a realistic manner, for the program to communicate reasonably with the doctor, it is necessary to give some idea of the precision of these numbers. One of the better techniques is to use "error-bars". This can help transform what appears to be a definitive decision:

Cut off head: 40%

Give aspirin: 30%

Cut off foot: 20%

vs:

-Treatment- 0 10 20 30 40 50 60 70 80 90 100

Cut off head: |———————————-X—-|

Give aspirin: |————X————|

Cut off foot: |—-X————|

As you can see, this makes it much more clear that the program really hasn't decided much of anything at all.

It should also be clear from my example that in addition to the numerical information, an explanation of the reasoning process together [sic] may well be warranted, to check for any unwarranted assumptions, and other things to look out for. (Such as the need for reattaching the head after repairs are effected, and the assumption that the patient is a robot.)

(The disease in question, of course, is "headache.")

In real life, a doctor giving a second opinion isn't just going to give a number. He's going to give reasons, and an idea how sure he is of the appropriateness of a particular treatment and alternative treatments and even perhaps alternative diagnosis to consider. [Or maybe the insurance industry has this process reduced to a coded number now too, in which case, the Risks should be obvious.]

The deceptive problems of encoding preferences and subjective evaluations into numbers is, of course, a pervasive problem in other areas. Indeed, the entire area of risk analysis is rife with it, as I've pointed out indirectly in other messages. It's so much easier to calculate with simple numbers that this is a very tempting trap to fall into. But we must resist the temptation to manufacture certainty where non[e] exists. Whether we are computer professionals, scientists, pollsters, journalists, or newspaper readers, I think being careful with these issues is a matter of professional integrity. It's an integrity that is all too often lacking, out of ignorance, sloppiness, desire to persuade, or desire to be persuaded.[8]

17.9 Chapter Summary

This chapter contains a number of cases from real life concerning power. The first (Google and Chinese Censorship case) involves Google's cooperation with the government of the People's Republic of China in censoring search requests for information on the Web in exchange for the right to operate its business in China. The second (Demon Worship case) involves a request for information on what newsgroups employees are reading so it can be seen if they are violating company policy. The third (System Privileges case) concerns ethical use of system privileges. The fourth (The Computer Goes to Court case) concerns use of computers to send evidence to jurors. The fifth (The Computer Becomes the Court case) involves the replacement of jurors with a computer system to decide cases. The sixth (File Transfer case) deals with how ethically to handle a case in which an employee at one company says a file has been transferred successfully to another company, but an employee at the other company claims not to have received it. The seventh (Fix Bug case) involves the discovery of a programming error in code you wrote and what the ethical response to it should be on your part. The eighth (Life-and-Death Computer case) involves several postings that point out the risks of letting software skew predictions of survival for patients after treatment.

17.10 Your Turn

Question 1. Use the ethical decision-making process described in Chapter 6 to solve the cases in this chapter, as directed by your instructor. Answer any additional questions contained in the cases.

EIGHTEEN

A Miscellaneous Collection of Cases

18.1 Mail Inspection Case

(© 1996 by John Halleck, used with permission)

Due to hardware problems, the mail to your site has to be remailed. (This involves checking each letter in the dead letter queue, checking to see to whom it should have been sent, and running a program to put it into the user's mailbox.) While doing this you end up seeing the contents of several messages. What should you do (if anything) in the following cases?

- A message seems to be bragging about getting away with some fraud.
- A message is giving information you know to be false about someone you know.
- A message is telling another user false information about you.
- A message seems to be setting up a drug deal.
- A message that gives you a personal advantage.

18.2 Fake Sale Case

(© 1996 by John Halleck, used with permission)

You are asked to write a program to print tags for a sale. Your boss asks you to put out tags that have a price sufficiently high that a 10% discount marked on it brings it back to the original price. Do you do this?

18.3 Numerically Unstable Case

(© 1996 by John Halleck, used with permission)

A user comes by with a question about running his/her program on your machine. You notice that the methods that the program employs are numerically unstable (i.e., the answers have lots of digits, but only the first is significant [i.e., correct]). The user claims that his/her thesis depends on the first three digits of the answer. The user finally finds a way of getting your machine to give the "same" answer, although he/she admits that he/she knows the answer is bogus.

- Do you say anything to the thesis committee?
- Years later you get an information request from a prospective employer of this user. Do you say anything now?
- Your boss tells you that your company is planning to hire this person, what do you say now?

18.4 Edited File Case

(© 1996 by John Halleck, used with permission)

During the normal routine of tracking down software problems you are forced to check the contents of some users' files. You find a file that is in the process of being edited to be the user's own program, from a program of another student. What should you do? You find a file that shows that the customer is cheating on their taxes. Should you do anything? You find proof that the user is bilking YOUR company. Now what? You note that somebody you are interested in getting to know better has a file of her/his favorite sexual fantasies. Do you use this knowledge when you finally get a date with her/him?

18.5 Class Project Case

(© 1996 by John Halleck, used with permission)

You are hired part time to write a program. You later find out that this is the quarter project in a class that the person who hired you is enrolled in. Now what?

18.6 Hide from the IRS Case

(© 1996 by John Halleck, used with permission)

You are writing an accounting program. The person that wants it asks you to add some features to hide some accounts from the IRS. What do you do?

18.7 Ignore the Problem Case

(© 1996 by John Halleck, used with permission)

You find a potentially serious problem in some monitoring software that you wrote. Your boss says to ignore it, if there is a problem the customer will complain soon enough if it affects her/him. Do you take any action? The software is monitoring patients in a hospital, does this change your actions?

18.8 Chapter Summary

This chapter contains a miscellaneous collection of cases. The first (Mail Inspection case) involves mail that must be resent, some contents of this mail are observed by you – the Postmaster. What do you do about the ethical dilemmas presented by some of these contents? The second (Fake Sale case) involves your boss asking you to print tags for a sale and make it appear that a 10% discount is being given when, actually, the items are not being discounted at all. The third (Numerically Unstable case) involves a student who is running a bogus program on your machine for his/her thesis. You are asked what you would do with this knowledge if faced with several different situations. The fourth (Edited File case) involves a case that requires you to check some users' files. During this process you are confronted with a number of ethically challenging dilemmas and asked what you would do when faced with each dilemma. The fifth (Class Project case) involves your being hired to write a program and discovering it is a course requirement for the student who hired you. The sixth (Hide from the IRS case) involves your writing a program for a client who asks you to put some features in it that will hide certain accounts from the IRS. The seventh (Ignore the Problem case) supposes that you find a potentially serious problem in some software you wrote. Your boss tells you to ignore it – that the customer will complain about it if it causes a problem. Do you do this, even if it might involve a life-threatening situation?

18.9 Your Turn

Question 1. Use the ethical decision-making process described in Chapter 6 to solve the cases in this chapter, as directed by your instructor. Answer any additional questions contained in the cases.

NINETEEN

Parasitic Computing Case

19.1 Introduction

The last chapter of this book is reserved for the treatment of a unique computer ethics dilemma. Few dilemmas can literally be called "computer" ethics dilemmas. This is because most such dilemmas are not restricted only to the use of computers. They often can employ some other medium. For instance, the action of a bank teller pilfering a bank account by shorting each deposit a fraction of a cent through the use of a computer is not a unique computer ethics crime. This crime could also have been committed without the use of a computer.

The dilemma to be described in this chapter involves a proof-of-concept experiment performed by four faculty members at the University of Notre Dame. The four were Vincent Freeh and Jay Brockman of the Department of Computer Science and Engineering, and Albert-Laszlo Barabasi and Hawoong Jeong of the Department of Physics. This dilemma might best be introduced in the researchers' own words:

Parasitic computing is an example of a potential technology that could be viewed simultaneously as a threat or healthy addition to the online universe. On the Internet, reliable communication is guaranteed by a standard set of protocols, used by all computers. These protocols can be exploited to compute with the communication infrastructure, transforming the Internet into a distributed computer in which servers unwittingly perform computation on behalf of a remote node. In this model, one machine forces target computers to solve a piece of a complex computational problem merely by engaging them in standard communication.

Parasitic computing raises important questions about the ownership of the resources connected to the Internet and challenges current computing paradigms. The purpose of our work is to raise awareness of the existence of these issues, before they could be exploited. By publishing our work we wish to bring the Internet's various existing vulnerabilities to the attention of both the scientific community and the society at large, so that the ethical, legal and scientific ramifications raised by it can be resolved.

Our implementation of parasitic computing is not efficient. If it is made efficient, it could offer unlimited computational power. How should it be dealt with then? Should it be allowed under controlled circumstances? These are issues that the community must address shortly.[1]

19.2 The TCP/IP Protocol

Before addressing questions of ethics regarding this issue, it is necessary to consider a few technical details concerning how a computer communicates with other computers on the Internet. The protocol that enables such communication is called TCP/IP. More precisely, TCP/IP involves two protocols that cooperate to make the Internet work. The first of these protocols is the Transmission Control Protocol, known as TCP. The second is the Internet Protocol, known as IP. TCP and IP are part of a suite of layers that compose the Internet protocol suite. The bottom layer in this suite is generally known as the Network interface or Network access layer. It is sometimes divided into two layers, the first known as the Data-link layer and the second known as the Physical layer. Some of the functions performed in this layer are encapsulation of IP datagrams into frames to be transmitted by the network and mapping IP addresses to physical hardware addresses. The next layer up from the Network interface layer is the Internet layer. This is the layer in which IP operates. Above this layer is the Transport layer. TCP operates in this layer. The top level of the suite is the Application layer. Protocols such as HTTP (Hypertext Transfer Protocol), FTP (File Transfer Protocol), and IMAP (Internet Message Access Protocol) operate in this layer[2] (see Fig. 19.1).

19.3 Communication on the Internet

Here is how the Internet protocol suite works to facilitate communication on the Internet. When a user wishes to connect with another server, that

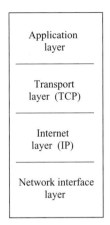

Figure 19.1 Layers in the Internet protocol suite

user enters the target server's address (the Uniform Resource Locator or URL) into the user's browser, including the page that the user wishes to view (e.g., http://www.loc.gov/index.html). The browser establishes a TCP connection to the server and then issues an HTTP request over the TCP connection. TCP at the Transport layer of the sending computer breaks the request into packets and numbers them. After the packets are broken up and numbered, they are sent to the Internet layer where IP sends them over the Internet to their destination. Each of these packets might travel to the target server over any number of diverse routes. When the HTTP request reaches the target server the fragmented packets are reassembled and checked for integrity at the recipient's end. If the reassembled packets forming the request are complete, the target server issues a response to the sender. If some packets are missing or corrupted they are dropped and the receiving node waits for the sending node to retransmit the message.

An important component in the parasitic computing experiment is the Checksum function of TCP. Checksum is the means that TCP uses to verify that all of the packets that compose a message arrive at their destination, and that they arrive intact. The sending node computes a checksum and sends it with the message. When it arrives, the receiving node also computes a checksum and compares it with that of the sending node. If the two checksums do not agree, the message is either corrupt or packets are missing. The interesting thing about the checksum from the standpoint of the parasitic computing experiment is that, since the checksum function is capable of doing arithmetic, it can be exploited to force the receiving node to do computation without the receiving node's knowledge or consent.

The researchers showed how the exploitation of the checksum function was possible by solving an NP-complete satisfiability problem (i.e., a problem in complexity theory using Boolean variables to determine if a given expression evaluates as true). They constructed messages containing possible solutions and sent them to recipient nodes located in North America, Europe, and Asia. They used the checksum function to force the recipient computers to determine whether the possible solution the message contained was indeed a correct solution. If it was, the message was sent by the receiving computer to the Application layer of the receiving computer's Internet protocol suite. The receiving computer reacted to this message as if it were an HTTP request, but because it was not a valid request it sent back a reply such as "page not found." The parasitic (sending) node interpreted this reply as indicating that the message contained a valid solution to the problem. Messages were constructed so that invalid solutions do not pass the checksum match. The receiving computer judged that these messages were corrupted and dropped them. The parasitic node, receiving no reply to these messages, interpreted them as containing invalid solutions. The preceding is a relatively brief sketch of how the checksum function was exploited in this experiment. Two other related matters need to be mentioned, the question of false negatives and the question of efficiency. With regard to false negatives, there is the possibility that a correct solution is not sent back to the parasitic node. Ordinarily the checksum function would take care of this, but the researchers changed the checksum's basic purpose so it cannot do this. The researchers tested for false negatives by repeatedly sending the correct solution to several nodes in North America, Europe, and Asia and found that the rate of false negatives ranged from 1 in about 100 to less than 1 in 17,000. With regard to efficiency, the researchers point out that for the experiment to be efficient the computation sent out by the parasitic node would have to increase until the computation-to-communication ratio is larger than the amount of cycles needed to solve the problem on its own rather than exporting it. The researchers say it remains to be seen whether a high-level implementation of a parasitic computer could be efficient. Further details may be found in a 2001 article entitled "Parasitic computing" authored by the researchers in the scientific journal *Nature.*[3]

19.4 Ethical Issues in Parasitic Computing

The quotation from the researchers at the beginning of this chapter indicates that they were aware of the ethical issues involved in this case. How, then, do they defend against the criticism of many people who say that they were violating the property rights of the owners of the targeted servers when they forced these servers to perform computation without the owners' knowledge or permission? The researchers, in the *Nature* article mentioned in Section 19.3, reply as follows. "Unlike 'cracking' (breaking into a computer) or computer viruses, however, parasitic computing does not compromise the security of the targeted servers, and accesses only those parts of the servers that have been made explicitly available for Internet communication."[4]

While it may access only the parts of servers that have been made explicitly available for Internet communication, parasitic computing is still using the cycles of those servers without the permission of their owners. The ACM (Association for Computing Machinery) Code of Ethics and Professional Conduct, in section 2.8, states: "Theft or destruction of tangible and electronic property is prohibited by imperative 1.2 – 'Avoid harm to others.' Trespassing and unauthorized use of a computer or communication system is addressed by this imperative. Trespassing includes accessing communication networks and computer systems, or accounts and/or files associated with those systems, without explicit authorization to do so. Individuals and organizations have the right to restrict access to their systems so long as they do not violate the discrimination principle (see 1.4). No one should enter or use another's computer system, software, or data files without permission. One must always have appropriate approval before using system resources, including communication ports, file space, other system peripherals, and computer time."[5] The parts of this section that seem to apply to the case at hand are these: First, "Trespassing includes accessing communication networks and computer systems . . . without explicit authorization to do so." Second, "No one should enter or use another's computer system . . . without permission. Third, "One must always have appropriate approval before using system resources, including communication ports, file space, other system peripherals, and computer time." These three statements would make it appear that parasitic computing could be in violation of the ACM Code. As we saw in Chapter 3 (Philosophic Belief Systems), this Code would be characterized as having an Idealistic view. It follows the belief that certain actions are always right or always wrong, no matter what the motivation for doing them might be.

There is, however, another way to view the ethics of parasitic computing. One might take a more Pragmatic approach to it. This approach is seen in the "no harm, no foul" position of your author and his colleague Charles Crowell of the University of Notre Dame:

> The principal reason for our "harm being the arbiter of abuse" position in relation to parasitic computing lies in the shared nature of the Internet as a public resource. Traditional views of ownership rights involving the idea that an owner has sole control over use and profit from personal property (Calabresi & Melamed, 1972) do not apply strictly, in our opinion, when personal and public property are juxtaposed in a dependency relationship as they are in the context of computers being connected to the Internet. Because the act of connecting to the Internet in order to receive communication services is optional and elective, such action necessarily involves an implicit consent to a form of property sharing that trumps sole propriety. This act is analogous to placing a mailbox on the public easement in front of one's house in order to receive postal service. In these instances, personal property (mailboxes or TCP/IP layers) are made explicitly available to the public so that valued communication services thereby can be obtained. The dependency of the private upon the public arises here because one's personal communications in these instances must pass through a public handling system. Of necessity, this means that one's mailbox or TCP/IP protocol is subject to public interrogation, which amounts to a kind of shared relationship between owner and public.[6]

This suggestion that the "private property" model of ownership in the context of Internet communication might be subject to a new interpretation offers an alternative to the view that parasitic computing is unethical.

Consider also these reflections of Vincent Freeh, one of the parasitic computing experimenters: "In class recently while I was typing in the URL for the course page, a student said, 'Just Google it.' It turns out

Figure 19.2 Vinton G. Cerf

that he uses Google instead of bookmarks. This is not strictly the service Google provides. Similarly, to log on to my university's wireless I have to type a password to a web page. In order to get the web page to come up, I often go to Google. In both cases, Google is used for a different purpose than was intended and in a way that does not benefit Google. It is hard for me to see a qualitative difference between these uses and parasitic computing."[7]

It seems that after six years, there is still no clear judgment on the subject of the ethics of parasitic computing. Perhaps the concluding word for now should be given by one of the inventors of the TCP/IP protocol, Vinton G. Cerf. He has said that the researchers' work: "is pretty clever and I am impressed with the thinking behind it. Ethics, however, suggests that one mount a campaign to get volunteers to provide cycles. One should also consider that compute cycles are highly perishable – if you don't use [them], they evaporate. So some justification might be found if the arriving packets had lowest possible priority for use of the computing cycles."[8] In a subsequent communication, however, Cerf made clear: "Please note that I would not condone the use of parasitic computing on machines whose owners had NOT authorized such use."[9]

19.5 Chapter Summary

This chapter dealt with the parasitic computing experiment conducted at the University of Notre Dame in 2001. It recounted the technical details of the experiment and considered its ethical significance.

19.6 Your Turn

Question 1. Do you agree that, according to imperative 2.8 of the ACM Code of Ethics and Professional Conduct, the experiment was unethical? Why or why not?

Question 2. Do you agree with the following position stated by Barger and Crowell? Why or why not? "Traditional views of ownership rights involving the idea that an owner has sole control over use and profit from personal property do not apply strictly, in our opinion, when personal and public property are juxtaposed in a dependency relationship as they are in the context of computers being connected to the Internet. Because the act of connecting to the Internet in order to receive communication services is optional and elective, such action necessarily involves an implicit consent to a form of property sharing that trumps sole propriety."[10]

Question 3. If you disagree with the position stated in the previous question, do you also disagree with the statement in the first paragraph of this chapter that parasitic computing is a unique computer ethics dilemma? Why or why not?

Question 4. What do you think of Vinton Cerf's implicit suggestion that a compromise might eventually be worked out, premised on the understanding that arriving packets sent to the target computer by the parasitic computer be given the lowest possible priority for use of the computing cycles of the target computer?

Appendix

Topics for Presentations, Discussions, and Papers

Accountability of bloggers – A blog is a Web site containing analyses, opinions, and sometimes hyperlinks. What is the accountability of the owner of the blog for this material?

Carnivore's use by the FBI – Carnivore is an investigative device used to monitor e-mail and other electronic communications by means of "packet sniffing." It has raised privacy concerns.

Computer viruses – Programs that enter a computer through trickery or stealth, infecting it and usually corrupting its data and/or affecting its operation.

Credit card fraud online – Often involves "spoofing" (see Web spoofing) to obtain personal information that will enable illicit use of a credit card.

Cybersquatting – Usually involves investing in domain names that might in turn be sold to companies for a higher price than was originally paid.

Data mining – The practice of sifting through large amounts of data in search of information that might be used for commercial purposes, for example, to target potential customers.

Dating on the Internet – Involves using the Internet to find and make contact with other people for romantic purposes. The anonymity afforded by the Internet can make this a dangerous activity, however.

Fake ID manufacture and sale with computers – Involves use of Internet technology to sell fake identification cards (e.g., drivers' licenses). These are often described by the online sales sites as "novelty" cards to avoid criminal liability for their sale.

Gambling on the Internet – Involves wagering on sports events or games of chance. This activity often involves offshore sites and runs the risk of inauthentic practices that make the odds of winning (or being paid off) much less than they are at a physical casino or sports facility.

Hacking and Cracking – Hacking is an activity engaged in to test one's own knowledge and skill, usually for noncriminal purposes. Cracking is an activity engaged in for destructive and/or criminal purposes.

How socioeconomic class affects access to the Internet – Notice that this topic is *not* "How the Internet affects socioeconomic class," but rather "How one's access to the Internet is affected by socioeconomic class."

Open-source software – Software for which the source code is available for public inspection and modification.

Parental control of Internet use – Can involve a number of practices by which parents monitor, direct, and limit their children's access to and use of the Internet.

Pornography and censorship on the Internet – This topic concerns the control of access over the Internet to material that would cause sexual arousal.

Prescription drug sales on the Internet – This topic concerns such issues as the purity of drugs being sold, whether a medical doctor must prescribe them, how much they cost, and whether they can be obtained from foreign countries.

Posting "wanted" posters for abortion doctors on the Internet – This topic concerns the de facto incitement to murder physicians who perform abortion by posting their names and addresses on the Internet.

Privacy of personal health data on the Internet – This concerns preserving the privacy of personal data on the Internet, in this case, medical data.

Sale and auction of ovaries online – Regarding the ethics of selling personal parts of the human anatomy, in this case ovaries, on the Internet.

Sale of college degrees online – Deals with the ethics of "degree mills" selling academic degrees on the Internet without requiring the completion of study usually specified for their award.

Sale of term papers on the Internet –Involves the ethical danger that term papers will be sold over the Internet to students who will submit them as their own work.

The information technology gap between developed and developing countries – Covers the concerns presented in Chapter 10 on Computer Ethics and International Development.

Unsolicited e-mail (spam) – Spam is the Internet equivalent of "junk mail." Besides being unsolicited, it also has the danger of being a means for transmitting viruses and identity theft attempts.

Web spoofing – Involves disguising an attack Web site to look like a legitimate site that you are seeking to contact. After you contact the disguised site, possibly through clicking on a fake link, you may be asked for private information that will be transmitted to the attack site.

Notes

1. Introduction

1. J. J. O'Connor and E. F. Robertson, "Babbage biography," <http://www-groups.dcs.st-and.ac.uk/~history/Biographies/Babbage.html> (22 June 2007).
2. J. J. O'Connor and E. F. Robertson, "Hollerith biography," <http://www-groups.dcs.st-and.ac.uk/~history/Biographies/Hollerith.html> (22 June 2007).
3. Mary Bellis, "Howard Aiken and Grace Hopper – Inventors of the Mark I Computer," <http://inventors.about.com/library/weekly/aa052198.htm> (21 July 2007).
4. Alexander Randall 5th, "Q&A – A lost interview with ENIAC inventor J. Presper Eckert," <http://www.computerworld.com/hardwaretopics/hardware/story/0,10801,108568,00.html?source=NLT_AM&nid=108568> (30 December 2006).
5. Institute of Electrical and Electronics Engineers, Inc. (IEEE), "timeline.pdf," <http://www.computer.org/portal/cms_docs_ieeecs/ieeecs/about/history/timeline.pdf> (21 July 2007).
6. John Horgan, *New York Times*, Science Desk, Tuesday, 10 November 1998, sec. D, p. 5, National Edition.
7. Heinz von Foerster, "Responsibilities of Competence," *Journal of Cybernetics* 2, no. 2 (1972): 1–6, <http://mlab.uiah.fi/~timo/vonfoerster/> (12 January 2007).
8. James H. Moor, "What is computer ethics?" *Metaphilosophy*, 16, no. 4 (October 1985): 266–75.
9. Deborah G. Johnson, *Computer Ethics*, 2d ed. (Englewood Cliffs, NJ: Prentice Hall, 1994), p. 10.
10. Mary Gatta and Mary Trigg, *Bridging the gap: Gender equity in science, engineering and technology* (New Brunswick, NJ: Rutgers University, 2001). <http://www.chr.up.ac.za/ggp/coursematerial/2007/good_gov/elize/Gap%20gender%20and%20science.pdf> (28 December 2007).

11. "Department of State Washington File: Text: Research on Children, Learning and Computers," <http://canberra.usembassy.gov/hyper/2001/0130/epf206.htm> (30 December 2006).
12. Herman Tavani, "The uniqueness debate in computer ethics: What exactly is at issue, and why does it matter?" *Ethics and Information Technology* 4 (2002): 37–54.
13. Luciano Floridi and J. W. Sanders, "Mapping the foundationalist debate in computer ethics," *Ethics and Information Technology* 4 (2002): 7–8.
14. Tavani, 50–51.

2. The Computer as a Humanizing Agent

1. Alfred Bork, "Interactive learning," *American Journal of Physics*, 47, no. 1 (January 1979): 580–606.
2. John Seeley Brown, "Reflecting on Global Creation Networks and the Architecture and Rationale of the Firm in the 21st Century," lecture sponsored by the O'Brien-Smith Leadership Program at the Mendoza College of Business, University of Notre Dame, September 22, 2006.
3. Thomas Dwyer, "Some thoughts on computers and greatness in teaching," *SIGCUE: Topics in Instructional Computing* 1 (January 1975): 76–80.

3. Philosophic Belief Systems

1. William Halverson, *A Concise Introduction to Philosophy*, 4th ed. (New York: Random House, 1981), p. 340.
2. Plato, *The Republic*, Benjamin Jowett, trans. (New York: P. F. Collier and Son, 1901), pp. 253–91.
3. Geoffrey Sayre-McCord, "Kant's Grounding for the Metaphysics of Morals: A Very Brief Selective Summary of Sections I and II," <http://www.unc.edu/~gsmunc/phil22/Kantsum.pdf> (3 January 2007).
4. Matt McCormick, "Immanuel Kant – Metaphysics," *Internet Encyclopedia of Philosophy*, <http://www.iep.utm.edu/k/kantmeta.htm#H8> (3 January 2007).
5. Plato, *Crito, or, The Duty of a Citizen*, trans. by Henry Cary, <http://www.gutenberg.org/etext/13726> (2 August 2007).
6. "RBC Financial Group – RBC Letter," <http://www.rbc.com/responsibility/letter/september2006.html> (4 January 2007).
7. John R. Searle, "The Problem of Consciousness," <http://www.ecs.soton.ac.uk/~harnad/Papers/Py104/searle.prob.html> (4 January 2007).
8. Marvin Minsky, "N.Y. Times interview," 28 July 1998, personal e-mail (28 July 1998).
9. Aristotle, Nicomachean Ethics, Book I, section 8, paragraph 2, http://classics.mit.edu/Aristotle/nicomachaen.1.i.html> (9 July 2007).
10. Ibid., Book II, section 9, paragraph 1.

11. William James, *Pragmatism: A New Name for Some Old Ways of Thinking* (New York: Longmans, Green and Co., 1907), p. xi.
12. Ibid., 49–55.
13. William James, "The Moral Philosopher and the Moral Life," *International Journal of Ethics*, 1, no. 3 (April 1891): 330–54.
14. Fyodor Dostoevsky, *The Brothers Karamazov*, trans. by Constance Garnett (Melbourne: W. Heinemann, 1912).
15. Ludwig Wittgenstein, *Tractatus Logico-Philosophicus*, trans. by D. F. Pears and B. F. McGuinness (London: Routledge & Kegan Paul, 1961), Proposition 7.0, 151.
16. Ibid., Propositions 6.4–6.422, 145, 147.

4. A Philosophic Inventory

1. Colvin Ross, "An educational philosophical inventory," *Journal of Educational Thought*, 4, no. 1 (1970): 20–26. Consecutive pages available online in four separate files: <http://ux1.eiu.edu/~rnbarger/ross-p20-p21.tif> (30 December 2006), <http://ux1.eiu.edu/~rnbarger/ross-p22-p23.tif> (30 December 2006), <http://ux1.eiu.edu/~rnbarger/ross-p24-p25.tif> (30 December 2006), and <http://ux1.eiu.edu/~rnbarger/ross-p26.tif> (30 December 2006).
2. Josephine C. Barger, Robert N. Barger, and John J. Rearden, "Relationship of students' philosophic orientation to academic field of study." (Paper presented at the annual meeting of the American Educational Studies Association, Chicago, Illinois, October 25–29, 1989), <http://ux1.eiu.edu/~rnbarger/aesa1989.html> (30 December 2006).

5. The Possibility of a Unified Ethical Theory

1. James H. Moor, "Just consequentialism and computing" *Ethics and Information Technology* 1 (1999): 65–9.
2. Ibid., 65.
3. Ibid., 66.
4. Bernard Gert, *Morality: Its Nature and Justification* (Oxford: Oxford University Press, 1998).
5. Moor, "Just consequentialism," 67.

6. The Ethical Decision-Making Process

1. John Rawls, *A Theory of Justice*, rev. ed. (Cambridge, MA: Belknap Press of Harvard University Press, 1999).
2. Bill Carter, *New York Times*, 13 January 2000, Business/Financial Desk, Late Edition – Final, sec. C, p. 1, col. 5.

9. Computer-Related Codes of Ethics

1. Illinois Institute of Technology, "Codes of Ethics Online – Computing and Information Systems," <http://ethics.iit.edu/codes/computer.html> (1 July 2007).
2. Association for Computing Machinery, "ACM: Code of Ethics," <http://www.acm.org/constitution/code.html> (23 March 2007).
3. Association for Computing Machinery and Institute for Electrical and Electronics Engineers, "Software Engineering Code of Ethics and Professional Practice," <http://www.acm.org/serving/se/code.htm> (23 March 2007).
4. Computer Ethics Institute, "The Ten Commandments of Computer Ethics," <http://www3.brookings.edu/its/cei/TheTenCommandmentsOfComputer Ethics.pdf> (18 June 2007).

10. Computer Ethics and International Development

1. World Summit on the Information Society (WSIS), "Basic Information about WSIS," <http://www.itu.int/wsis/basic/faqs.asp> (3 April 2007).
2. World Summit on the Information Society, "Geneva Plan of Action," <http://www.itu.int/wsis/docs/geneva/official/poa.html> (3 April 2007).
3. World Summit on the Information Society, "Geneva Declaration of Principles," <http://www.itu.int/wsis/docs/geneva/official/dop.html> (3 April 2007).
4. World Summit on the Information Society, "Tunis Commitment," <http://www.itu.int/wsis/docs2/tunis/off/7.html> (25 July 2007).
5. World Summit on the Information Society, "Tunis Agenda for the Information Society," <http://www.itu.int/wsis/docs2/tunis/off/6rev1.html> (3 April 2007).

11. Robotics and Ethics

1. Roboethics Roadmap, EURON (EUropean RObotics research Network) Roboethics Atelier, Genoa, 27th of February – 3rd of March, 2006, Scuola di Robotica, (Project coordinator) Dr. Gianmarco Veruggio, 5.
2. Ibid., 6–7.
3. Ibid., 25.
4. Ibid., 11–12.
5. Ibid., 22.
6. Isaac Asimov, "Runaround," *Astounding Science-Fiction*, March, 1942, 94–103.
7. Roboethics Roadmap, 26–27.
8. Ibid., 29.
9. Michael Anderson, Susan Leigh Anderson, and Chris Armen, "Towards Machine Ethics," <http://people.cs.uu.nl/virginia/aotp/papers/ Towards%20Machine%20Ethics.pdf> (20 August 2007).

10. Ibid.
11. John Rawls, *A Theory of Justice*, rev. ed. (Cambridge, MA: Belknap Press of Harvard University Press, 1999).
12. Anderson, Anderson, and Armen, "Toward Machine Ethics."

12. Theft and Piracy Concerns

1. "Trademark Cyberpiracy Prevention/Anticybersquatting Consumer Protection Act," <http://www.domainhandbook.com/tcpa.html> (8 August 2007).
2. "Underground-Review.com – Fake Id Novelty Free Template Cards Driver License Review," <http://www.underground-review.com/> (8 August 2007).
3. "Deter. Detect. Defend. Avoid ID Theft," <http://www.ftc.gov/bcp/edu/microsites/idtheft/> (8 August 2007).
4. "CIPO – Patent – 40598," <http://patents1.ic.gc.ca/details?patent_number= 40598> (9 August 2007).
5. "U.S. Senate: Reference Home > Constitution of the United States," <http://www.senate.gov/civics/constitution_item/constitution.htm#a1> (9 August 2007).
6. "RIAA," <http://www.riaa.com/newsitem.php?news_ear_filter=&resultpage =5&id=0BB7A35D-544B-2DD2-F374-4F680D6BAE9B> (9 August 2007).
7. "Home | Open Source Initiative," <http://www.opensource.org/> (10 August 2007).
8. "Linux Online – About the Linux Operating System," <http://www.linux. org/info/> (10 August 2007).
9. M. David Ermann, Mary B. Williams, and Michele S. Shauf, eds. *Computers, Ethics, and Society* (Oxford: Oxford University Press, 1997), 234–35.
10. "Dilbert Comic Strip Archive – Dilbert.com," <http://www.unitedmedia. com/comics/dilbert/archive/dilbert-20070803.html> (10 August 2007).
11. "Pharming: Is your trusted Web site a clever fake?" <http://www.microsoft. com/protect/yourself/phishing/pharming.mspx> (11 August 2007).
12. "OnGuard Online – Phishing," <http://onguardonline.gov/phishing.html> (11 August 2007).
13. "Farmers Bank, N.A." <http://www.farmersbankna.com/site/fraud_alert. html> (11 August 2007).
14. "Diplomas for Sale, Vicki Mabrey Reports on Online Diploma Mills – CBS News." <http://www.cbsnews.com/stories/2004/11/08/60II/ main654319.shtml> (13 August 2007).
15. "Aspen State Teacher's [sic] College," <http://www.aspenstate.org/pages/ 1/index.htm> (13 August 2007).
16. "win06nl.pdf [application/pdf Object]," <http://aspenhistory.org/win06nl. pdf> (13 August 2007).
17. "Federal Bureau of Investigation – Press Release," <http://www.fbi.gov/ pressrel/pressrel03/spoofing072103.htm> (9 October 2007).

14. Privacy Concerns

1. "Javascript Injection | TestingSecurity.com," <http://www.testingsecurity.com/how-to-test/injection-vulnerabilities/Javascript-Injection> (22 August 2007).
2. Jon Swartz and Theresa Howard, "Facebook plans to offer targeted ads," USA Today, 27 August 2007, <http://www.usatoday.com/tech/news/computersecurity/ 2007–08–26-facebook_N.htm?csp=34> (27 August 2007).
3. "US-CERT Cyber Security Tip ST04–015 – Understanding Denial-of-Service Attacks," <http://www.us-cert.gov/cas/tips/ST04–015.html> (22 August 2007).
4. "CDT | Center for Democracy and Technology," <http://www.cdt.org/> (22 August 2007).
5. "Department of Homeland Security | Preserving our Freedoms, Protecting America," < http://www.dhs.gov/index.shtm> (23 August 2007).
6. "EFF: Privacy," <http://www.eff.org/Privacy/> (22 August 2007).
7. "EPIC Archive – Privacy," <http://www.epic.org/privacy/> (22 August 2007).
8. " US-CERT: Control Systems – Cyber Threat Source Descriptions," < http://www.us-cert.gov/control_systems/csthreats.html> (23 August 2007).
9. "994.pdf [application/pdf Object]," <http://homes.cerias.purdue.edu/~spaf/tech-reps/994.pdf> (24 August 2007).
10. Ibid.
11. "Virus Basics," <http://www.us-cert.gov/reading_room/virus.html> (25 August 2007).
12. "p 22-denning.pdf [application/pdf Object," <http://delivery.acm.org/10.1145/110000/102869/p22-denning.pdf?key1=102869&key2=8939518811&coll=portal&dl=ACM&CFID=33002936&CFTOKEN=88469102> (26 August 2007).
13. "The Risks Digest Volume 9: Issue 62," <http://catless.ncl.ac.uk/Risks/9.62.html#subj7> (26 August 2007).
14. "frontline: hackers: who are hackers: notable hacks," <http://www.pbs.org/wgbh/pages/frontline/shows/hackers/whoare/notable.html> (26 August 2007).

16. Power Concerns

1. "MEDIA; White House Approves Pass for Blogger – New York Times," <http://query.nytimes.com/gst/fullpage.html?res=9C03E2DD1E3DF934A35750C0A9639C8B63&sec =&spon=> (2 September 2007).
2. "A Bloggers' Code of Ethics – CyberJournalist.net – Online News Association – Ethics and Credibility," <http://www.cyberjournalist.net/news/000215.php> (2 September 2007).
3. *Schenck v. United States*, 249 U.S. 47 (1919).
4. "freedomforum.org: Abortion foes' wanted posters, Web site are 'true threats'," <http://www.freedomforum.org/templates/document.asp?documentID=16266> (19 September 2007).

5. "ABC News: 'Cyberchondria': Point, Click, Sick," < http://abcnews.go.com/GMA/OnCall/story?id=3190086&page=1> (10 September 2007).
6. Ibid.
7. "The Risks Digest Volume 17: Issue 12," <http://catless.ncl.ac.uk/Risks/17.12.html#subj6> (10 September 2007).
8. "Ivan Goldberg discusses Internet Addiction," <http://www.psycom.net/iasg.html> (12 September 2007).
9. "Challenger Accident," <http://www.fas.org/spp/51L.html> (17 September 2007).
10. "The Risks Digest, Volume 6: Issue 20," <http://catless.ncl.ac.uk/Risks/6.20.html> (19 September 2007).

17. Cases Concerning Power

1. Declan McCullagh, No booze or jokes for Googlers in China | CNET News.com, <http://news.com.com/No+booze+or+jokes+for+Googlers+in+China/+page+1/2100–1030_3–6031727.html?tag=item> (28 April 2007).
2. Ibid., <http://news.com.com/No+booze+or+jokes+for+Googlers+in+China+-+page+2/2100–1030_3–6031727–2.html?tag=st.num> (28 April 2007).
3. Ibid., <http://news.com.com/No+booze+or+jokes+for+Googlers+in+China+-+page+3/2100–1030_3–6031727–3.html?tag=st.num> (28 April 2007).
4. "Google: Web Search Help Center," <http://www.google.com/support/bin/answer.py?answer=17795> (28 April 2007).
5. "Google Censorship FAQ, March 2, 2007," <http://blog.outer-court.com/archive/2007–03–02-n19.html> (28 April 2007).
6. "The Risks Digest, Volume 13: Issue 1," <http://catless.ncl.ac.uk/Risks/13.01.html> (21 September 2007).
7. "The Risks Digest, Volume 13: Issue 2," <http://catless.ncl.ac.uk/Risks/13.02.html> (21 September 2007).
8. Ibid.

19. The Parasitic Computing Case

1. Vincent Freeh et al., "Parasitic computing," <http://www.nd.edu/~parasite/> (5 April 2007).
2. "Network Access Layer," <http://www.pku.edu.cn/academic/research/computer-center/tc/html/TC0200.html> (5 April 2007).
3. Albert-Laszlo Barabasi et al., "Parasitic computing," *Nature* Vol. 412 (30 August 2001): 894–97, <http://www.nd.edu/~parasite/nature.pdf> (5 April 2007).
4. Ibid., 895.
5. "ACM: Code of Ethics," <http://www.acm.org/constitution/code.html> (6 April 2007).

6. Robert N. Barger and Charles R. Crowell, "Ethics of 'Parasitic Computing': Fair Use or Abuse of TCP/IP over the Internet?" in *Information Ethics: Privacy and Intellectual Property*, ed. by Lee Freeman and A. Graham Peace (Hershey, PA: Information Science Publishing, 2005), p. 156.

7. Vincent W. Freeh, "Re: Use of quote by you," 26 April 2007, personal e-mail (26 April 2007).

8. Vinton G. Cerf, "Re: Inquiry from WorldCom website," 12 September 2003, personal e-mail (12 September 2003).

9. Vinton G. Cerf, "Re: Permission to use a quote from you," 21 September 2003, personal e-mail (21 September 2003).

10. Barger and Crowell, p. 156.

Selected Bibliography

Printed Sources

Barabasi, Albert-Laszlo, Vincent W. Freeh, Hawoong Jeong, and Jay B. Brockman. "Parasitic Computing." *Nature* 412 (30 August 2001): 894–97.

Barger, Robert N., and Charles R. Crowell. "Ethics of 'Parasitic Computing': Fair Use or Abuse of TCP/IP Over the Internet?" In *Information Ethics: Privacy and Intellectual Property*, edited by Lee A. Freeman and A. Graham Peace, 143–61. Hershey, PA: Information Science Publishing, 2005.

Bork, Alfred. "Interactive learning." *American Journal of Physics* 47, no. 1 (January 1979): 580–606.

Calabresi, G., and D. A. Melamed. "Property rules, liability rules and inalienability: One view of the cathedral." *Harvard Business Review* 85 (1972): 1089–1128.

Dostoevsky, Fyodor. *The Brothers Karamazov*. Translated by Constance Garnett. Melbourne: W. Heinemann, 1912.

Dwyer, Thomas. "Some thoughts on computers and greatness in teaching." *SIGCUE: Topics in Instructional Computing* 1 (January 1975): 76–80.

Ermann, M. David, Mary B. Williams, and Michele S. Shauf, eds. *Computers, Ethics, and Society*. Oxford: Oxford University Press, 1997.

Floridi, Luciano, and J. W. Sanders. "Artificial Evil and the Foundations of Computer Ethics." *Ethics and Information Technology 3(1)* (2001): 55–66.

Floridi, Luciano, and J. W. Sanders. "Mapping the foundationalist debate in computer ethics." *Ethics and Information Technology* 4 (2002): 1–9.

Gert, Bernard. *Morality: Its Nature and Justification*. Oxford: Oxford University Press, 1998.

Halverson, William. *A Concise Introduction to Philosophy*, 4th ed. New York: Random House, 1981.

James, William. "The Moral Philosopher and the Moral Life." *International Journal of Ethics*, 1, no. 3 (April 1891): 330–54.

Johnson, Deborah G. *Computer Ethics*, 2nd ed. Englewood Cliffs, NJ: Prentice Hall, 1994.

Moor, James H. "What is computer ethics?" *Metaphilosophy* 16, no. 4 (October 1985): 266–75.

————. "Just consequentialism and computing." *Ethics and Information Technology* 1 (1999): 65–9.

Plato. *The Works of Plato.* Edited by Erwin Edman. Translated by Benjamin Jowett. New York: Random House, 1927. pp. 91–106.

————. *The Republic.* Translated by Benjamin Jowett. New York: P. F. Collier and Son, 1901. pp. 253–91.

Rawls, John. *A Theory of Justice,* rev. ed. Cambridge, MA: Belnap Press of Harvard University Press, 1999.

Ross, Colvin. "An educational philosophical inventory." *Journal of Educational Thought 4,* no. 1 (1970): 20–6.

Tavani, Herman. "The uniqueness debate in computer ethics: What exactly is at issue, and why does it matter?" *Ethics and Information Technology 4* (2002): 37–54.

Wittgenstein, Ludwig. *Tractatus Logico-Philosophicus.* Translated by D. F. Pears and B. F. McGuinness. London: Routledge & Kegan Paul, 1961.

Electronic sources

Anderson, Michael, Susan Leigh Anderson, and Chris Armen. "Towards Machine Ethics." <http://people.cs.uu.nl/virginia/aotp/papers/Towards%20Machine%20Ethics.pdf>.

Aristotle. Nicomachean Ethics. Translated by W. D. Ross. <http://classics.mit.edu/Aristotle/nicomachaen.1.i.html>.

Association for Computing Machinery, Inc. "ACM: Code of Ethics." <http://www.acm.org/constitution/code.html>.

Association for Computing Machinery, Inc. and the Institute for Electrical and Electronics Engineers, Inc. "Software Engineering Code of Ethics and Professional Practice." <http://www.acm.org/serving/se/code.htm>.

Barger, Josephine C., Robert N. Barger, and John J. Rearden. "Relationship of students' philosophic orientation to academic field of study." Paper presented at the annual meeting of the American Educational Studies Association, Chicago, October 25–29, 1989. <http://ux1.eiu.edu/~rnbarger/aesa1989.html>.

Computer Ethics Institute, "The Ten Commandments of Computer Ethics." <http://www3.brookings.edu/its/cei/TheTenCommandmentsOfComputerEthics.pdf>.

"Department of State Washington File: Text: Research on Children, Learning and Computers." <http://canberra.usembassy.gov/hyper/2001/0130/epf206.htm>.

Freeh, Vincent, Albert-Laszlo Barabasi, Hawoong Jeong, and Jay Brockman. "Parasitic computing." <http://www.nd.edu/~parasite/>.

Gatta, Mary, and Mary Trigg. "Bridging the gap: Gender equity in science, engineering and technology." New Brunswick, NJ: Rutgers University, 2001. <http://www.chr.up.ac.za/ggp/coursematerial/2007/good_gov/elize/Gap%20gender%20and%20science.pdf>.

Google Censorship FAQ." March 2, 2007. <http://blog.outer-court.com/archive/2007-03-02-n19.html>.

"Google: Web Search Help Center." <http://www.google.com/support/bin/answer.py?answer=17795>.

Illinois Institute of Technology. "Codes of Ethics Online – Computing and Information Systems." <http://ethics.iit.edu/codes/computer.html>.

James, William. *Pragmatism: A New Name for Some Old Ways of Thinking.* New York: Longmans, Green and Co., 1907. <http://www.4literature.net/William_James/Pragmatism/>.

McCormick, Matt. "Immanuel Kant – Metaphysics." *Internet Encyclopedia of Philosophy,* <http://www.iep.utm.edu/k/kantmeta.htm#H8>.

McCullagh, Declan. "No booze or jokes for Googlers in China | CNET News.com." <http://news.com.com/No+booze+or+jokes+for+Googlers+in+China+-page+1/2100–1030_3–6031727.html?tag=item>.

———. "No booze or jokes for Googlers in China – page 2 | CNET News.com." <http://news.com.com/No+booze+or+jokes+for+Googlers+in+China+-+page+2/2100–1030_3–6031727–2.html?tag=st.num>.

———. "No booze or jokes for Googlers in China – page 3 | CNET News.com." <http://news.com.com/No+booze+or+jokes+for+Googlers+in+China+-+page+3/2100–1030_3–6031727–3.html?tag=st.num>.

"Network Access Layer," <http://www.pku.edu.cn/academic/research/computer-center/tc/html/TC0200.html>.

O'Connor, J. J. and E. F. Robertson. "Babbage biography." <http://www-groups.dcs.st-and.ac.uk/~history/Biographies/Babbage.html>.

———. "Mathematicians/Hollerith." <http://www-groups.dcs.st-andrews.ac.uk/%7Ehistory/Mathematicians/Hollerith.html>.

Randall, Alexander, 5th. "Q&A – A lost interview with ENIAC inventor J. Presper Eckert." <http://www.computerworld.com/hardwaretopics/hardware/story/0,10801,108568,00.html?source=NLT_AM&nid=108568>.

"RBC [Royal Bank of Canada] Financial Group – RBC Letter." <http://www.rbc.com/responsibility/letter/september2006.html>.

Sayre-McCord, Geoffrey. "Kant's Grounding for the Metaphysics of Morals: A Very Brief Selective Summary of Sections I and II." <http://www.unc.edu/~gsmunc/phil22/Kantsum.pdf>.

Searle, John R. "The Problem of Consciousness." <http://www.ecs.soton.ac.uk/~harnad/Papers/Py104/searle.prob.html>.

von Foerster, Heinz. "Responsibilities of Competence," *Journal of Cybernetics* 2, no.2 (1972): 1–6, <http://mlab.uiah.fi/~timo/vonfoerster/>.

World Summit on the Information Society (WSIS). "Basic Information about WSIS." <http://www.itu.int/wsis/basic/faqs.asp>.

———. "Geneva Declaration of Principles." <http://www.itu.int/wsis/docs/geneva/official/dop.html>.

———. "Geneva Plan of Action. < http://www.itu.int/wsis/docs/geneva/official/poa.html>.

———. "Tunis Commitment." < http://www.itu.int/wsis/docs2/tunis/off/7.html>.

———. "Tunis Agenda for the Information Society." <http://www. itu.int/wsis/docs2/tunis/off/6rev1.html>.

Index